MICHELLE LOPEZ

IDENTITY
IDENTITY
IDENTITY
IDENTITY

SEEING YOURSELF THROUGH GOD'S EYES

CONTENTS

INTRODUCTION

I CAN REMEMBER A TIME when the news reported about good things and found good stories to focus on. Then it appeared to me, there was a shift and more and more what you saw on the news were the bad things that happened. Local news began to tell of all the wrecks and crime in the area making it seem like it was happening all the time. Now, I am not trying to lessen the impact and heartache of those. Nor say, the media is bad and never reports anything good. However, I want to show how a picture can be presented that highlights certain things and then people began to focus on only those things spreading fear. Is there a picture we are to focus on? And another way to operate in other than fear? As a believer and follower of Jesus Christ, God provides us with an answer in Philippians 4:8 in AMP: ***"Finally, believers, whatever is true, whatever is honorable and worthy of respect, whatever is right and confirmed by God's Word, whatever is pure and wholesome, whatever is lovely and brings peace, whatever is admirable and of good repute; if there is any excellence, if there is anything worthy of praise, think continually on these things [center your mind on them, and implant them in your heart]."***

I have heard stories from the point of view of those who served in the Vietnam War. And how the media's coverage of the war caused a negative backlash for them which carried over once they returned home. Perhaps, this was a turning point where media was given access to see and show war to the public in a way to dictate public opinion and use people of influence to assist in this cause. It seemed from the perspective of those who had served in the war and all they went through that their serving their country was not seen as honorable due to some media coverage and from those opposing the war. But is there another point of view, another perspective?

On the flip side, media has been used to shed light on things that need to have light shed on. Media has shown corruption in various areas and made it to where action was demanded for justice to be taken. People are no longer able to hide in the shadows of their ugliness and hatred and horrors they inflict on others. This was seen at a greater level after World War II when people began to see, thanks to media coverage, the things that the Nazis had done to the Jews and others as the aftermath of war began to reveal what had taken place in the concentration camps. Is there more to be revealed?

And today we still have media and many different media coverages from national to local but now we have social media and media through the internet. Social media has been on the rise where every phone has video and camera ability with a quick upload or even live feed which can be immediately shared across the web with people able to voice their opinions. Anyone can put whatever they want out there on the internet and it can go worldwide quickly. And when people were getting killed and it appeared to be over the color of their skin it hit social media and took off. I saw different reports, different posts, different comments. I saw the hurt, anger, pain and I felt it too. Not to the same degree as someone whose gone through it personally, but I still felt what I felt. My heart went out to those I know and to those I do not and to my friends because they need and deserve to be treated the same as anyone else and not be treated differently only because their skin tone is darker, meaning their labeled black and not white by the world's system. The enemy, satan, has really used the lie of race to do his evil work and so many have stepped into his snare. But is there another opinion? Another voice to be heard and heard even across the world wide web? What is the answer?

You see I say skin tone is darker rather than put a world label of black or African American or white or any other labels because I think that is part of the problem. Rather than looking to understand or appreciate different cultures or ways of living, or diversities in how people look, I believe satan has used people to create divisions and bring distractions that God never intended. Pulling the church into a world system defying the reason the church is to exist. And not looking at what God says. What is the reason the church exists? Why all the labels? What is God saying?

Somewhere the thought was put into action that it is okay to label and categorize people. It became accepted and became accepted in the church. And I believe there is another more acceptable correct way which is what has led to my writing this book, along with the help of Holy Spirit (God's Spirit). Hopefully, you did not allow yourself to be offended and put this book down already because God has been prompting me to write this for some time. And I am being obedient in finally writing this. I believe there have been lies Christians (believers and followers of Jesus Christ) have believed and bought into, and some have gotten swept up into the culture of the world rather than understanding to Whom Christians belong and that Christians are not to allow anyone to define them except God. How does God define people?

I realize we do not have the best history in America due to the Civil War and how people were put into slavery based on their skin color and how it took America way too long to bring equality among people with darker skin tones compared to lighter skin tones. And there is still much work to be done in that area because of how systems have been put in place to create divisions and some systems have been well hidden. It is hard for me to look back at America's history and other countries and see how badly people have been treated all because someone thought others deserved to be treated that way based completely on their skin color being different or they were a different culture and people wanted to establish dominance over others. People can elevate themselves in status while making others look less valued and some can do so with an eerie ease. Yet, what does God say?

When social media and media was imploding with racial tensions across America and it did not look like we had come that far in racial relations in this country, I kept praying and seeking God for answers. I kept seeing responses from people I know, some who are Christian. And there were responses I saw where I was not able to tell Christian from non-Christian which should not be the case. I kept thinking we are supposed to be leading people to Jesus and people are supposed to be seeing Jesus in us through our actions, through our words, through our responses, through how we live. I continued praying and seeking God and then I heard God say, "Identity."

Hearing that word "Identity" was not what I expected, not that I especially had any expectations on what God would say other than my expectation that He would speak to me and give an answer to my prayer and time of seeking Him. Sometimes, God speaks to me in sharing only one word. Then, as I pray and seek Him more, He reveals more to what the one word He shared means. This time was no different and as I continually sought Him as to what He meant by "Identity" I heard Him say, "The issue with race is an identity issue and it starts with My people.

My Word holds the answers. My people need to know who they are and to Whom they belong. It begins with them."

This book comes from an ongoing prayer and seeking God for answers. And what He has revealed to me is captured through these pages. It is a picture that highlights and focuses on identity through God and His Word and not through the world or any other lens. It is His side, His solution as seen through His eyes. It is His report, His news which is Good News. This Good News is a report that was given in person and can be found recorded in the Bible, God's Word. It is a news cast that is ongoing and still provides Good News today and for all days, to be heard and received by anyone who hears and believes. In Luke 2:8-11 TPT, we can find this Good News: ***"That night, in a field near Bethlehem, shepherds were watching over their flocks. Suddenly, an angel of the Lord appeared in radiant splendor before them, lighting up the field with the blazing glory of God, and the shepherds were terrified! But the angel reassured them, saying, 'Do not be afraid, for I have come to bring you good news, the most joyous news the world has ever heard! And it is for everyone everywhere! For today in Bethlehem a rescuer was born for you. He is the Lord Yahweh, the Messiah.'"*** A rescuer was born for us is God's News and a news worthy of being told and retold, a news that is life changing and relevant every day. It was a God News delivered personally from God to the world. It is a God News still in need of being personally delivered from God to the world. However, God has chosen His children to be a part of His delivery team.

I have always heard that there are two sides to each story, especially when there is a conflict. How many times have you seen arguments arise and people begin to take sides because they have heard one side of the story? Perhaps, they know that person so it is easy to be emotionally attached and take a side. Or they may even know the opposing side, and even more are drawn to one side over the other. Sometimes conclusions are quickly drawn without all the information being gathered. However, the Lord spoke to me one day and He said, "There is a third side to every story. And it is My side." I remember that revelation hitting me in a powerful way because I had only seen situations in twofold. I immediately thanked Him for telling me and sharing His knowledge. I thanked Him again because He had shown me early on in my walk with Him that I was to look to Him and His Word for my answers. He showed me that my answer and how I was to respond and how I was to act was found in His Word regardless of anything or anyone else, including myself. Yet, I had not seen it to this degree until He shared with me that every story has His side. There is more than one side to politics, there is His side. There is more than one side to racial problems, there is His side. There is more than one side to religion, there is His side. There is more than one side to what any media platform tells, there is His side. There is more than one side to every conflict, there is His side. There is more than one side to every story, there is His side. There is more than one side to every solution, there is His side. And you can go on with that train of thought because it ends with, there is His side. Do you know what His side is? Will you choose His side, regardless of popularity? Can you see His news as the Good News it is? Will you choose His Good News over any other news you hear? For God's side of the story is seeing everything through His eyes, especially regarding who you are, regarding your identity.

I grow increasingly thankful for God and how personal He is and how much He wants to reveal to us and how much He wants to show us and have us learn His side. It is a side that will go on for eternity and a side that will help us this side of eternity. A side that is victorious, full of love, and full of wisdom. A side that I am learning more and more is the best side, the right and correct side for all situations and all times regardless. And I grow increasingly thankful for His Word, both His written Word which is the Bible and His Rhema Word which is how He speaks things to us today from His heart to ours and sometimes shows us a Rhema Word in the Bible. I always want to be willing and eager to hear Him, expecting Him to show me things and to remain teachable.

For those who are grammar people, and I am to a certain extent, you will see satan written in lower caps throughout this book. It is not a mistake but done with the intent to verify that he does not have the authority over God's people unless they give it to him. Not following the world's standards for writing etiquette may seem silly or trivial but not to me. I want satan and others to know that through Jesus Christ, and thanks to Him, you have authority over satan and all he has charge over. To me, it is a visual reminder to see his name in lower caps. And the opposite, as any time I refer to God and His Word, I will be capitalizing anything relating to Him like I have in this sentence. I always want to honor God and the things relating to Him and for me to do so in writing is one way I honor Him.

I will also be referencing the Bible as God's Word because it is His Word. Some people see the Bible as another book, especially other religions. Yet, it is far more which is the main reason you will be reading it as God's Word. I want to emphasize the importance of His Word and that His Word is far greater than what anyone else says. God used men to write and transcribe His Word, but it came from Him and He used His Spirit to help men convey what He was saying. God's Word is also Jesus made flesh, which was a huge revelation for me and something I always want to keep in the forefront of remembrance and have reverence of.

As Christians, our identity is found in God's Word and His Word should be our benchmark, our compass, our guide, our way of life, and our way of how we are to see ourselves and others. So, we begin "Identity," created in God's image, seeing ourselves through God's eyes, seeing ourselves according to His side of the story.

CHAPTER 1

God's Side is Him

GOD'S SIDE OF THE STORY starts with Him and His news. To know His side of the story, is to know Him and His Word. His news is worthy of being told and retold because His news changes lives, now and for eternity. His news touches the natural and the spiritual. And to tell this Good News of God and Who He is, God has given us His news, His script, His message by giving us His Word. God tells us in John 1:1-2,4 GNT: ***"In the beginning the Word already existed; the Word was with God and the Word was God. From the very beginning the Word was with God. The Word was the source of life, and this life brought light to people."*** God's Word existed before us, His Word was with Him, and His Word was Him; therefore, we should place more importance and value on His Word than anything else, especially over any report or news from man. By willingly sharing His Word with us, God has also willingly shared Himself with us so we can know Him and then know ourselves. We can fellowship with Him and grow in our fellowship with Him through His Word and spending time with Him. We can always find God's side of the story in His Word where we can always find Him. God wants His side of the story to become our side of the story in every area of our life so we can see everything through His eyes and respond accordingly. God has always existed even before we or anything else we see on earth existed. Exodus 3:14 NLT says: ***"God replied to Moses, 'I AM WHO I AM. Say this to the people of Israel: I AM has sent me to you.'"*** God told Moses to tell the people of Israel that He is I AM. He was letting them know that He has always and will always exist, He is eternal in nature, He is the source of all things, He is unwavering, and always reliable. He was wanting them to know He could be trusted now and for all eternity. And He wants us to know as well. He is still I AM WHO I AM, He is still I AM. He is still there for us and always will be. He remains reliable and unwavering and trustworthy and He wants us to fully be persuaded so we are not persuaded by any news or story that is contrary.

By understanding God, we can then have a firm foundation to understand who we are and how He created us, and we can understand our identity and how we are to identify. A foundation that cannot be shaken and can withstand any attack, even from ourselves. Attacks come from satan or people he is influencing and not from God. God seems to get blamed for a lot of things like the weather, wars, sickness, and disease among other things. Yet, God is not the author of these things. 1 John 1:5 NLT reveals to us: ***"This is the message we heard from Jesus and now declare to you: God is light, and there is no darkness in Him at all."*** Jesus Himself came proclaiming that God is light and He is void of darkness. The reality of this impacted His disciples and they continued delivering this message, this news: God is light, and there is no darkness in Him at all. They received God's news about Him and were telling others what they had heard and believed. It is important that we hear God's news, especially about Him, believe His news and tell His news to others. How many stories do you tell in one day, how many conversations do you have, and how many of those involve telling God's news, telling His side of the story? How many times do you let people know how He sees their situation, what His answer is? If someone is having problems, do you tell them what God's Word says about their problems? Or do you agree with their problems and what they may be saying? Or do you agree with God and what He is saying regarding their problems? Even if the person may not agree with God, do you still agree with God? Jesus was telling and showing Who God is and His disciples followed suit, they picked up where He left off and we are to do the same because we are His disciples and we are God's children.

Not only is God light but He created light as seen in Genesis 1:3 NLT when He said: ***"Let there be light, and there was light."*** And in Genesis 1:1 NLT we see: ***"In the beginning God created the heavens and the earth."*** God is the Creator. How much more should we believe Him and see like Him? John 1:3 NLT tells us: ***"God created everything through Him, and nothing was created except through Him."*** And Isaiah 44:24 NLT says: ***"This is what the Lord says – Your Redeemer and Creator: 'I am the Lord, Who, made all things. I alone stretched out the heavens. Who was with Me when I made the earth?"*** No man was with Him, so we should believe no man over God. We should want to know Who God is and Who we are to Him because He created us. We should believe what God says, so much so, that we are never moved by any reports or news of man. We should see so clearly as God sees that we always respond as He sees because we respond with His Good

News, because what God says we also say. We allow ourselves to believe God and what He says no matter what. Why then would we not want to believe or even find out God's side of any story and then believe and live out His side of the story over man's? When we see or hear something, He should be the first we go to and ask Him how He sees and how He wants us to see and respond. John 4:24 NKJV tells us: ***"For God is a Spirit, and those who worship Him must worship in spirit and truth."*** He exists outside of time and beyond this earthen place for He is greater. God declares in Isaiah 46:9 NKJV: ***"For I am God, and there is none like Me."*** God is not like people so He should be the One Who we look to for our answers. Because Proverbs 29:25 NLT says: ***"fearing people is a dangerous trap, but trusting the Lord means safety."*** By trusting in God and His Good News, His side of the story, we will find safety. His side of the story is the safe side, it is the correct side, and it is the side that can be trusted. For Psalms 118:8 NLT tells us: ***"It is better to take refuge in the Lord than to trust in people."*** In Numbers 23:19-20 NLT it says: ***"God is not a man, so He does not lie. He is not human, so He does not change His mind. Has He ever spoken and failed to act? Has He ever promised and not carried it through?"*** God provides the answers in Hebrews 6:16-18 NLT: ***"Now when people take an oath, they call on someone greater than themselves to hold them to it. And without any question that oath is binding. God also bound Himself with an oath, so that those who received the promise could be perfectly sure that He would never change His mind. So, God has given both His promise and His oath. These two things are unchangeable because it is impossible for God to lie. Therefore, we who have fled to Him for refuge can have great confidence as we hold to the hope that lies before us."*** I find it very refreshing to know that not only will God never lie but He is unable to lie. God's very nature is Truth. Regardless of what any person may say and then not do, this is not how God operates or will ever operate. What He says in His Word should become what we say, should become how we live and conduct our lives. God's Word should always be our life's blueprint, our news, our story, for how we are to live our lives. When God speaks to us, we can trust Him and trust what He says. Those who God chose to speak to, like Moses, knew God could always be trusted. Now God is wanting to speak directly to everyone and anyone who will listen and then be obedient to what He says. He is speaking, are we listening? We should be asking and listening because He wants to speak to us and tell us His side so we can see everything through His eyes. It is refreshing to know there is Someone Who is always wanting to speak to us and always wanting to provide us with the correct answers.

Isaiah 40:8 NKJV declares: ***"The grass withers, the flower fades, but the Word of our God stands forever."*** And GNT says: ***"Yes, grass withers and flowers fade, but the Word of our God endures forever."*** God's Word will stand and endure forever when those things within this world will wither and fade. Matthew 24:35 GNT informs us: ***"Heaven and earth will pass away, but My Words will never pass away."*** The NLT says: ***"Heaven and earth will disappear, but My Words will never disappear."*** Heaven and earth will come to an end but not God's Words. God's Word tells us in Isaiah 55:11 NLT that He sends out His Word ***"and it always produces fruit [and] it will accomplish all [He wants] it to, and it will prosper everywhere [He] sends it."*** The NKJV says God's Word ***"goes forth from [His] mouth; it shall not return to [Him] void."*** God's Word is valid, good, legal, binding and is ever working and will always be that way and no other way. All reports that have been told, all news that has been reported, all reports and news yet to be told and even all reports and news that are archived from being previously told and reported will all pass away, will all disappear, will not withstand for eternity but God's Word, His News, will. How much more should we then want to rely on His News and His News alone for how we are to live, think, speak, and even respond to other news and reports? We should want to know, trust, and lean on God's News which is not temporary and will last forever. Two sides to every story will not remain forever but a third side, which is God's side, will never fade away but will last forever. God tells us in Isaiah 55:8-11 NKJV: ***"For My thoughts are not your thoughts, nor are your ways My ways, says the Lord. For as the heavens are higher than the earth, so are My ways higher than your ways, and My thoughts than your thoughts. For as the rain comes down, and the snow from heaven, and do not return there, but water the earth, and make it bring forth and bud, that it may give seed to the sower and bread to the eater, so shall My Word be that goes forth from My mouth; it shall not return to Me void, but it shall accomplish what I please, and it shall prosper in the thing for which I sent it."*** When rain and snow fall to the ground, they hit their intended target, the ground, where they remain. God has sent us His Word and He is not taking it back because we are His intended targets. He knows how important His Word is and how important His Word is to our lives. His Word directs us to Him, to His ways, and to His thoughts. God's ways and God's thoughts are higher and better than ours; yet, in His goodness, in His love, He wants to share His ways and thoughts with us and He has and it is in His Word. He sends His thoughts and ways down to us through His Word which brings the nourishment and sustenance we need to thrive and have an abundant life here on earth, so we can live according to His ways. His Word is like water that is needed for the earth which is essential and vital for sustaining life. His Word is like a seed which is important for the sower so it can be sewn to produce a harvest that brings forth food that is good and good for us. And His Word is like the bread that is made into the food that tastes good and is good for us which can nourish and provide life. God's Word accomplishes all God intends His Word to accomplish for us and He has shared the Good News of His Word with us. We must do our part in accepting God's Word into our own lives and living our lives according to God's Word, according to His side of the story.

I remember my paternal great-grandmother making homemade bread. The aroma filled the house and there was always a sense of excitement and anticipation before the bread came out of the oven. There were times I would stand in her kitchen quietly waiting for the bread to finishing cooking. Waiting for it to be sliced so I could partake of what I knew would taste good, a taste I had grown accustomed to and looked forward to upon my visits with her. It was like you could taste the added love, the added care, the added passion that she put into making the bread. I remember wanting to and eating it as soon as it came out of the oven, letting no time waste as it was placed before me. And the satisfaction I felt afterward created a warmth, a soothing for my soul, because she was right there with me watching and sometimes eating a slice with me. I enjoyed my time with her and I enjoyed partaking of what she had made and wanted to share with me. Even more so, God has provided us with His Word, crafted with His love, His goodness, the very essence of Himself, filled with His thoughts and ways which He has made obtainable to us. His Word that brings us life and nourishment to meet our every need while here on earth. When we look at His Word, we can see Him and know how much He loves us and how much He has shared Himself with us. When we are in His Word, we are with Him, we are spending time with Him developing and deepening our fellowship with Him. It is as if I were sitting with my paternal great-grandmother sharing a piece of bread with her except with God it is much, much more intimate and precious when we are in His Word and are spending time with Him. Because His bread, His Word, touches more than just the natural, His Word supersedes the natural and will sustain our life for eternity. His Word came from Him so His Word should be more important to us than any other word, any other reports, or any other news. His Word is intimate and His love letter to us, individually and collectively all at the same time. And His Word is powerful and authoritative to accomplish mighty things for us and through us for ourselves as well as for others and for His Kingdom on earth. God and His Word cannot be separated, accepting Him is accepting His Word and vice versus. He has given us His Word to let us know who we are and who we are to Him. His Word helps us properly gain our rightful identity and not fall short in accepting any false identities other sources want to hand us. His Word helps us focus on who we truly are and are to be and not be distracted in settling for counterfeits. We can think and walk in our identity as God intends because we can know God's thoughts and ways through His Word and they are good and loving toward us. We can receive His thoughts and ways as our own believing and relying on His side of the story, learning to see everything through His eyes regardless of any other news or stories being told. His story is the best story providing us with the best life, providing us with our rightful identity.

God's side of the story also begins with Him, Who He is and that He is the Good News. His news never changes rather His news stays steady and constant because God remains steady and constant. He declares this in Malachi 3:6a NKJV: ***"For I am the Lord, I do not change."*** I find it so inspiring to know with all the many changes that happen in life, God will remain the same. He can always be counted on and is always available. God's side of the story is always good because God is always good. God is good and anything that comes from Him is good, including us. For James 1:17 TPT says: ***"Every gift God freely gives us is good and perfect, streaming down from the Father of lights, Who shines from the heavens with no hidden shadow or darkness and is never subject to change."*** Because God is good and He made us, we should respond to ourselves and others in the same goodness that comes from God. Everything that comes from God is good because God is good. We came from God so we are good and should live our lives from this perspective. If something is bad, it did not nor will it ever come from God. For those who are not acting good, we should pray on their behalf that they come to know God and be able to partake of His goodness for themselves, by living out God's goodness in their lives, and then expressing His goodness to others. Psalms 119:68 NLT says: ***"You [God] are good and do only good; teach me Your decrees."*** And TPT says: ***"Everything You [God] do is beautiful, flowing from Your goodness; teach me the power of Your wonderful Words!"*** God wants us to know He is good but also teach us about His goodness, teach us His Word, teach us His side of the story, teach us so we can see ourselves through His eyes, so we can participate in His goodness, participate in His Word, each and every day. God knows that this is for our benefit, for our well-being, for our good. Creating us was a part of God's beautiful work, a part of His goodness, and that is how we need to see ourselves and others, even those who test this by their unbeautiful and not good actions. Those who are doing evil do not know how they were created nor do they know God, Who, created them. They do not know His goodness, His character, His ways, His Word. They are listening to the wrong voice(s), the wrong stories, and are living apart from God, Who, is good and will always be good. God wants us to see them through His eyes and seek Him and His ways for how we are to respond. Firmly, allowing Him to establish our true identity helps us see people as God sees and helps us respond accordingly.

Psalms 34:8 MSG tells us: ***"Open your mouth and taste, open your eyes and see – how good God is. Blessed are you who run to Him."*** The NLT says: ***"Taste and see that the Lord is good. Oh, the joys of those who take refuge in Him."*** And the end of this verse in the NKJV says: ***"Blessed is the man who trusts in Him!"*** See God's goodness is tangible, and it can become personal for anyone who is willing to make the effort to get to know God. In doing so, you get to know how good God is and how blessed you are in trusting in God and His goodness. Psalms 100:5 NKJV says: ***"For the Lord is good; His mercy is everlasting, and His truth endures to all generations."*** We can not only trust God's goodness for ourselves, but it can be a place of safety, a shelter from trouble or danger. We can find out how good God is and how His goodness will have a major and positive impact on our lives because God wants to share His goodness and all that His goodness affords us. God wants to reveal Who He is, and He wants us to experience Him and all He has for us. If you are tasting something, you are experiencing something directly for yourself, you are deciding based on your own experience. It becomes a personal experience. I can tell you how good my paternal great-grandmother's bread was and I can go into specific details about it. I can even share the recipe with you. I can make the bread sound and look tasteful to you but until you taste the bread yourself you cannot fully understand nor appreciate the taste of the bread. You may have tasted other breads (believed other stories, other news, other reports) and think you know something about bread. You may dismiss the importance of this bread thinking all bread is the same or that you already have experienced the best bread. But until you actually decide for yourself to try this bread you will never know how good, how satisfying, how wonderfully set apart this bread is and that it is the bread for you (God's news, His story, His report, God Himself). God is wanting to share His goodness with you, He wants you to experience Who He is for yourself and to do so on a personal and intimate level. James 4:9 NKJV says: ***"Draw near to God and He will draw near to you."*** Whenever you draw near to someone, you get closer to the person. And if this person is then drawing closer to you, the two of you will come to an intimate closeness. Once you get closer to someone, you get to know that person better and it becomes a mutual fellowship. God wants you to know Him better and He wants you to get close to Him and He wants to get close to you. God wants intimacy with you. He wants to share Himself, all He is and all He has with you. Taking a piece of bread, placing it up to and then in your mouth, and chewing it so you can experience the goodness of the bread's taste, makes it personal, makes it tangible. God wants you to do so even more with Him. And He has provided His Word as one means of experiencing Him and Who He is.

It is imperative that we trust God and trust His side of the story at all times. For in doing so, there is safety and protection, there is guidance and instruction. The more we get to know God, the more we realize how much He wants to share His goodness with us and how much He can be trusted. We have to do our part by following His leading, following His prompting, and following His Word. Proverbs 3:5-8 NKJV tells us: ***"Trust in the Lord with all your heart and lean not on your own understanding; in all your ways acknowledge Him, and He will direct your paths. Do not be wise in your own eyes; fear the Lord and depart from evil. It will be health to your flesh, and strength to your bones."*** The NLT informs us: ***"Trust in the Lord with all your heart; do not de-***

pend on your own understanding. Seek His will in all you do, and He will show you which path to take. Do not be impressed with your own wisdom. Instead, fear the Lord and turn away from evil. Then you will have healing for your body and strength for your bones." Now that is a side I want to get on and remain on. But I have my part. God gives us a free will for which I am thankful but even more thankful that I now use my free will to follow God and His understanding rather than my own. Even in writing this book, I have had to not lean on my own understanding but His. I must daily make the choices to allow Him to direct me in all I do and then follow His directions. I must continually rely on Him and how He thinks over relying on myself and how I think. And I can find this out in His Word, in spending time fellowshipping with Him, spending time in prayer, spending time worshiping Him. Oh, how many decisions and mistakes I have made because I made the choices and then lived out those choices without knowing or having a full understanding of God and following His side of the story. And even with all I know I still am realizing how much I still need to learn but am grateful He remains willing to teach me. How many choices do most people go through in their daily walk without including God? How many are you? How many am I? I have finally learned to not withhold any part of my life from God nor any decision no matter how big or small. Throughout my day I have learned to be mindful of Him and include Him in my ongoing everyday decisions which has proven to be a wonderful life change. Even though there are days I seem to master and other days I could do better, my heart remains yielded to Him and wanting to include Him in my daily life. I remember I was just learning to listen to God and seek Him throughout my day. I was working at a job that called for long hours and required me to be on call. On this day, I had already worked well past a full workday and I had gotten called to a hospital late one evening.

Once I left, the evening had turned to early morning and there was no one that was out, and on the streets, but me. At that hour, the red lights were turned to work where the lights would flash yellow for the main road going through town and the lights on the roads crossing the main road would flash red. If someone was on a road that intersected with the main road, this person was to stop. There was only one main road that ran through this town, and this was the road I had pulled out on when I left the hospital. I was a few red lights from a road that ran from down town when I heard the Spirit of the Lord, within me, tell me to stop at this light. I immediately thought, in my very tired mind, why stop because the light is flashing yellow, and you do not have to stop on yellow, and I just want to get home. I was still a good distance from this light and had two lights to pass through before this light. And again, I heard the Spirit of the Lord tell me to stop at this specific light, even though it was flashing yellow, and I was the only person on the road. There literally was still no one on the road but me and it had been that way since leaving the hospital. I finally stopped leaning on my own understanding, even though I wanted to get home and get some much-needed rest, and thought to myself I am just going to stop at this light like the Lord told me to. And I even thought I am going to stop even if someone sees me, though there still was not anyone else around that I could see. Now to the right of this intersection was downtown and there were buildings that prohibited you from seeing downtown as you approached the intersection. So, as I approached this light, I slowed down and came to a stop just like I would have done had the light turned red. And just as I came to a complete stop and was behind the white line like you are supposed to be at a red light, a semi-truck came speeding through the light from my right even though the light from that direction was red and the truck was supposed to stop. The semi-truck was going at such a speed that the driver had to be speeding all the way through downtown and may have even thought that he or she was the only one on the road at that time. Up until then, I had been the only person on the road and was actually surprised to see the semi-truck. I realized, even though I did not know this semi-truck was going to be speeding through this light rather than stopping, God knew. He knew we would both be on the road approaching the same intersection and He was prompting me to stop, even though the flashing light indicated yield. Had I just yielded I would not have noticed the semi-truck and would have been going through the intersection as the semi-truck speed through. I was thankful that I had not listened to my own understanding that morning, especially in my tired state, but had listened to His prompting and leading me to stop. I would like to say I have been successfully listening to His leading and prompting since but I have missed it on several occasions. I am thankful that when I do, He is always gracious to forgive me and provide me with a second chance. He does not right me off as being imperfect but He keeps leading and prompting me. I have learned more and more to recognize His leading and prompting even in what appears to be the small things. What helps is to be continually mindful of Him and His wanting to lead and guide me. And it is equally helpful to have an understanding of Who He is and who I am in Him. My identity I have learned comes from Him so what others think of me, what others may say about me, or how others see me, matters not. What matters is how He sees me, what He says about me, and what He thinks about me. He is the One Who is to direct my path and He will always direct me correctly, properly, safely and according to His ways, according to His Word, according to His side of the story. I must ensure I know His ways, His Word and His side of the story and that I see myself through His eyes and my actions line up accordingly.

Psalms 37:3-5 AMPC tells us: *"Trust (lean on, rely on, and be confident) in the Lord and do good; so, shall you dwell in the land and feed surely on His faithfulness, and truly you shall be fed. Delight yourself also in the Lord, and He will give you the desires and secret petitions of your heart. Commit your way to the Lord [roll and repose each care of your load on Him]; trust (lean on, rely one, and be confident) also in Him and He will bring it to pass."* And TPT says: *"Keep trusting in the Lord and do what is right in His eyes. Fix your heart on the promises of God, and you will dwell in the land, feasting on His faithfulness. Find your delight and true pleasure in Yahweh [God], and He will give you what you desire the most. Give God the right to direct your life; and as you trust Him along the way, you will find He pulled it off perfectly!"* God always knows what is best for us in every area and in every detail of our lives. He can see all things, including seeing ahead and knowing that it is for our safety to stop at a flashing yellow light early one morning when it appears that there is no one else on the road. He knows how we need to respond in situations and events. He knows how we are to respond to other people and their responses and even to other stories and news. He knows how we are to live and conduct ourselves in this world. He knows His side is always correct and the best side for me. I have to always trust Him, always lean on, rely on, and be confident in Him. I have to always do good. He is good but I have to do my part in doing good, regardless if others are not. My trust in Him has to be ongoing, continual, never wavering but constant. As I trust Him, trust His side of the story and see things as He does, my desires change to become like His, I begin to want what He wants and my ways begin to line up to match His ways. By following God, I get to partake of His faithfulness and can experience the fullness of His promises right here and right now in my life. God's thoughts are higher than mine and He has a path He wants me on. He has a path He wants everyone on. Jeremiah 29:11 NLT tell us: ***"For I know the plans I have for you, says the Lord. They are plans for good and not for disaster, to give you a future and a hope."*** It makes sense that a good God would have good plans for us but we must be willing to seek Him for what those plans are and then take the necessary steps to get on His plans. When I do, I am on the plan for a good life full of hope and a future. There was a time in my life where I was not fully seeking God, especially in every area of my life, so I was not seeing the good in all areas of my life. God began using the goodness of His Word, His story to draw me by using Jeremiah 29:11. I began to hold my life up to His Word and began to seek God through this specific passage of His Word. I began to realize God can be trusted and so can His Word, but I had to get to know God and His Word for myself, I had to be willing to get on the right path, His path. I had to be willing to follow His plan, to follow His side of the story. Psalms 119:105 TPT says: ***"Truth's shining light guides me in my choices and decisions; the revelation of Your Word makes my pathway clear."*** And the NLT reveals: ***"Your Word is a lamp to guide my feet and a light for my path."*** God provides all the guidance and direction we need for the path He has for us. It does not matter what it may look like all around us, God will highlight, make it clear, make it where we can see His path above any other path. And He does this through His Word. He highlights the choices and decisions we need to make that is best for us in any situation. Decisions that will keep us safe, keep us in good health, keep us prospering in this world, keeps us moving forward, and moving His Kingdom forward. God not only directs us through His Word, but His blessings follow when we trust God and then follow Him, follow His Word, follow His side of the story. Many want a blessing like it is a handout, but the blessings come from God and doing things His way. And for me I have found God and

His Word are the true blessing. The more I get into His Word, the more I seek Him and spend time with Him, the more I am blessed. Jeremiah 17:7 NLT states: ***"But blessed are those who trust in the Lord and have made the Lord their hope and confidence."*** By trusting God and having my hope and confidence in Him, I am blessed. And Isaiah 26:4 NLT says: ***"Trust in the Lord always, for the Lord is the eternal Rock."*** I always am on solid ground when I trust God. My feet remain firmly placed and secure. No matter any shaking that may occur around me or any news that may report otherwise, I will remain unshaken and unmoved because God is unshaken and unmoved and I trust Him and His news, I trust His report. And Psalms 37:5 NLT tells us: ***"Commit everything you do to the Lord. Trust Him and He will help you."*** When I commit everything I do to Him, I trust and know He will always help me. When other reports indicate otherwise, I trust and know His help is always there for me. Because Psalms 115:11 NLT lets us know: ***"All who fear the Lord, trust the Lord. He is your helper and your shield."*** When I honor and reverence God for Who He is, I know and trust Him. I recognize His role in my life to help and protect me, to shield me from the enemy and his attacks because I am following Him and His Word, I am believing Him and His side of the story. God can be trusted over anyone, He can be trusted at all times, His Word holds true over anyone else's, and this will always hold true.

I find it comforting to know that God can always be trusted, He is always my refuge, He is always my place of comfort, He is always my place of safety, and He is always my helper. Psalms 46:1-3 TPT says: ***"God, You, are such a safe and powerful place to find refuge! You are a proven help in time of trouble – more than enough and always available whenever I need You. So, we will never fear even if every structure of support were to crumble***

away. We will not fear even when the earth quakes and shakes, moving mountains and casting them into the sea. For the raging roar of the stormy winds and crashing waves cannot erode our faith in You. Pause in His presence." A greater part of knowing who I am is knowing Who He is. I gain confidence in my identity being in Him, being His child, being His daughter as I gain confidence in knowing God, knowing His Word, knowing how much He can be trusted no matter what I may see going on around me. God is not moved so I learn to not be moved. Stories come and go, news comes and goes, opinions come and go, ideologies come and go, social norms come and go, but not God, He remains the same and He remains trustworthy and so does His side of the story. Psalms 91:2 TPT tells me: ***"He is the hope that holds me and the stronghold to shelter me, the only God for me, and my great confidence."*** And the AMPC says: ***"I will say of the Lord, He is my Refuge and my Fortress, my God; on Him I lean and rely, and in Him I [confidently] trust!"*** Not only must I trust God and put my confidence in Him but I must say I do. My words have to line up with His Words as I talk about Who my God is and what He does for me. I say, out loud, I trust my God, Who, is always there for me, I place my confidence in Him for He is my Fortress, He is Who I go to for help, He is Who I lean and rely on. I must talk about God's news over any other news and place my trust only in His news. I say it, I hear it, I believe it. And nothing else I hear or see will I believe over God and what He says. Nor do I go about saying what those other news and stories are saying or doing but I continue to say what God says and what God does. I make what God says, His side of the story, the final authority in my life and in every area regardless of any other news, any other reports, or any other side. It has brought me peace and it can bring anyone peace, true peace, peace not known by the world or any other news. Isaiah 26:3-4 GW says:

"With perfect peace You will protect those whose minds cannot be changed, because they trust You. Trust the Lord always, because the Lord, the Lord alone, is an everlasting rock." And Philippians 4:6-7 GW says: ***"Never worry about anything. But in every situation let God know what you need in prayers and requests while giving thanks. Then God's peace, which goes beyond anything we can imagine, will guard your thoughts and emotions through Christ Jesus."*** When we learn God can be trusted, we learn there is no need to worry because we know God will come through for us each and every time. We know we can go to Him in prayer and make our requests to Him because He is always faithful to answer. So rather than being moved by any other news or reports, we remain peaceful and thankful because God responds to His own, God always responds to His children. Knowing we are His child, knowing our identity is in Him, helps keep us grounded and understanding God will come through for us each and every time. God always keeps His Word and God always keeps His promises to us, which He lets us know through His Word and through directly communicating with us. Psalms 28:7 TPT says: ***"Yahweh [God] is my strength and my wraparound shield. When I fully trust in You, help is on the way. I jump for joy and burst forth with ecstatic, passionate praise! I will sing songs of what You mean to me!"*** We can sing forth fully confident in knowing God will always be there for us and is protective of His children. He wants us to always realize He is and continually remind ourselves. It is imperative we keep His Word, keep what He tells us before us because the world has many distractions and stories that can contradict God's. We must be fully persuaded at all times that God remains faithful to His children and He and His Word can be trusted. It provides us with strength when we do and keeps us focused on God and His side of the story. God wants us to know Him as well as He knows Himself. God wants us to see things as

He does at all times. 2 Thessalonians 3:3 AMPC says: ***"Yet the Lord is faithful, and He will strengthen [you] and set you on a firm foundation and guard you from the evil [one]."*** And Deuteronomy 32:4 NKJV tells us: ***"He is the Rock, His work is perfect; for all His ways are justice, a God of truth and without injustice; righteous and upright is He."*** And the NLT says: ***"He is a faithful God Who does no wrong; how just and upright He is!"*** And the GNT lets us know: ***"The Lord is your mighty defender, perfect and just in all His ways; Your God is faithful and true; He does what is right and fair."*** And Deuteronomy 7:9 NLT says: ***"Understand, therefore, that the Lord your God is indeed God. He is the faithful God Who keeps His covenant for a thousand generations and lavishes His unfailing love on those who love Him and obey His commands."*** No matter how many times other people have failed us, God will not. He means what He says every time and He is consistent in what He says every time. His very nature is moral, right, and fair and He sets the standard of what is moral, right, and fair. It is His standard He wants us to understand as His children and then learn to walk in the same standard as He does. He wants us to accept His standard as our own.

God wants us to learn His thoughts and His ways so we can then walk in His ways because we have learned to think like He does. He has shared all this with us in His Word. He has shared His plan with us but in His goodness and love He has given us the free will to choose. God knows there will be many stories, news, and influences trying to convince us to not go with Him but He still trusts us to make the right choice. He has given us the means to do so. God fully understands Romans 6:23 NKJV: ***"For the wages of sin is death, but the gift of God is eternal life in Christ Jesus our Lord."*** And TPT says: ***"For sin's meager wages is death, but God's lavish gift is eternal, found in your union with***

our Lord Jesus, the Anointed One." God knows the cost of choosing the wrong side, of choosing to not go with His side. Yet, He has given us a way out, He has given us a payout because He paid for our sins upfront through Jesus' death on the cross, His descent into hell and then His resurrection. God gave us the gift in His Son which enabled us the gift of repentance. He is just waiting for people to repent and turn to Him and receive the gift of His Son, Jesus Christ. God has been alive much longer than us, the ones He created. He has watched how we turned away from Him and turned to sin, how we can and have been deceived by satan, ourselves, and others. And He wants us to know Him and His side of the story because it is for our good. He wants us to see through His eyes, see ourselves as His precious children, and how precious we are to Him. 2 Petter 3:9 AMPC tells us: ***"The Lord does not delay and is not tardy or slow about what He promises, according to some people's conception of slowness, but He is long-suffering (extraordinarily patient) toward you, not desiring that any should perish, but that all should turn to repentance."*** And the GNT says: ***"The Lord is not slow to do what He has promised, as some think. Instead, He is patient with you, because He does not want anyone to be destroyed, but wants all to turn away from their sins."*** Notice, it says God wants all to turn away from sin, He wants all to repent because He does not want anyone to perish. God did not pick a sin or sins that someone had done and say that person did not deserve to repent. Nor did God pick out a person He thought did not deserve repentance. Instead, He gave us all the gift of repentance just as He gave us all the gift of His Son, Jesus. God knew the cost and wanted to provide the freedom from death and He did. We repent by changing how we think about sin to how God thinks about sin. When we change how we think about sin, we then change how we act by acting like God would act and not sin. We have to see sin like God sees sin and then respond to sin like God responds. In essence, we exchange our thoughts for God's and our ways for His ways. When we realize our identity as God sees us, we realize we need to think and act like our Father. We realize we will be giving up death for life. We make the choice to want to think and act like our Father, God, over how the world and satan wants us to think and act. And then we make the choice to think and act like our Father, God.

As we make the choice to think and act like God, we do not want people to go on sinning because God does not want anyone to go on sinning. We see the cost as God sees. We see the benefits of not sinning as God sees. We see the exchange we made for death to life as He sees. We see how Jesus provided the way as God sees. We see how repentance lets people turn away from sin and turn to Jesus and follow His and God's ways. And we want the same for others just as God does. We exchange our will to His will regarding not wanting anyone to perish. To help make this point clearer, the Lord recalled to my remembrance a story I heard through Kenneth Copeland Ministries. I tell this story to not evoke any fear nor any other emotion but to emphasize how God has His side to a story, even this story. And how God wants us to seek Him for His side especially if no one is reporting His side. He may need us to report His side so others can know Him and can begin following Him and His ways. I want people to see how God can operate, how we can operate when we know who we are in Him. This story is from 1981 when Stephen Morin, who was on the FBI's ten most wanted list for being a serial killer, kidnapped Margy Palm in San Antonio, Texas. Though Margy described Stephen as looking "like a rapid dog" and there was a "strong satanic presence" on him, God was about to work in his life. Even though Stephen had done some horrible things and was planning on continuing, God had different plans. God saw

Stephen as someone He did not desire should perish, but that he should turn to repentance. What Stephen did not know was Margy knew who she was through God's eyes. When Margy left her home that day, Holy Spirit had prompted her to bring some tapes from Kenneth Copeland's teachings and a scripture book. And when Stephen kidnapped her, she could tangibly feel the fear gripping her but she did not yield to the fear. Rather, she asked Stephen if he knew Jesus and began to share Jesus with him. Margy even boldly prayed for Stephen taking authority over the demonic influence he was under. She read from her scripture book and played some of Kenneth Copeland's teachings and Stephen heard what Jesus had done for him because of God's love. Unknown to Margy, at that time, Stephen heard an audible voice that said, "This is the last time I am going to call you." Stephen then gave his life to Jesus and became saved and redeemed from all of his sins. Margy could see a tangible change come over him. The darkness that filled his eyes was gone and was replaced with God's light and love. Stephen's ex-wife had faithfully been praying for him. And now "grace had taken one of the worst in society and washed him white as snow." Stephen emptied his gun of the bullets, let Margy go, and wanted to turn himself in. After he was picked up by the police, he willingly accepted the judgment for his crimes and went to death row, but he went a changed man. He met Kenneth Copeland who continued to mentor him. Stephen continually got into God's Word, learning more about God's side of the story that had now become his side of the story, and he told others about God, His Word, and His Son even while on death row. He had exchanged death for life. Though his life was sentenced to death for crimes he committed, he was experiencing, and would for eternity, God's ways and His abundant life.

Most people would see this story only from the natural point and only from the sides that were reporting the story. People would have heard the news and responded through their emotions and how they felt after hearing the news. Only by hearing the story through Kenneth Copeland Ministries did I know the story according to God's side as seen through God's eyes. God in His justness does not want anyone harmed nor does He want anyone harming others. Death and destruction are satan's ways and his nature. Margy could see the "strong satanic influence" Stephen was under and how his appearance reflected this. God does not approve of people being serial killers after all He is the One who put "thou shalt not kill" as number six in His ten commandments. Stephen's ex-wife had faithfully been praying for Stephen and had not given up on him being saved. Her prayers were going to a good, loving, faithful, and trustworthy God. God does not approve of people being kidnapped nor is it ever His will. However, Margy finding herself in that situation did not yield to the fear she was feeling. Instead, she yielded to the Spirit of God she knew and took her authority over satan's influence in Stephen's life. She saw God's side of the story and knew there was more to what she was seeing and feeling in the natural. Margy told Stephen about Jesus because she knew Jesus could change his life. She shared teachings about Jesus because her life had been changed and she knew who she was to God. She knew how to act and respond like God's child. God wanted Stephen to repent and turn to Jesus. God saw Stephen as worthy of being saved though He did let him know He was giving him one more chance. God did not want Stephen to continue hurting and killing others. And Stephen had a choice and he chose to repent and accept Jesus. He had heard Margy pray and talk about Jesus and he had heard the tapes of Kenneth Copeland teachings. Kenneth Copeland, who was already cooperating with God and His ways, was spreading God's Word to others through teaching and preaching. And seeing this story through God's eyes, Kenneth Copeland went on to mentor Stephen while he was in prison. God needs people, He needs us, to know and cooperate with Him and His side of the story. God does not want anyone to perish, it is a part of His goodness, it is a part of His will, it is a part of His ways, it is a part of His side of the story. He understands the end game and that it is for eternity. He knows all that we see now will one day be no more and there will be those who will spend eternity with Him or spend eternity without Him. God wants everyone to turn away from evil, from sin, and turn toward Him and the life they can have through His Son, Jesus. God wants us to experience His goodness now and live in His goodness by living in His ways, by seeing through His eyes, by knowing who we are in Him. Yet, He will not look at evil forever allowing evil to prevail. He will have a say and step in, especially when those who do know Him pray and know how to pray.

Lamentations 3:22-23 NLT tells us: ***"The faithful love of the Lord never ends! His mercies never cease. Great is His faithfulness; His mercies begin afresh each morning."*** The ESV says: ***"The steadfast love of the Lord never ceases; His mercies never come to an end; they are new every morning; great is [His] faithfulness."*** And the GNT says: ***"The Lord's unfailing love and mercy still continue."*** While the MSG says: ***"God's loyal love could not have run out, His merciful love could not have dried up. They are created new every morning. How great Your faithfulness!"*** God shows us mercy by not giving us the judgments, the punishment we deserve but rather extending His love to us. We did not deserve Jesus and what He did for us but God sent Him anyway and Jesus did what He did for us anyway. God is loyal and faithful, and His love is not like man's. I believe people are searching for what is missing in their lives and trying to fill what is missing with all types of things which can sometimes lead to death and destruction. And sometimes people are hurting and trying to get the pain to stop while searching for ways or means to do this. Yet, what is missing in their lives is God and He is the One Who can heal the pain and hurt. He is the One Who leads to Jesus because Jesus is the One Who leads them back to God. Fellowship with God and being in right standing with Him is a part of being God's child and understanding this is a part of our identity.

God extends His forgiveness to us because of His love for us. Being forgiven of our sins, allows us to get close to God. He sees us as forgiven and wants us to see ourselves the same. He wants us to see ourselves through His eyes, through what Jesus provided for us, and how we regain our rightful standing with Him. God makes it simple when man can make it hard. God spoke to Stephen who yielded to Him and was saved not because he was good but because God is. Stephen was able to change his identity by becoming God's child. He did not have to clean himself up because the blood of Jesus did that for him. All he had to do was repent and receive Jesus and begin walking in his new identity. When he did, he received God's forgiveness. All any of us have to do is repent and receive Jesus and begin walking in our new identity. When we do, we receive God's forgiveness, the moment we repent. We have to change the way we see and think about ourselves to the way God sees us and thinks about us. He sees us through the finished work of what Jesus did for us and He receives and accepts us as His child, which we are. Picture a baby being born and then handed to his father. The father does not hesitate in taking his child. He does not have to think about it or make the child wait, even to be cleaned up. His love for the child is already there, he has given his child his name, he has fully accepted the child into the family and sees the child as his own. He plans on teaching his child what he knows and letting him know what it means to be a part of the family. He is looking forward to spending time with him and enjoy watching him grow. When the father looks at his child, he sees the child that he loves. When God looks at us, He sees the child that He loves. He is not looking at our mess ups like we or others may rather He is looking at His child He loves, His child who He wants to grow up in His ways, to know what it means to be a part of His family, a child who He can spend time with and wants to spend time with Him. God wants a mutual fellowship with His children which we can have with Him any time we want. Psalms 86:5 NLT says: ***"O Lord, You are so good, so ready to forgive, so full of unfailing love for all who ask for Your help."*** And the AMPC says: ***"For You, O Lord are good, and ready to forgive [our trespasses, sending them away, letting them go completely and forever]; and You are abundant in mercy and loving-kindness to all those who call upon You."*** Anyone can call upon God and receive His goodness, His love, His mercy but you must be willing to call upon Him and you must then receive from Him. People and people's love can be circumstantial or conditional. You can be liked or not liked by people based on your looks or what you have to offer or not offer or if you have a title or any number of factors. But God's love remains the same, steady, love that you can always count on. A steady love that gave us Jesus releasing God's forgiveness to us. God has always and will always be here for us. Deuteronomy 31:8 NLT tells us: ***"Do not be afraid or discouraged, for the Lord will personally go ahead of you. He will be with you; He will neither fail you nor abandon you."*** GNT says: ***"The Lord Himself will lead you and be with you. He will not fail you or abandon you, so do not lose courage or be afraid."*** There is no reason to ever fear or be discouraged because God is always with us and is always willing to lead and guide us. No matter what news or stories that may bring fear or discouragement we have God's News, we have His side to the story so we can remain encouraged and full of His love. We can remain rest assured knowing who we are and that our identity is in being God's child. We know Him and we know He takes care of His children.

Our role to play in all this is to not believe any lies regardless of how convincing they may appear. We have to make a firm commitment to always go with God and with what He says. People can be drawn into believing lies told by news, stories, teachings, or reports given that contradict God and His ways. People can act out in various ways because they have believed the lies or they have been hurt and are responding from the hurt. People can see God as they see people and not truly realize Who God is and who they are to Him. However, it is imperative that we realize Who God is and trust in Him regardless. We must fully understand we are His children and all that goes with being His child and then not allow ourselves to hand over our rights as His children. I can be given a will with all the rights and possessions listed in the will. Instead of accepting and getting all the will offers me, I make the choice to sign everything over to someone else. I can think I did not deserve it or I can believe there is something better and this is in the way of getting what I think is better or I can think any number of other things other than this is mine and I receive it. I must choose to listen to God in every instance no matter what may be said that contradicts what God is saying or Who He is or who I am as His child. James 4:8 NLT says: ***"Come close to God, and God will come close to you. Wash your hands, you sinners, purify your hearts, for your loyalty is divided between God and the world."*** I do not wash myself to be clean and acceptable to God, the blood of Jesus did that for me. Rather, I wash myself of sin and following the world's way and satan's way of doing things. I can keep my hands dirty by continuing to make the decision to sin or I can wash my hands by making the decision to not sin. I can draw close to God instead knowing He will draw close to me. In this closeness, I can get to know Him, His nature, His ways, and accept His love for me which compels me to want to please Him and not this world or anyone else, especially if they are being influenced by satan. The RIV says: ***"Come extremely close to the presence of God, and He will respond by coming extremely close to you. And to those of you who are blowing it in so many ways – I mean, you are sinning and really missing the mark of what God approves and wants for your lives – it is time for you to come clean! You need to make a decision to do whatever is necessary to cleanse your hands – and by hands, I mean your entire lives. Oh, you double-minded – those of you who cannot seem to make up your mind to live single-minded for God alone and free from the world; It is time for you to make a final decision to purposefully cleanse and sanctify yourselves – and I mean all the way to the very deepest parts of your inner beings."*** God understands what sin does to someone, He understands what it means to be apart from Him, He understands what being in love with the world does to a person and He does not want this for His children. God understands what following the father of this world, satan (the devil), means and how crafty he can be to make this world and the ways of this world look appealing and attractive. But God sees through the lie and wants us to see through the lie as well. He knows it is for our good, our safety, and our well-being when we do.

God knew satan before he became satan. God created him as an angelic being, who was to worship God. However, he turned from God and turned to evil becoming prideful by thinking he could replace God. There are many stories, news reports, religions, and ways of man today trying to do the same. As

God's children, we must remain firmly grounded and rooted in our identity and not be swayed away from God and His Truth, away from God and His ways, away from God and His Word, away from God and His side of the story. We must always be swayed to see ourselves and how we are to live, how we are to believe, how we are to act, how we are to talk according to God's way and how God sees. We must never allow rejection to get in our way by knowing God will never reject us. Jesus Himself was rejected even by those who should have recognized Him as God's Son. We need to see ourselves as God's children just as Jesus did and live in our identity as God's children just as Jesus did, even if it may cause some to reject us. We must accept and love Jesus as much as we accept and love God and reject the god of this world, satan (the devil), along with his ways, just as God and Jesus reject him and his ways. John 8:42-44 GNT makes the point: ***"If God were your Father, you would love Me, for I proceed forth and came from God; nor have I come of Myself, but He sent Me. Why do you not understand My speech? Because you are not able to listen to My Word. You are the children of your father, the devil, and you want to follow your father's desires. From the very beginning he was a murderer and has never been on the side of truth because there is no truth in him. When he tells a lie, he is only doing what is natural to him, because he is a liar and the father of all lies."*** Whenever a lie is being told, no matter how big or small, because a lie remains a lie, satan is behind it. If a child of God is involved in a lie, he or she has just stepped over into satan's realm, his territory, and is partnering with satan by being involved in the lie. You can be God's child and still make choices to line up with satan and his lies over God in certain situations or in believing differently about something. It is like you are traveling down a road, you know you are you, you know what family you belong to, and you make a decision to veer slightly off course. You can easily realize this and redirect yourself back on the right road. Or you can decide to keep going, decide to keep believing satan's lies, so you travel further and further away from your original road and destination. You can see other people traveling on this same road and think it must be okay or you can even encounter some friends so you decide to keep traveling down this other road. You can keep going on and on until you do not recognize the territory you are traveling through but you have accepted this as your new road and have not considered where it leads. And at some point, you go so far that you fail to even recognize yourself but have adapted to your surroundings by liking and accepting what the new territory has to offer. But when you repent, you change your course back to the correct road, back to God's path, back to His ways. You can make the choice to not take any side roads but remain on the road, remain on the path by continually choosing God and His ways over any other ways, over the ways of this world, over the ways of satan. By believing God's Truth over satan's lies, including about yourself, you remain secure on the correct road that provides life and life full of abundance.

God sent Jesus to reveal the way we are to go, to direct us down the right road. And Jesus came to lead the way we are to go by showing us the correct road, by leading us to God, by revealing God to us, and revealing who we are to God. Jesus came to show us God's side of the story and how we are to see things through His eyes. God knew to know Him we must get to know and accept Jesus, His Son. And Jesus knew He had to go do what God wanted Him to do. He knew He had to show us how we can live by God's Truth, live in God's ways. Jesus came to let us know that His side of the story is God's side of the story, making it only One side, God's. He came to show us how He knew Who He was because His identity was firm in Him being God's Son, even when others failed to believe. And He, as well as God, wants us to be equally firm in our identity in being God's son, in being God's daughter, even when others may not see us the same way or may reject us. Jesus knew He could only carry out God's plan to bring us back into being in right standing with God. We must fully understand and receive God's love for us and not allow any other love, or any lies about love, to take precedent. Because Romans 5:8 NKJV tells us: ***"But God demonstrates His own love toward us, in that while we were still sinners, Christ died for us."*** Jesus did what only He could do for us because God loves us that much. And regardless of what story or news or any attempts to influence us, we must stand firm in who we are in God and who we are through Jesus. 1 John 3:1 NKJV lets us know: ***"Behold, what manner of love the Father [God] has bestowed on us, that we should be called children of God! Therefore, the world does not know us, because it did not know Him"*** As God's children, we are supposed to be set apart from the world because God's children are to look and sound like Him and not the world. God's children are to believe like Him and live like His Son, Jesus. Ephesians 5:1 NKJV says: ***"Therefore, be imitators of God as dear children."*** We are to see God as being our Father just as Jesus did and then live like we are His children, just as Jesus did. He wants us to receive and live in God's love just like He did. Jesus fully understood Psalms 136: 1-4 NLT that says: ***"Give thanks to the Lord, for He is good! His faithful love endures forever. Give thanks to the God of gods. His faithful love endures forever. Give thanks to the Lord of lords. His faithful love endures forever. Give thanks to Him Who alone does mighty miracles. His faithful love endures forever."*** When we can understand God and Who He is, we can understand who we are. We can begin to see every story, every news, every report through God's eyes, according to His side. We can live our lives by living in and only in God's ways continually giving thanks to Him.

CHAPTER 2

Jesus the Ultimate Influencer

IT MAKES A DIFFERENCE who you allow to influence you. With all the various influences in society, especially with the rise of the internet and technology, there are many stories, many news reports, many opinions, and many sides for everything regardless of the topic. Yet, God always has His side for everything and every topic. You can look up one thing and find many opinions, many sides telling you how to believe and sometimes these opinions and sides can change with time. Take coffee for instance. You find many reports that coffee is just as good for you as it is bad for you. There are even reports on when you should drink it and how many cups per day. There are varying opinions of how you should process coffee and which coffee is better. There are even reports on who should drink it and who should avoid it. However, coffee is still coffee, so is coffee bad or good or even something else? Do you add up all the good reports versus the bad reports and the most reports on one side wins? Do you allow your opinion of coffee to be based on popular opinion or based on personal experience or because of someone you know or according to where you live? Do you even like coffee? If you do like coffee, can you image anyone else not liking coffee? If you drink coffee, how do you like your coffee because there are different types, blends, and roasts of coffee? And what about culture, does it play a role? What if more people like coffee than those who do not or the reverse? Does God have something to say? Where does Jesus enter the mix or does He? Do They care about coffee?

I started drinking coffee when I was two and it was because of the influence from both of my grandmothers. I grew up spending a lot of time with both and split a lot of my summers between staying with them. They lived in the same town so my sharing my time with them was made easy. At that time, I was the youngest grandchild for my maternal grandmother and the only grandchild for my paternal grandmother. Both grandmothers liked their coffee and would both give me almost anything I wanted. My wanting to try coffee was a definite yes when I asked them. Not only did I get to try it, but I liked it. And now I was getting to drink coffee with them both. Thus, a long journey with me and coffee started with many, many mornings beginning my day with coffee and many of my days consisting of drinking coffee throughout the day. Decades of drinking coffee and thinking that I needed coffee to start the day and my wanting my day to start with coffee. I liked, liked, liked coffee. I liked the smell, the feel of the cup in my hands, the taste, I liked the whole experience of it. Until one day, I heard the Lord, God, ask me if I would give up coffee. And though I had a long-standing relationship with coffee because I was well into adulthood, I immediately heard myself answer with a yes. Followed by but I need Your help. I had heard if you stopped drinking coffee it would give you headaches and you should not just stop drinking it but taper off and how breaking habits were hard and sometimes people could not do it. And then there were the thoughts of well now how do I relate to my coffee drinking friends, how do I start my day, how am I going to function in the morning, can this really be done because I have been drinking coffee since I was two, and my whole adult life has been spent drinking lots and lots of coffee, not to mention, I really like it. Yet, Jesus. He did exactly what God asked of Him and He is my example. I had started to learn (am still learning) that He is more than enough. I had started to learn (am still learning) to allow Him to be the One Who influences me, especially given the magnitude of His ultimate sacrifice that He made for me, personally, and for anyone else who will accept Him and what He has done. Because I had started the journey of learning and understanding 2 Corinthians 5:15 NLT: ***"He died for everyone so that those who receive His new life will no longer live for themselves. Instead, they will live for Christ, Who, died and was raised for them."*** Jesus did not just die for me so I could go on and live my life unchanged, live my life for myself, live my life how the world, through the influence of satan, says I should live. Nor live according to what I like and want to do regardless of what God may say. Jesus died for me out of love so I could live and not die so I could live the good, fruitful life God always planned for me to live. Jesus showed that I can live for God and He showed how vast and wonderful that life is. He showed me to not buy into satan's lies and the lies displayed through other reports or stories but to believe in and live out the truth of God. And I can do this by allowing Jesus to be my influencer. And Jesus wants to be everyone's influencer.

Now I am by no means giving an opinion on coffee and whether or not you should drink it. God spoke directly to me and I only do what He tells me. Please keep drinking coffee if you like it and know that He does not tell everyone to stop drinking it. If you enjoy it, enjoy it. Have a cup while you are reading. Nor am I looking to compare Jesus to coffee though I have seen various memes, signs and shirts that make such references as "give me coffee and Jesus" or "I just need coffee and Jesus" or "I start my day with coffee and Jesus." Nor am I looking to poke fun of anyone or slam some marketing strategy but I have learned to value my Jesus above all and give Him His proper honor in my life, give Him His proper honor in my speech, give Him His proper honor in my likes and dislikes, give Him His proper honor in my decisions regardless of how big or small and regardless of others' opinions. I am not flawless in this but my heart is all in to wanting to be, to wanting to do right by Jesus and wanting to learn His ways, His side of the story so I can make His ways, His side of the story my own because His side is God's side. I want Him to be my ultimate influencer in all things. Jesus always followed God. Knowing Jesus did I can. Even if that side is, God wanting me to give up something that I like, like coffee, because He asked me to. And doing so without knowing the reason He had asked. He did not say why and to this day I have not felt led to ask why. This coming from someone who was the why kid growing up because I was always asking why to everything even on into adulthood. I now value what God says and what Jesus says above needing to know the why behind it. Because though I was still a sinner, Jesus died for me. Though I deserved to die Jesus, Who, did not deserve to die chose and did die for me. Jesus made a choice to submit His will to God's. God had a plan for us and Jesus was a part of that plan. And when Jesus was faced with the reality of the final part of the plan starting to unfold, He did not fall under the pressure, but Jesus declared in Luke 22:42 NLT: ***"Father, if You are willing, please take this cup of suffering away from Me. Yet I want Your will to be done, not Mine."*** Jesus does not want me to fall under the pressures of this world, this culture, nor satan and his lies and tactics. Nor does Jesus want me to be influenced by what may be considered popular or unpopular, what is socially acceptable or not acceptable, nor by any other influences except Him. He wants my identity to be so grounded in Who He is and what He has done for me that I remain as unmoved in this world and it's influences as He did. Because Jesus' side of the story always remains the same as God's side of the story.

John 5:19 NLT says: ***"So Jesus explained, 'I tell you the truth, the Son can do nothing by Himself. He does only what He sees the Father doing. Whatever the Father does, the Son also does."*** Jesus made God His ultimate influencer allowing God to influence every decision and every area of His life, including submitting His will to God's. Because Jesus will only do what God does, He wants to be our influencer. Jesus was so confidant in being God's Son that He knew it was important to follow God and do as God did. Philippians 2:5-8 TPT tell us: ***"And consider the example that Jesus, the Anointed One, has set before us. Let His mindset become your motivation. He existed in the form of God, yet He gave no thought to seizing equality with God as His supreme prize. Instead, He emptied himself of His outward glory by reducing Himself to the form of a lowly servant. He became human! He humbled Himself and became vulnerable, choosing to be revealed as a man and was obedient. He was a perfect example, even in His death—a criminal's death by crucifixion!"*** The MSG says: ***"Think of yourselves the way Christ Jesus thought of Himself. He had equal status with God but did not think so much of Himself that He had to cling to the advantages of that status no matter what. Not at all.***

When the time came, He set aside the privileges of deity and took on the status of a slave, became human! Having become human, He stayed human. It was an incredibly humbling process. He did not claim special privileges. Instead, He lived a selfless, obedient life and then died a selfless, obedient death—and the worst kind of death at that—a crucifixion." And verse 6 in GNT says: ***"He always had the nature of God."*** Knowing Jesus has God's nature should make me want to make Him my ultimate influencer. 2 Corinthians 5:21 NLT tells us: ***"For God made Christ, Who, never sinned, to be the sin offering for our sin, so that we could be made right with God through Christ."*** Jesus did what He did so I could be made right with God. Thank You, God, and thank You, Jesus. Through God's and Jesus' combined story, I was able to be saved so my story could be written anew. So, I could live out my new story by thriving in who I am as God's child thanks to Jesus. Allowing Him to define me rather than anyone else. Because Acts 17:28 TPT says: ***"It is through Him [Jesus] that we live and function and have our identity, just as your own poets have said, 'Our lineage comes from Him.'"*** Jesus changed the very origin of my ancestry to God's. My genealogy now reads: God, Jesus, and me. I have full access to God and all He has and all He is and all He has for me thanks to Jesus. Jesus made a way and it is only through Him. I have to fully accept and walk in this new genealogy. I have to walk in my new identity as God's child.

Regardless of the world having many opinions, reports, sides, cultures, and even religions about how they see you or want to define you, it does not matter. Nor does what they say about God, who He is and how to get to Him matter. It only matters what Jesus says. John 14:6 TPT makes it clear: ***"Jesus explained, 'I am the Way, the Truth, and I am the Life. No one comes next to the Father except through union with Me. To know Me is to know***

My Father too. And the MSG says: ***"Jesus said, 'I am the Road, also the Truth, also the Life. No one gets to the Father apart from Me. If you really knew Me, you would know My Father as well.'"*** There is only one way to God and it is through Jesus, there are no exceptions, there are no alternative plans, there are no other stories, there is no one else that will get you to God but Jesus; it is through Jesus that you can obtain the life God intends for you to have and it is a life to be lived now and for eternity. To live apart from Jesus is to live apart from God. John 17:3 NLT tells us: ***"And this is the way to have eternal life – to know You, the only true God, and Jesus Christ, the One You sent to earth."*** The GNT informs us: ***"And eternal life means to know You, the only true God, and to know Jesus Christ, Whom You sent."*** We can begin our eternal journey now by knowing Jesus, Whom God sent directly to you, to me, to anyone who will receive Him. And by knowing Jesus we can know God Who is the One true God. By understanding and getting to know Jesus and God, we get to know ourselves because our lineage comes from Them. Through Jesus, we can know God's report, His side of the story over all others because Jesus came to reveal God's side of the story to us. And it is a good life leading to good things. Not believing Jesus and not living your life influenced by Him can lead to a bad life and bad things. In John 10:9 NKJV, Jesus tells us: ***"I am the door. If anyone enters by Me, he will be saved and will go in and out and find pasture."*** The world and all their news and stories, with satan who often is behind influencing them, wants bad for us, wants harm for us, and often craftily disguises his plans to make them look good, make them look pleasing, and sometimes popular. For it is revealed in John 10:10 NKJV: ***"The thief [satan] does not come except to steal, and to kill, and to destroy. I [Jesus] have come that they [you and me] have it [life] more abundantly."*** The AMPC says: ***"I [Jesus] came that they may have and enjoy life,***

and have it in abundance (to the full, till it overflows). The NKJV says: ***"I [Jesus] have come that they may have life, and that they may have it more abundantly."*** And TPT says: ***"But I [Jesus] have come to give you everything in abundance, more than you expect – life in its fullness until you overflow!"*** Jesus' side of the story is that He came to give us a life, a life now here on earth, that is amply supplied, a life that is abounding, and is greatly plentiful in every area of our lives. Jesus came to give us a life that is so full and overflowing that we have more than enough to share with others around us. He supplies us so we can be fully supplied and be able to supply others. He gives so we can receive and can give to others. The world's side of the story will say take and take and take, even at the cost of others. Jesus' side tells us He gave His all and gifted us His best in all we need so we can then give to others, not from lacking, but from an abundant supply and giving our best. Have you ever done a gift exchange and gone out and gotten the best gift? There was a price limit but you spent a couple dollars more because you knew the person receiving the gift would really like what you bought and it would really mean something to that person. And then in return you got a gift that did not cost but a couple of dollars compared to the price limit and you knew no thought or real attention went into buying your gift because not only did it have a far less value it ended up being something that did not even come close to what you liked or what you would have bought for yourself. People often give less but take more. They want to get the really, nice gift while giving the really, not so nice gift. Would you go buy a brand-new coat and give it away or would you give your old coat away and then buy yourself a new one? Yet, God did not withhold anything from us, He gave His best in giving us His Son. He knew it was going to take His best and He willingly gave knowing we would not be able to give anything in return but only be willing to receive His best, Jesus. There was and is nothing we can or could give God to do what Jesus did. Nor anything we could do except what Jesus did. And Jesus willing became God's best gift and carried out God's plan, God's side of the story all for you and all for me. He chose to be God's plan for us. How then can I not make the choice to allow Jesus to be the One Who influences me so that I play my part in carrying out God's plan, carrying out God's side of the story, showing God's side of the story in how I live my life each and every day? Jesus made the choice to live according to God's side of the story, living as God sees, so I can choose to do the same. I can trust God and I can trust Jesus with my life by following Jesus because it leads to the best and truly good life. 1 Corinthians 1:9 NKJV tells us: ***"God is faithful, by Whom you were called into the fellowship of His Son, Jesus Christ our Lord."*** And the GNT says: ***"God is to be trusted, the God Who called you to have fellowship with His Son Jesus Christ, our Lord."*** And the MSG says: "***God, Who, got you started in this spiritual adventure, shares with us the life of His Son and our Master Jesus. He will never give up on you. Never forget that.***" He will never give up on anyone. He will always be a good, sharing, caring, and loving God and so will Jesus. And Jesus wants us to follow Him by doing the same.

What news and reports you believe has an impact on your life. God, through Jesus, wants you to always believe and respond according to His side of the story. He understands the importance of having a belief system in place so when you are presented with facts and information that goes against God's Truth, His Word, His Ways, you will remain steadfast in following God and following Jesus. Psalms 119:1-5 NLT tells us: ***"Joyful are people of integrity, who follow the instruction of the Lord. Joyful are those who obey His laws and search for Him with all their heart. They do not compromise with evil, and they walk only in His paths.***

You have charged us to keep your commandments carefully. Oh, that my actions would consistently reflect your decrees!" Jesus showed His love for His Father God by doing what God told Him to do and upholding what God said was right and wrong and not what man, or even the religious leaders of that time, or what any cultural norms said was right or wrong. What God said was the final and only say for Jesus. God's commands became Jesus' commands. And Jesus wants that to be how we live. He made it clear in John 14:21 NLT: ***"Those who accept My commandments and obey them are the ones who love Me. And because they love Me, My Father will love them. And I will love them and reveal Myself to each of them."*** And in John 15:9-10 NLT: ***"I have loved you even as the Father has loved Me. Remain in My love. When you obey My Father's commandments, you remain in My love, just as I obey My Father's commandments and remain in His love."*** We position ourselves to fully receive the combined love of God the Father and Jesus the Son when we allow Jesus to be the One to influence us and our decisions and we follow God's commands as He did. What Jesus says reigns above what anyone else says, regardless of the role someone has in our life. Jesus will always follow God and His ways and will always direct us to do the same, no exceptions.

When satan appeared to Adam and Eve, he gave them a different report, a different type of story, a different type of news that contradicted God. Yet, Eve engaged in a conversation with satan and allowed herself to question what God had said. While Adam stood by listening without saying anything. The result was that Adam and Eve were deceived and acted on this deception (see Genesis 3). They did so by going against God's side of the story thus creating their own side of the story which then lined up with satan's side. This marked the separation of man from God due to the sin agreement Adam and Eve entered with satan. They forfeited their God given authority and bought the lie of satan. This is still being played out today. People are buying the lies of satan and acting on those lies by believing the wrong side of the story. Thankfully, Jesus came to establish what was lost by Adam and Eve. When satan appeared to Jesus, he gave Jesus a different report, a different type of story, a different type of news. Yet, Jesus immediately answered satan with God's Word. He did not engage in pleasantries. Jesus knew God's Word, God's side of the story and had already made God's side His side. Jesus was not going to be moved by what satan said. And Jesus did not just pick out anything in God's Word to say but He said exactly what was needed to counter what satan had said. Jesus spoke the Truth of God's Word over the lie of satan. Jesus knew a lie to God is a lie and there are no small lies or partial lies because to God all lies are lies. Jesus also knew about satan and what he stands for and how he is against God. Jesus knew satan will try to deceive people, often doing so with slight suggestions that may sound appealing. Jesus knew about God's Kingdom and God's Word and He knew how greater God's Kingdom and God's Word was over all else. And unlike Adam and Eve, Jesus had been alone in the wilderness for forty days without any food. When satan said to Jesus, ***"If you are the Son of God, command that these stones become bread."*** Jesus immediately said, ***"It is written, 'Man shall not live by bread alone, but by every word that proceeds from the mouth of God.'"*** (see Matthew 4:1-11 NKJV) Jesus walked on this earth as a man, who felt hunger and tiredness, but He knew the value of God's Word, of God's side over satan's side or any other side. He knew not to yield to any feelings or anything that was temporary. Jesus knew Who He was and He did not have to prove Himself to satan. Two more times satan tried to get Jesus to go against God's Words and His side of the story and two more times Jesus immediately answered satan with what God's Word said compared to what satan was saying. And satan immediately left. And satan will do the same when we do the same as Jesus. Jesus knew the power of God's Word over satan and that there was no comparison nor will there ever be. And Jesus knew He came to be our example, to be our influencer over satan and his lies. Jesus came to fully restore what was lost by Adam and Eve and give us back the authority we have in this earth, even over satan. Jesus came to be our bread, to bring us life, the life more abundant.

This world is not rooting for you or me nor is satan. Even though the world (culture norms, media, among other things) tell us how to live, how to act, how to "just be you", how to "do what feels good", or "feels right to you", we are always to do what Jesus did and follow God's commands, follow Jesus' commands. Regardless of how popular something may be or how many people may approve (including how many social media likes you may get), no means no to God and no means no to Jesus. If God tells us not to do something, it means Jesus is saying the same, and we are to say the same. No matter how popular or how much approval someone has, only Jesus could have done for us what He did. So, it stands to reason, Jesus should always be the One we follow and allow to be our influencer. Romans 5:8-11 NLT tells us: ***"When we were utterly helpless, Christ came at just the right time and died for us sinners. Now, most people would not be willing to die for an upright person, though someone might perhaps be willing to die for a person who is especially good. But God showed His great love for us by sending Christ to die for us while we were still sinners. And since we have been made right in God's sight by the blood of Christ, He will certainly save us from God's condemnation. For since our friendship with God was restored by the death of His Son while we were still His enemies,***

we will certainly be saved through the life of His Son. So now we can rejoice in our wonderful new relationship with God because our Lord Jesus Christ has made us friends of God." God knew we needed saving and Jesus knew too. Two wills merging into One for our benefit. Both knowing there was only One plan and One way for this to occur, only one story and that story was through Jesus. We should be friends with God, friends with Jesus and not friends with this world nor allow any friends in this world to get us to agree to anything that goes against God and His ways. Because 1 Peter 3:18 NLT tells us: ***"Christ suffered for our sins once for all time. He never sinned, but He died for sinners to bring you safely home to God. He suffered physical death, but He was raised to life in the Spirit."*** Jesus did what only Jesus could do for us even when we did not deserve it. How can we not realize and then allow Jesus to be our influencer in all things? How can I not accept Him fully and all He did for me? God's side of the story is made easy in how one receives Jesus. God does not make it complicated or make it religious or set up a bunch of rules. He tells us how in Romans 10:9 NLT: ***"If you openly declare that Jesus is Lord and believe in your heart that God raised Him from the dead, you will be saved."*** Yes, when we do just that, we will be saved regardless of where we were born or currently live, regardless of our social status, regardless of our skin tone, regardless of our culture, regardless of what religion we may have believed prior, regardless if we believed God truly existed before, regardless of our age or gender, regardless of how we have sinned or for how long, and regardless if we have been rejected by others or who may accept us. We must believe what God said knowing that settles it regardless if someone says something different, even if that someone has a title that may give them some prominence or authority in this world or even in a church. God's side of the story is what we choose to believe each and every time. Romans 10:9-13 GNT even tell us: ***"If you confess that Jesus is Lord and believe that God raised Him from death, you will be saved. For it is by our faith that we are put right with God; it is by our confession that we are saved."*** Because once you make this declaration, you are made right with God immediately, even though you may not feel like it or even be recognized as such. We must go by what God says and what Jesus says. 1 John 4:15 GNT lets us know: ***"If we declare that Jesus is the Son of God, we live in union with God and God lives in union with us."*** And TPT says: ***"Those who give thanks that Jesus is the Son of God live in God, and God lives in them."*** We are to be thankful for Jesus and give thanks for Who He is and what He has done for us. When we realize Jesus is the One Who made it possible for us to become God's children, it should bring us to be thankful and give Him the proper thanks by verbalizing to Him and to God our thankfulness. As we do, it keeps in the forefront of our thoughts who we are and all we have thanks to Him. Jesus became the big Brother Who stepped in and took care of the business, that only He could take care of, on behalf of His younger siblings. He looked at us as His siblings long before going to the cross for us. It was like we were held captive, far away on an unknown island, completely lost and unaware of what Jesus was about to do, and there was only one way out, there was only one way home. And this only way was Jesus, our big Brother, Who was going to have to exchange His life for ours, He was going to have to die by going to the cross, going to hell, and then He would be raised back to life. He understood fully what it would cost but He understood even more what it would mean and do for us because we would be set free and be able to come home, be able to see our Father God, and have fellowship with Him. So, Jesus did it, He paid the price for us to be released and now we are thankful. We lift our voices in thanksgiving to Him for what He did for us. And when we do, it helps us realize how we share a mutual relationship with God, all thanks to Jesus. And it is a mutual relationship in which we can develop and have an intimate fellowship.

Once we are saved, once we get set free, thanks to Jesus, we can receive any healing or anything else we need. Because when Jesus went through everything He did for us, He provided us with more than the assurance that we would be set free from death and hell. He provided us with the more abundant life mentioned previously, because saved means so much more than just saved from sin. One must look at the word saved from the original translation which was in Greek because the New Testament of God's Word was originally written in Greek. And the word saved in Greek is the word *sozo* which means to rescue, protect, keep alive, preserve life, deliver, heal, and be made whole. Knowing that opens a whole new understanding of what you receive when you receive Jesus by declaring Him to be Lord and believing God raised Him from the dead because you will be saved, rescued, protected, kept alive, have a preserved life, delivered, healed, and be made whole. Hallelujah, that is worthy of shouting about and worthy of making Jesus the One Who is your ultimate influencer, and worthy of giving Him thanks. No one can do what Jesus has done. Before there were any news reports or other sides of the story God had already prepared and written His and written Jesus' side as He describes in Romans 8:29 NLT: ***"For God knew His people in advance, and He chose them to become like His Son, so that His Son would be the firstborn among many brothers and sisters."*** God knew what we would need and made the preparations ahead of time. God knew He needed to send Jesus, our big Brother, to free us from sin and provide us with the *sozo* life. And Jesus agreed and willingly complied with God's preparations. For God tells us in John 1:12-13 NKJV: "***But as many as received***

Him, to them He gave the right to become children of God, to those who believe in His name: who were born, not of blood, nor of the will of the flesh nor of the will of man, but of God." When you receive Jesus, you receive a new birth and your new identity. And it is in this new birth and new identity that God intends for us to live. Jesus showed us how we are to live and He is to be the One Who influences us. We must learn and understand that we died with Jesus and we were raised again to new life with Jesus. We must grab a hold of that revelation not with our intellect, or in the natural, but receive it in the supernatural with the help of God's Spirit and allowing how we see ourselves to line up with how He sees us, to line up with the finished work of Jesus, to line up with God's News, to line up with God's side of the story, rather than any other news or reports or sides. Because Romans 6:4-8 GW tells us: ***"When we were baptized into His death, we were placed into the tomb with Him. As Christ was brought back from death to life by the glorious power of the Father, so we, too, should live a new kind of life. If we have become united with Him in a death like His, certainly we will also be united with Him when we come back to life as He did. We know the person we used to be was crucified with Him to put an end to sin in our bodies. Because of this we are no longer slaves to sin. The person who has died has been freed from sin. If we have died with Christ, we believe that we will also live with Him."*** We should be changed through Jesus' influence in our lives and that change, those changes, should be evident to us and others, should be evident to God. We should make our will God's will just like Jesus did, just like He showed us. We should be growing in our understanding that we died when Jesus died and that old person no longer exists and when Jesus was raised up again so were we raised up as a new person, to live a new life thanks to Jesus. We should be growing up in our new life and our new identity. I can do as Jesus and do as Galatians

5:24 NKJV says: "***And those who are Christ's have crucified the flesh with its passions and desires.***" Because Galatians 2:20 NKJV informs me: ***"I have been crucified with Christ; it is no longer I who live, but Christ lives in me; and the life which I now live in the flesh I live by faith in the Son of God, Who, loved me and gave Himself for me."*** While Colossians 3:1-2 TPT tells me: ***"Christ's resurrection is your resurrection too. This is why we are to yearn for all that is above, for that is where Christ sits enthroned at the place of all power, honor, and authority! Yes, feast on all the treasures of the heavenly realm and fill your thoughts with heavenly realities, and not with the distractions of the natural realm."*** Jesus lived out His life showing us how to live out our lives. He showed us it can be done; He showed us it is God's side of the story for us to live in His ways and not the world's way, not based on any other news or side of the story.

Even before His crucifixion, people tried to kill Jesus because He was speaking God's Truth and living in God's Truth; He was speaking God's Kingdom and living out God's Kingdom. His life practice was to share God's side in every story, in every situation, everywhere He went and to everyone who would listen. He never wavered, never changed but always remained consistent, always remained persistent. He kept His focus on God and His ways and did not allow culture, religion, man's views, man's ways, or anything else distract Him or convince Him to change His story, which was God's story, to change His ways, which were God's ways. And He wants us to follow His lead, follow His influence and no other. Jesus kept His focus and He wants us to do the same. He wants us to keep our focus on Him, on His ways, on God's Kingdom, and on God's Word. He wants us to keep our focus on our identity in being God's children and Him being our big Brother. Mark 1:15 TPT tells us: ***"His message was this: 'At last***

the fulfillment of the age has come! It is time for God's Kingdom to be experienced in its fullness! Turn your lives back to God and put your trust in the hope-filled gospel!'" And GNT says: ***"The right time has come and the Kingdom of God is near! Turn away from your sins and believe the Good News!"*** To believe the Good News is to believe Jesus because Jesus is the Good News. He did not only come to preach and teach us the Good News, God's Word, but to preach and teach us about Himself because Jesus is God's Word, Jesus is God's Good News in the flesh. Once I gained this knowledge, this revelation, it opened-up God's Word to me as truly being the Living Word of God, it made me look at God's Word completely different, and it made me see Jesus completely different. I truly began to understand that God's Word is not just another book as I had heard others say or that God's Word was something to supplement other literature or that God's Word was just another religious teaching. It made me realize how much God's Word stands alone as God's Word, as God's side of the story, as being Jesus Himself and that God's Word speaks for Himself, speaks about Himself. John 1:14 MSG tells us: ***"The Word became flesh and blood, and moved into the neighborhood. We saw the glory with our own eyes, the one-of-a-kind glory, like Father, like Son, generous inside and out, true from start to finish."*** And the NLT says: ***"So, the Word became human and made His home among us. He was full of unfailing love and faithfulness. And we have seen His glory, the glory of the Father's one and only Son."*** And the GNT says: ***"The Word became a human being and, full of grace and truth, lived among us. We saw His glory, the glory which He received as the Father's only Son."*** God's Word came down from heaven in the fullness of Jesus Himself and walked out God's Word here on earth. God's Word and Jesus are One and the Same just as God's side of the story and Jesus' side of the story are One and the Same. When we allow God's Word to influence us, we are allowing Jesus Himself to influence us. We can look at the entirety of God's Word and entirely see Jesus. Knowing this should even more persuade us to allow Jesus, and only Jesus, be the One Who is our influencer. Jesus was John 1:1-2 where He was with God in the beginning. We could read John 1:1-2 TPT this way: ***"In the beginning the Living Expression [Jesus] was already there. And the Living Expression [Jesus] was with God, yet fully God. They [God and Jesus] were together – face-to-face, in the very beginning."*** I want to make Jesus my ultimate influencer because He was with God face-to-face before I or anything else existed. He was God's Good News (God's Word), He willingly came down to be God's Good News (God's Word) in Person (in the flesh) on earth so He could show me God's love and God's Kingdom and do what only He could do to make me God's child, to establish my identity as God's daughter. And They want me to make Jesus my ultimate influencer and anyone else who is a believer and follower of Jesus.

Jesus knew God's love and goodness firsthand and He wanted to share God's love and goodness with us. He wanted us to know His Father like He did and He wanted to share His Father with us. Jesus wanted His Father to become our Father. Jesus demonstrated the loving, good, and giving nature of God because He knew the loving, good, and giving nature of God. Jesus knew John 3:16 ESV: ***"For God so loved the world, that He gave His only Son, that whoever believes in Him should not perish but have eternal life."*** And the TPT says: ***"For here is the way God loved the world – He gave His only, unique Son as a gift. So now everyone who believes in Him will never perish but experience everlasting life."*** Jesus was God's gift to us. God did not want anyone to perish so He sent Jesus and Jesus did not want anyone to perish so He came to be our gift. Jesus knew what all came with Him being our gift because He knew there would be a gift exchange. Jesus would be exchanging His life for ours so we could have the gift of being God's children. Jesus already knew the gift of being God's Son and He wants us to share in this gift. Jesus knew God intimately and was in direct fellowship with Him and He wanted us to have the same. Jesus knew God was giving us an everlasting life so Jesus came to give us an everlasting life. Jesus knew without Him, just as God did, it would not end well for us. He wanted to change our ending by changing our life now and for eternity. Jesus came to give us the *sozo* life, to give us the more abundant life, that God wanted us to have all along. Jesus made what was not possible, possible, for us. He made and showed the way because He became the way and remains the way. Romans 8:3-6 GW shares with us: ***"It is impossible to do what God's standards demand because of the weakness our human nature has. But God sent His Son to have a human nature as sinners have and to pay for sin. That way God condemned sin in our corrupt nature. Therefore, we, who do not live by our corrupt nature but by our spiritual nature, are able to meet God's standards in Moses' Teachings. Those who live by the corrupt nature have the corrupt nature's attitude. But those who live by the spiritual nature have the spiritual nature's attitude. The corrupt nature's attitude leads to death. But the spiritual nature's attitude leads to life and peace."*** Jesus came to give us our spiritual nature so we can live here on earth as He did. He is our example because He lived by His spiritual nature and He wants us to continually look to Him so we can live as He did. We can live influenced by our spiritual nature that we received when we became born again. When we were born again, we no longer have just our natural nature but now our spiritual. We are no longer just a physical side but now we have a spiritual side, a side we can learn to live by over our natural just like Jesus.

Ephesians 4:21-22, 24 NLT: ***"Since you have heard about Jesus and have learned the truth that comes from Him, throw off your old sinful nature and your former way of life, which is corrupted by lust and deception. Put on your new nature, created to be like God—truly righteous and holy."*** We have the ability to not walk in our former ways of sin but to walk in our new nature as God's children, to walk in our true identity. Just like throwing off a nasty, dirty, stained blanket, I can do the same with my old sinful nature. I choose to not want that blanket on me anymore so I throw it off and I can because I now have my new life in Christ Jesus. So, I take that old blanket and throw if off of me. I then pick up this new blanket that has been made specifically for me. I put that blanket on me and now this blanket covers me. When I look at myself, I now see this blanket that was hand-made for me, a blanket that looks like Jesus' blanket. It is a matching set given to me by God and Jesus came to deliver it to me. This blanket is made with Jesus' precious blood which now covers me. Any time I mess up I can repent and change my thoughts and line up my ways to not mess up in this area again. And it is like I had never messed up. I removed my new blanket and started acting like I had my old blanket, but I realized that was a mistake, so I repent and quickly get my new blanket again. And, it was like I never took off my new blanket but had it with me the whole time. I now see the value of my new blanket (my new nature, my true identity) and I no longer want to remove my new blanket for the reason I messed up. Colossians 3:10 TPT says: ***"For you have acquired new creation life which is continually being renewed into the likeness of the One Who created you; giving you the full revelation of God."*** By letting Jesus, our big Brother, be our influencer, He can show us how we can live like God's children on earth. He can show us how we can grow as God's children and continually learn of His ways. He can show us how to live in our new nature and live comfortably like we have had our new blanket (our new nature) all along because our identity is firmly rooted in being God's child.

CHAPTER 3

Holy Spirit is Your Source

IMAGINE YOU ARE A REPORTER looking for your big story, your big break and one day you get it. You get an insider, who gives you all the intel, all the information you need to report the story that will be told and retold for centuries. This story will propel you forward in a manner like no other. Your source is invaluable to you. You realize without your source you would not be able to report this story nor bring it to life with such detail, clarity, and creditability. As you write the story, your source is right there with you giving you all the information, play by play, word by word, that you need. It will be your face everyone sees when the story surfaces, but you know all the insight and knowledge came from your source that no one else will see. Then the day approaches for your story to be revealed and you hope it is seen and retold over and over again as people believe what you have written, all thanks to your source. And thanks to God, we have such a source but even better, even greater, even more helpful, even more insightful, even more loyal, and even more trustworthy than any source of man. Because God has provided us with Holy Spirit, to be His inside Person, to be our source while we are here on earth. God has given us His Spirit so we could have Someone giving us the intel we need when we need it. Holy Spirit is God's greatest Source Who is here to help us write the story of our lives according to how God created us, according to how we are to live as His children on earth. And we write our story with Him, Holy Spirit, by how we live for God, by how we live for Jesus.

While on earth, Jesus' source was Holy Spirit and He is the same Holy Spirit God gives us. Jesus knew Who He was and how He was created. He knew God's plan for Him and Holy Spirit helped Him. One of the main things Jesus revealed to us was how we can co-labor with Holy Spirit, how we can allow Him to be our source, and He can help us live like heaven on earth. Holy Spirit can provide us with God's side of the story in every situation helping us to not get deceived by other stories or influences, especially regarding our identity. Holy Spirit is our inside source Who gives us play by play God's plan for our lives and provides us with the revelation and knowledge of God's Word. He can point out when something contradicts God's Word so we will not be fooled and led astray. Holy Spirit helps bring to life God's Word and helps show us how to live out God's Word in our lives. Holy Spirit helps reveal and lead us to Jesus so we can live like He did, here and now, so we can believe like Jesus, here and now. Holy Spirit can help us not buy into any other story that would lead us away from who we are according to God, according to how He created us, according to God's side of the story. Holy Spirit can help reveal our rightful identity to us and help us live out our identity all based on God's side of the story about us and not based on any other story. Holy Spirit can help us see ourselves as God does, through His eyes. Holy Spirit can help keep us grounded in our identity as God's children regardless of any pull or any other voices vying for our attention. We can learn to know Holy Spirit's voice and how to follow Him and His leading.

In navigating through life, we can find some source as recommended by the world, we can even choose to be our own source, or we can choose God's source (Holy Spirit). Jesus choose God's source and it worked out well for Him. And Jesus wants us to make the same choice. It took me awhile to make the right choice in allowing Holy Spirit His proper place in my life and allowing Him to be my source. I grew up in church or rather grew up to know church. It was a place you were to go on Sundays or any other time there was a service. The church seemed to set guidelines and rules you were to follow. And if you were to change churches, especially denominations, the rules and guidelines could change as well. From my perspective, it seemed like there was an ongoing list of things you were not allowed to do but really no explanation as to why. And being the kid who was prone to always ask why, I was often thinking why. I truly tried to do what I thought was good but I saw many who were not which just added more confusion to the mix. But all the while, I was really trying in my own strength, in my own way to live like I thought a Christian was to live. I enjoyed church for the most part though I kept seeing different standards of how people lived and how they acted when at church, even from those who were called pastors. Society would have said I was doing okay so no need to make any changes. Yet, I had no understanding of Holy Spirit and Who He is and how He was here to help me. I knew He was a part of the Trinity, which consisted of the Father, the Son, and the Holy Ghost as He was sometimes referenced instead of Holy Spirit. And any time the

Trinity was mentioned it was to let me know that They were all three in One with the focus always on God and Jesus. It was as if Holy Spirit was a part of God's business but He was a silent partner Who was truly silent. He was listed as being One of the owners right after Jesus but you only dealt with God or Jesus. If Holy Spirit was ever explained, I must have not been paying attention or I was not in service that day. Even though I had made the decision to accept Jesus as a child, I did not have any real understanding of where to go from there nor that Holy Spirit was to be my Helper. I was told Jesus came to live in my heart when I got saved and being saved meant I would not be going to hell. And I knew I did not want to go to hell. I had been in that service when hell had been described. Most of the preaching I had heard did not involve much of God's Word being taught but was mainly a nice message filled with man's viewpoints, man's sayings, and man's quotes. I had no understanding of how God created me, though I did have times when I did talk to Him, because I really did want to do what was right. I just did not consult Him with consistency, or bring Him into all of my life decisions. I did not know my identity was now in God, as being His child, and I was to live accordingly. I did not understand how I was to live more like being His child and how He wanted me to live over my natural parents, especially if they were not teaching me His ways and how to live in His ways. All the while, I had Holy Spirit Who is the One that comes to live inside you when you get born again. He was not to be the silent partner after all. I had no idea I was trying to be a Christian from mostly a soul and sometimes flesh perspective. When I was not going by my feelings, I was going by my own thoughts, and at other times yielded to my flesh. Yet, I had Holy Spirit Who was willing to be my source and provide me with all the help I needed. I thought when I somehow knew something or somehow knew not to do something that it was my subconscious at work, some sixth sense in operation, I was having a premonition, or it was even God choosing to talk at certain times. Yet, Holy Spirit has His voice and way of directing and leading. And, He wants me to recognize Him and allow Him to lead me. I had no idea He was the One Who led Jesus and would do the same with me. Sounds almost silly now knowing what I know as I write this book.

Before the very foundation of this world began, Holy Spirit was here waiting on God to speak, waiting on God to move, waiting on being our source to help us just like He was waiting on Jesus to help Him. In Genesis 1:2 NLT, it tells us: "***The earth was formless and empty, and darkness covered the deep waters. And the Spirit of God was hovering over the surface of the waters.***" Even though the earth had yet to take on any shape, any form because God had yet to speak it into existence, Holy Spirit was here already in position waiting to help. He was waiting on God to speak so He could move, waiting to be Who God needed Him to be. And Holy Spirit is still here to help us (God's children), to help us speak like Jesus, and to help us live like Jesus. Holy Spirit is our source for helping establish within us who we are and how we were created because He comes from God, our Father. He will always lead us to Jesus, to God's Word, and to God Himself. Holy Spirit will always remind us we are God's children, what that means, and how we are to put that into action in our lives.

Holy Spirit was a part of God's plan for us. He had already set it up where we would not be alone here on earth. He knew what Jesus was going to be able to do for us and He knew what Holy Spirit was going to be able to do for us. Holy Spirit is not an object or an it but He is a Person, just like Jesus. But unlike Jesus, Holy Spirit can be ever present all over the earth. Holy Spirit lives in those who believe in Jesus helping them any time they need help and guiding them in the ways of God, providing revelation of God's Word, and showing them how to remain set a part from the world. Holy Spirit helps show us God's side of the story each and every time regardless of any other story being told. He helps us see things through God's eyes, including ourselves. Holy Spirit remains the same just like God and just like Jesus. And He is full of God's love and goodness. It is so refreshing to know God cares about us that He gave us Holy Spirit, which is His Spirit, to help us live in the victory and the authority we are to live in as God's children. He gave us a source that helps us learn, understand, and then live like Jesus.

Thanks to Holy Spirit and His help we are not empty or void, but we have Him with us and in us. 1 John 4:13 NLT says: ***"And God has given us His Spirit as proof that we live in Him and He in us."*** Holy Spirit is our source on the inside of us helping verify we are God's children. He serves as God's seal of approval that we are a part of God's family. In the natural, there are ways of identifying a person as being a part of a certain family. For instance, you can share the same last name, you can share similar physical traits such as eye color, you may even sound similar when talking, you can share the same values, or you can live in the same home. Holy Spirit shares the same home with us because He is in us, we are His home. Holy Spirit helps identify us as God's children and provide us with all the information needed regarding God's family. 1 Corinthians 2:12 NKJV tells us: ***"Now we have received, not the spirit of the world, but the Spirit Who is from God, that we might know the things that have been freely given to us by God."*** We have the intel needed whenever we need thanks to Holy Spirit. He does not rely on natural things or natural sources and He is to be our source for all things. He can show us what to do and what not to do because He knows God's ways. He is always there prompting us but we have to be aware of Him, listen to Him, and then follow His leading. Holy Spirit can help us live the abundant life Jesus provided for us; He can help us live the *sozo* life by living like we are to live when we get born again, by living in our new nature. He can help us live our life like God wants and fulfill all we need before we leave the earth. He can help ensure we do not leave this life earlier than we are supposed to. Holy Spirit is our source straight from heaven helping bring heaven to earth while helping us live like heaven on earth. We can always know what to believe or not to believe because He will help us not be deceived. He helps keep us on track in following God's Word.

Jesus Himself was born with the help of Holy Spirit. God needed a human vessel for Jesus to be born on this earth. Yet, He only required the female because God was going to use Holy Spirit to cause the female to become pregnant, creating a miraculous conception that could not be duplicated. He took a pure vessel to bring forth an even purer vessel, Jesus. Jesus, Who would be born as a baby so He could become the unblemished, sinless, sacrifice for us. And He would be able to take back and reclaim everything stolen by satan and put us in right standing with God. And the seed for this to happen was Holy Spirit. God sent His angel, Gabriel, to appear to the female vessel He had chosen, named Mary. Gabriel explained to Mary God's plan, but Mary did not know how it would occur in the natural because God was going to do something supernatural, with the help of Holy Spirit, causing the supernatural to override the natural thus showing how His Kingdom can and is to rule the kingdom of this world. And as Mary asked Gabriel how she was going to get pregnant without a man because she only understood the natural way for this to occur, Gabriel told her God's power through Holy Spirit would cause her to become pregnant (see Luke 1:26-36). Luke 1:35 NLT tells us: ***"The angel replied, 'The Holy Spirit will come upon you, and the power of the Most High will overshadow you. So, the baby to be born will be holy, and He will be called the Son of God.'"*** And Matthew 1:18 NKJV tells us: ***"Now the birth of Jesus Christ was as follows: After His mother Mary was betrothed to Joseph, before they came together, she was found with child of the Holy Spirit."*** God also sent an angel to Joseph providing clarification to him regarding Holy Spirit's role in Mary's pregnancy. Matthew 1:20 NKJV reveals: ***"But while he thought about these things, behold, an angel of the Lord appeared to him in a dream saying, 'Joseph, son of David, do not be afraid to take to you Mary your wife, for that which is conceived in her is of the Holy Spirit.'"*** (see Matthew 1:18-23) God was to be Jesus' Father and Holy Spirit helped this come to pass. He merged heaven with earth allowing Jesus to step out from heaven and be born as a baby on earth. Holy Spirit is still helping God's plans come to pass, He is still helping God become the Father of many more sons and daughters. Holy Spirit is still moving in the earth helping with people being born again. And Holy Spirit is still helping God's sons and daughters after they are born again to move in the earth like God's children are supposed to.

Jesus Himself received Holy Spirit and started His ministry after this and continued in His ministry with the help of Holy Spirit. Jesus did not just come here to be born and then take off doing as He pleased because of Who He was. He did not think He was Jesus, God's Son, so He could set off doing what He wanted or what He thought was best. Jesus did what God wanted and spoke as God spoke with the help of Holy Spirit. Jesus went to John the Baptist so John could baptize Him because this was what God had foretold would happen and Jesus was fulfilling what God wanted (see Matthew 3:13-15). Then in Matthew 3:16 NLT we see: *"After, His baptism, as Jesus came up out of the water, the heavens were opened, and He saw the Spirit of God descending like a dove and settling on Him."* Luke 3:22 GNT says; *"And the Holy Spirit came down upon Him in bodily form like a dove."* Notice, Holy Spirit came in a bodily form that could be seen by John the Baptist. A part of God's plan for Jesus was to give Jesus, His Spirit, Holy Spirit. And a part of God's plan for us is to give us His Spirit, Holy Spirit. God then went on in Matthew 3:17 NLT to say: ***"This is My dearly loved Son, Who, brings Me great joy."*** And the NKJV says: ***"This is My beloved Son, in Whom I am well pleased."*** God sends His Spirit to His Son and then lets His Son and all who were there know Jesus is His dearly, loved, beloved Son and God is well pleased with Jesus Who brings Him great joy. Jesus allowed Himself to be in a place, according to God's plan, and Jesus received God's Spirit as part of God's plan for Him. He could have chosen to go somewhere else that day or He could have decided He knew God, He knew where He had come from, so He would just forgo receiving God's Spirit. Yet, He did not and He was in the exact place God wanted Him to be when He received Holy Spirit. Right after this, Jesus began following the lead of Holy Spirit, which included, Jesus withstanding being tempted by satan himself (see Luke 1:1-13). Jesus allowed Holy Spirit to be the source Who influenced Him when He was tempted and we can do the same. Luke 1:1 GNT says: ***"Jesus returned from the Jordan full of the Holy Spirit and was led by the Spirit into the desert."*** Luke 4:1 NJKV says: ***"Then Jesus, being filled with the Holy Spirit."*** Notice, it says Jesus was "full of the Holy Spirit" and "filled with Holy Spirit" and Holy Spirit led Him to go to the desert. Jesus did not decide to go to the desert on His own but by Holy Spirit leading Him and He was filled with and full of Holy Spirit when He went. Not only did He did not go on His own, but He did not go in His own strength. With the help of Holy Spirit, we can make sure we are not doing things on our own or in our own strength or because others have done something so we then think that is what we are to do as well. I have seen certain movements hit certain church circles and people will do things because those in their church circle are doing those things. However, we have a Helper, a Teacher, a Source Who can lead us in what we are to do or not to do regardless of what others may be doing, even in church. Jesus was not moved by what people were doing or not doing. He was only moved by what His Father was doing or not doing and Holy Spirit helped lead Him to do what His Father was doing and what His Father wanted Him to do. Jesus came as our example to show us God's ways and one of God's ways is receiving Holy Spirit and then following His leading. We do not take off and go into a desert for forty days or try and find the actual desert Jesus went to. We are not to decide to stop eating and fast for forty days unless Holy Spirit leads us to. We are to follow Holy Spirit's leading just as Jesus did. Holy Spirit will not mislead us but will always lead us correctly and directly as God intends and according to God's Word, according to God's ways. Holy Spirit will always lead us to God's best for us in every area of our lives. He will always show us God's side of the story regarding every situation, every news and report, and for any other stories being told. Holy Spirit will always reveal to us everything through God's eyes.

Just as Jesus went as Holy Spirit directed, Jesus spoke as Holy Spirit directed. Holy Spirit helped Jesus know what God was doing and what God was saying. Holy Spirit was not moved by satan showing up. He did not panic at the sight of satan. Holy Spirit is always at peace and He can help us always be at peace. When satan appeared to Jesus, Jesus replied to satan by saying God's Word; however, Jesus knew what to say because Holy Spirit was leading Him in what to say. Jesus did not just pick something out of God's Word rather Jesus spoke what Holy Spirit was telling Him to say. Holy Spirit was Jesus inside source letting Him know what Word to speak back to satan. Holy Spirit was helping show Jesus his current situation through God's eyes and He will always do the same for us. Finally, satan realized Jesus was not going to be moved or deceived so he fled. Holy Spirit will let us know what to say and when, including what specific Word of God to use and when. Holy Spirit's help is full proof every time, even over satan himself. There is no influence or story that will ever fool Holy Spirit so we can trust Him to help us not to be influenced or fooled by any story. Rather, He will help us to hold-fast to God's side of the story enabling us to see through God's eyes, especially regarding our identity. Ephesians 1:17 GNT tells us: ***"Ask the God of our Lord Jesus Christ, the glorious Father, to give you the Spirit, Who, will make you wise and reveal God to you, so that you will know Him."*** Holy Spirit can help us know God which can help us better understand our identity. He can help us get to know God as our Father and so much more. The more we get in tune with Holy Spirit, the more we can know what to do and how to respond to the world we live in. And even if satan himself were to appear to us, we would know how to respond. Notice, Jesus was not fearful of satan rather He remained calm and composed because He knew Who He was and to Whom He belonged and He knew He had Holy Spirit helping Him. It is the same for us. And it was the same for Smith Wigglesworth, who was a British Evangelist. There is a story of satan appearing to Smith, who I believe knew who he was and had a firm understanding of his identity as God's child. Smith had just laid down to sleep when he felt an evil presence come into his bedroom. Smith opened his eyes to see satan himself had appeared in his room. Smith responded by saying, "oh it's only you" and then rolled over and went to sleep. When we know who we are as God's child, we can be confident in our identity, we can be confident in how God created us, we can be confident in looking at satan and saying "oh it's just you" and go on about our business, go on about God's business. And Holy Spirit is in us going with us as our source, helping us all along the way.

Jesus was raised from the dead through the power of Holy Spirit which then revealed that Jesus is God's Son and our Lord. For Romans 1:4 NLT tells us: ***"And He was shown to be the Son of God when He was raised from the dead by the power of the Holy Spirit. He is Jesus Christ our Lord."*** In 1 Peter 3:18 NLT, it tells us Jesus ***"was raised to life in the Spirit."*** Holy Spirit helped reveal Jesus' identity by raising Jesus from the dead and Holy Spirit is here today to help reveal to us our identity, to reveal to us who we are and to Whom we belong. Holy Spirit is here to reveal God's side of the story as seen through God's eyes regarding our identity. Romans 8:11 TPT tells us: ***"Yes, God raised Jesus to life! And since God's Spirit of Resurrection lives in you, He will also raise your dying body to life by the same Spirit that breathes life into you!"*** And the NLT says: ***"The Spirit of God, Who, raised Jesus from the dead, lives in you. And just as God raised Jesus from the dead, He will give life to your mortal bodies by this same Spirit living within you."*** God raised Jesus by His Spirit, Holy Spirit, and He does the same for us when we receive Jesus as our Lord and Savior, Holy Spirit raises us up to new life, we get born again, and our spirit becomes alive so we will not have to touch death and go to hell. Holy Spirit then comes to live inside of us helping us to know what is acceptable and pleasing to God, helping us to know and live according to God's standards, helping us to not live like the world. Hell, with satan and all his demons, could not hold Jesus back from being raised from the dead thanks to the power of Holy Spirit. We have the same power living in us, helping us. And with His power and help, there is nothing satan and his demons can do to stop us from fulfilling what God has for us. We have to realize Who we are in God, Who we are in Christ Jesus, and Who we are with Holy Spirit in us. When we know our identity and operate in that identity, we operate as God created us to operate. All thanks to what Jesus did for us and all thanks for Holy Spirit helping us.

Jesus was helped by Holy Spirit and through Jesus' help we now have Holy Spirit. For Romans 8:3-6 TPT explains this: ***"For God achieved what the law was unable to accomplish, because the law was limited by the weakness of human nature. Yet God sent us His Son in human form to identify with human weakness. Clothed with humanity, God's Son gave His body to be the sin-offering so that God could once and for all condemn the guilt and power of sin. So now every righteous requirement of the law can be fulfilled through the Anointed One living His life in us. And we are free to live, not according to our flesh, but by the dynamic power of the Holy Spirit! Those who are motivated by the flesh only pursue what benefits themselves. But those who live by the impulses of the Holy Spirit are motivated to pursue spiritual realities. For the sense and reason of the flesh is death, but the mind-set controlled by the Spirit finds life and peace."*** Man would not, could not, cannot achieve for us what Jesus did and a greater part of what Jesus did for us was set it up for us to be able to have Holy Spirit as our Helper, our source while we are here on earth. Holy Spirit provides us with the ability to live out our life and to live out our identity as further clarified in Romans 8:9 TPT: ***"But when the Spirit of Christ empowers your life, you are not dominated by the flesh but by the Spirit. And if you are not joined to the Spirit of the Anointed One, you are not of Him."*** If we are of Jesus Christ, the Anointed One, we are joined to Holy Spirit and can live above our flesh and its desires thanks to our Helper, Holy Spirit, Who empowers us to do so. For Romans 8:12-13 TPT makes it clear: ***"So then, beloved ones, the flesh has no claims on us at all, and we have no further obligation to live in obedience to it. For when you live controlled by the flesh, you are about to die. But if the life of the Spirit puts to death the corrupt ways of the flesh, we then taste His abundant life."*** Holy Spirit is here to help us live by our spirit, which leads to a life that is abundant rather than living our life according to our flesh, which leads to a life of death. An abundant life, a life that is more valuable and plentiful and full of God and the things of God, is far better than the alternative. I have lived both and I will choose over and over again this life I have now in God, this life I have now in being and knowing who I am as His daughter.

Even with all the news, various stories, and different influences, we have a way to live in this life, in this time just as Jesus Christ lived, just as God created us to live and that is through the help and empowerment of Holy Spirit, our source. To live not by our flesh, but by our born-again spirit that is now equipped with the help of Holy Spirit, our Helper, our source, our power source. Holy Spirit is more powerful than satan or his demons or any spiritual force in this world because He is God's Spirit. He knew He could raise Jesus from the dead; He was just waiting on God to tell Him to. 1 John 4:4 NLT tells us: ***"But you belong to God, my dear children. You have already won a victory over those people, because the Spirit Who lives in you is greater than the spirit who lives in the world."*** The GNT says: ***"the Spirit Who is in you is more powerful than the spirit in those who belong to the world."*** And the MSG tells us: ***"the Spirit in you is far stronger than anything in the world."*** We have to believe it; Jesus did. He knew Holy Spirit was far stronger than anything in the world and He did not bow to anything in this world, including satan. Jesus knew Holy Spirit would raise Him from the dead when God said it was time. He knew Holy Spirit was here to help Him just as He knew Holy Spirit is here to help us. And I am so very thankful.

Jesus Himself spoke of Holy Spirit and Holy Spirit's importance to us so much so that He asked God to give us Holy Spirit. Jesus made a personal request for God, the Father, on our behalf. If Holy Spirit is not important in our daily life and our daily walk here on earth, then why did Jesus ask for Him to be here for us? In John 14:16-17 AMPC Jesus says: ***"And I will ask the Father, and He will give you another Comforter (Counselor, Helper, Intercessor, Advocate, Strengthener, and Standby), that He may remain with you forever."*** Holy Spirit is here to help reveal Jesus to us and all that Jesus did and spoke so we can know how we are to speak and live our lives. Holy Spirit is here to help provide revelation of God's Word so we can become doers of God's Word and live in the abundant life Jesus died to give us. John 14:26 AMPC says: ***"But the Comforter (Counselor, Helper, Intercessor, Advocate, Strengthener, Standby), the Holy Spirit, Whom the Father will send in My name [in My place, to represent Me and act on My behalf], He will teach you all things. And He will cause you to recall (will remind you of, bring to your remembrance) everything I have told you."*** Anything we need to know, any help or guidance or direction we need in life, Holy Spirit is here to help. He serves as Jesus' representative letting us know Jesus' opinion on all things, including how we are to live, think, and act. He is like our own built in personal navigational voice leading us, directing us, prompting us all along the way in our daily lives. He is there to help in the small details, the bigger decisions, and any and every area that we will allow Him access, any area where we will ask and listen to Him for His guidance, His prompting, allowing Him to be our source for information and for revelation. We can allow Him and have Him be our Comforter, Counselor, Helper, Intercessor, Advocate, Strengthener, and Standby. He wants to. God and Jesus want Him to. Holy Spirit is here to reveal to us all that Jesus revealed when He was here, to show us Who Jesus is, and how Jesus' life can be displayed in our life. Holy Spirit is here to reveal God's Kingdom to us so we can live like God's Kingdom here and now.

Holy Spirit anointed Jesus to do what Jesus did while He was here. Jesus did not anoint Himself or appoint someone else to anoint Him. Being baptized by John the Baptist did not anoint Jesus, rather Jesus was anointed when God sent His Spirit down from heaven to Jesus, then Jesus was anointed. Acts 10:38 NKJV tells us: ***"How God anointed Jesus of Nazareth with the Holy Spirit and with power, Who, went about doing good and healing all who were oppressed by the devil, for God was with Him."*** And Holy Spirit is here to anoint us to accomplish what we need to accomplish while we are here, to help us know and understand God's side of the story, and then help us live out God's side of the story, to help us go about doing good and healing all who are oppressed by the devil because Holy Spirit is with us, He is in us. Because Acts 1:8 GW informs us: "***But you will receive power when the Holy Spirit comes to you. Then you will be my witnesses to testify about me in Jerusalem, throughout Judea and Samaria, and to the ends of the earth.***" Jesus was God's witness while He was on earth and now we are to be God's witness, to be God's evidence and proof of God and His Kingdom while we are on earth, because it is a part of our identity, it is a part of us living out God's side of the story as seen through His eyes. We are to tell of God's Kingdom and we are to demonstrate God's Kingdom in all areas, places, and spheres of influences as Holy Spirit leads us. Holy Spirit led Jesus and He is here to lead us. He may tell you to go to the desert or He may tell you to stay away from the desert. He is the One Who anoints and empowers us to go and do as He leads.

Once Jesus completed His assignment on earth, He had to return to God, the Father, so we could have God, the Father's Spirit, as our Helper. Jesus tells us this in John 16:7-11 AMPC: ***"However, I am telling you nothing but the truth when I say it is profitable (good, expedient, advantageous) for you that I go away. Because if I do not go away, the Comforter (Counselor, Helper, Advocate, Intercessor, Strengthener, Standby) will not come to you [into close fellowship with you]; but if I go away, I will send Him to you [to be in close fellowship with you]. And when He comes, He will convict and convince the world and bring demonstration to it about sin and about righteousness (uprightness of heart and right standing with God) and about judgment: about sin, because they do not believe in Me [trust in, rely on, and adhere to Me]; about righteousness (uprightness of heart and right standing with God), because I go to My Father, and you will see Me no longer; about judgment, because the ruler (evil genius, prince) of this world [satan] is judged and condemned and sentence already passed upon him."*** Jesus told us He had to leave and it was better for us if He did so Holy Spirit could come. In verse 7 of the NLT, Jesus tells us: ***"But in fact, it is best for you that I go away, because if I do not, the Advocate will not come. If I do go away, then I will send Him to you."*** Jesus left to go back to God, our Father, but He did not leave us alone but left us with Holy Spirit Who is our Comforter, Counselor, Helper, Advocate, Intercessor, Strengthener, and Standby. Jesus knew there was only so much He could say and do while He was on earth, but He knew the Holy Spirit would be sent to help us and guide us into God's Truth, God's Word.

Holy Spirit would help us each step of the way as we learn about Jesus and His ways. Holy Spirit would be here helping us apply God's Truths and Jesus' ways in our lives. He would be the Spirit of Truth for us making sure we would not be distracted or persuaded to follow any lies, even ones presented as true. He would be our own personal Teacher, going One on one with us, providing us with the special attention needed to learn God's Truths and learn about Jesus and His ways by learning to apply God's Truths and Jesus' ways into our lives. Jesus further instructs us in John 16:13-15 GW: ***"When the Spirit of Truth comes, He will guide you into the full truth. He will not speak on His Own. He will speak what He hears and will tell you about things to come. He will give Me glory, because He will tell you what I say. Everything the Father says is also what I say. That is why I said, 'He will take what I say and tell it to you.'"*** Holy Spirit speaks as God speaks and says what Jesus says. When Holy Spirit speaks, He is giving us God's words or Jesus' words. His is always actively listening to Them so He can let us know what They are saying. And He gives us preciously what They say. Have you ever been given a message to deliver and you may have left out a word or two or even added a word or two? You may have thought you were giving the basis of the message so changing a word or two did not matter. Not with Holy Spirit, He will say exactly what is said to Him, nothing added and nothing left out. He can be trusted to be the perfect messenger each and every time. He will let us know when we see a report or any news just how God and Jesus would respond and want us to respond. Holy Spirit will not step over into reasoning or analyzing something with us. What God says goes and what Jesus says goes. Holy Spirit does not operate in gray areas trying to justify something nor should we.

We see so many stories and are bombarded with so many images because the world and those who live in and live like the world do not know God and His side of the story. They do not know Holy Spirit Who is sent here as our Helper. They will tell other stories that are apart from God and His side of the story and they will do and say things that goes against what Holy Spirit is revealing because He reveals God's side of the story. We are to be known for following God and His side of the story in all we do and all we say with the help of Holy Spirit. We have Holy Spirit Who will always support and will always recommend God and His story and will help us in doing the same. Holy Spirit will always point us to Jesus and show us how to love like Jesus because He first shows us how to love Jesus and receive the love Jesus has for us.

Holy Spirit helps us mature and grow in our knowledge of God and His Word and our knowledge of Jesus and His ways. He helps us to grow and grow up as God's children so we can become more and more like Jesus as we grow. He helps us to live set apart in this world living like we are God's children who know our identity as defined by Him. Romans 8:14-17 TPT: ***"The mature children of God are those who are moved by the impulses of the Holy Spirit. And you did not receive the 'spirit of religious duty,' leading you back into the fear of never being good enough. But you have received the 'Spirit of full acceptance,' enfolding you into the family of God. And you will never feel orphaned, for as He rises up within us, our spirits join Him in saying the words of tender affection, 'Beloved Father!' For the Holy Spirit makes God's Fatherhood real to us as He whispers into our innermost being, 'You are God's beloved child!' And since we are His true children, we qualify to share all His treasures, for indeed, we are heirs of God Himself. And since we are joined to Christ, we also inherit all that He is and all that He has. We will experience being***

***co-glorified with Him provided that we accept His sufferings as our own.*"** We are God's beloved children and that is how He sees us. We do not have to work or do anything to earn our status as His children. Just like a child gets born into a family and becomes a part of the family at birth so it is with us and God. When we got born again, we became God's children. It was a part of the deal of getting born again. But just like a child being born into a family in the natural there are things that come with being a part of the family. There are things that come with us being a part of God's family and He wants us to have all we get as His children. We get Holy Spirit as our Helper to help us receive all we are entitled to as God's children. And He helps us to know what to do with all we have, He explains what needs to be explained to us, He shows us what needs to be shown to us, and He is here every step of the way as we walk in all God has for us just because we are His children.

One of the things I have come to admire about my husband, Stephen, is he will always seek Holy Spirit on what to do and will only be persuaded by how Holy Spirit leads him. It matters not to him how popular something is or who may be doing the asking. There could be a thousand well known pastors doing the same thing but my husband will only be moved if Holy Spirit tells him to do it. And Holy Spirit always wants us to ask Him what to do in all situations because He always knows best and will always lead us to do what is best for us. There may be something that is good for me to do and Holy Spirit will not lead my husband to do it because it is not good for him. Holy Spirit is all knowing and He can see far ahead of us so He is the One we need to always seek and then follow. Before I knew my husband, I was needing help with a ministry I was involved in at the time. I was praying and seeking God regarding who I needed to fill a particular position in this ministry and about the characteristics I was needing from this person. After I had prayed, Holy Spirit led me to ask a specific person if he knew of anyone. I followed Holy Spirit's leading and went to this person to ask. Immediately upon asking, he said Stephen was the one I needed. Without hesitation, he began to tell me how Stephen follows Holy Spirit and if Holy Spirit told Stephen to lay down in the middle of the parking lot Stephen would obey Holy Spirit. He went on to tell me how following Holy Spirit was what mattered more to Stephen than following people or caring what they think. I remember thinking now this is the person I need if Holy Spirit confirms to him that he is to help me. And I remember thinking what a wonderful way for people to identify you. Before I even got to know Stephen, I had already heard how closely he follows Holy Spirit over anyone else including doing what Holy Spirit asks of him no matter how it may look to others. Holy Spirit then prompted me to ask Stephen if he would help and as I did ask him, Stephen's response was that he would pray and let me know. I have learned that when some people say they will pray about something that really is a brush off response because they have no intention of praying, no intention of seeking God and listening to Holy Spirit. But I could tell Stephen's response was different and that he was going to ask and then follow through with what he heard from Holy Spirit. It was not long after I had asked that he came back and let me know Holy Spirit had told him that he was to help. I am very thankful Holy Spirit did tell him to help me for many reasons because he was a tremendous blessing in the ministry. And one main reason is that it led us on our journey toward marriage. I was able to see his character and how he followed Holy Spirit. Holy Spirit can set up situations and accomplish so much that is for our good, for our benefit, if we will allow Him to be our Helper, our Source. If we will be listening for His leading and then follow His lead. I did not know Stephen when I had approached him to ask his help. I could have easily brushed it off and not only not asked Stephen but not even go up to ask the person Holy Spirit first asked me to speak to. Holy Spirit could have just told me to go to Stephen directly but He did not. I believe one of the reasons he led me to talk to the first person was so he could provide me with that description which Stephen would not have provided about himself. Holy Spirit always knows exactly the steps we need to take and all He requires is that we take them. It may be as simple as Him pointing out a specific person for us to ask a specific question to. And as we take the first step, He leads us to another step which provides for more leadings that will navigate us through life, a life filled with all God has to give and has already given us. A life lived with our Helper, our Comforter, our Counselor, our Advocate, our Intercessor, our Strengthener, our Standby, our Holy Spirit.

CHAPTER 4

Created in God's Image

WE LIVE IN A SOCIETY where an image of anything at any time can be uploaded onto some social media platform. Images are constantly streaming across cell phones, computers, and televisions. And with these images comes a variety of responses. Images telling you what and who is popular, what to wear and how you should look, what products to use, who to vote for, what and who you should and should not like, what you should do with your life, who you should be listening to, and so on and on go the various images. How many followers someone has can now make that person a social media influencer but is that person someone who should be seen as an example to follow? Anyone can make a video and now people are able to make money from their videos when a video goes viral. Who knew the term viral would be used in such a context? And many moments of time are spent on all these means of streaming images depicting the views of people all over the world. Many people allowing their emotions to get caught up in the responses and opinions of others as if their very life depended on those responses.

And even before all this modern technology there were still ways to get images out to people such as newspapers, magazines, and comic books. Even while driving, you do not have to drive far down most highways in America and you see images on billboards alerting you about various topics and providing you with advice. And of course, books are written in all types of genres from nonfiction to fiction. Then there is music that uses the airways to project images with the musicians creating their styles for their fans to follow, which now includes videos to create even more images. There is the radio used to broadcast news, sporting events, and other entertainment, including music. With the creation of Hollywood, more images of how to look and sound and act are projected through society telling everyone what is or who is popular and creating another venue of influence. And now people beyond Hollywood are creating their movies, shows, and displaying more images for people to see. Then there are various sports all over the world creating athletes who can use their platform to generate influence and depict more images. And we cannot forget the retail industry that has skyrocketed in providing even more images of what people need or do not need with all the marketing and advertising strategies and ways of getting those images out for people to see. Many people are getting caught up in having the latest version and most up to date product, especially those deemed in high demand and most popular. And let us not forget the gaming world and all those images. Simplicity has seemed to step aside to the more technologically advanced and the over stimulus of images always on display, always accessible. Even your neighbor or the person next to you is projecting some image, from what does this person look like, what is this person driving, where does this person live, and what does this person's home and yard look like. Your own family projects different types of images. Have you ever heard someone say you can tell they are a Lopez (fill in any family name) or you know whose child that is? You can look at how popular ancestry searches have become as people are searching for their family history and heritage and are willing to spend money to do so. Images are everywhere, even when you are not looking it is hard not to see all the images portrayed in society across the world. Images can be good things and can be used for good and images can be bad things and used for bad.

With all these images, it can sometimes set up a means for people to compare themselves to others and even compare themselves to the images they see. People can begin paying attention to people's opinions regarding themselves based on the images being portrayed. I was listening to a sermon on line one time and the pastor was telling a story about a couple he was counseling. The woman was comparing her husband to a male character on a television show she was watching. She had allowed an image to protrude from fantasy into her expectation of how she wanted her husband to be. She took an image that was not real and tried to make it a reality in their life and it was causing problems in their marriage. Current situations and past situations can also create images. I remember when my husband and I were dating I wanted to trust him and really see him for who he is but there was this inward turmoil going on within me. Then one day he said to me, "Do not let your past experiences dictate how you respond to me." Immediately, I realized what had been happening and that I was beginning to trust him and see that he could be trusted but then was carrying these images of past experiences of those who

I could not trust which had nothing to do with him or who he is. I had a choice to let go of all those old images and allow new images with him to take place and be in the moment with him so new images could be made.

Even with the continual bombardment of images, with some of those images specifically directed toward identity, it is God, Who, sets the standard and it is God, Who, established our identity because He made us in His image. In Genesis 1:26-28 GW: ***"Then God said, 'Let us make humans in Our image, in Our likeness. Let them rule the fish in the sea, the birds in the sky, the domestic animals all over the earth, and all the animals that crawl on the earth.' So, God created humans in His image. In the image of God, He created them, He created them male and female. God blessed them and said, 'Be fertile, increase in number, fill the earth, and be its master. Rule the fish in the sea, the birds in the sky, and all the animals that crawl on the earth."*** It is essential we know and understand we were created in God's image and He is the One Who is to define us. He is the One Who our identity is to come from because we are to believe His side of the story regarding who we are and how we were created. We were not made in the image of this world nor in the image of man, but we were made in the image of God Who made the heavens and the earth, Who made the animals and plants, Who made man. Our identity is in God and we are to see ourselves, see our image, through His eyes. It is wonderful to know that God Himself decided to create us, each person, each human, in His own image.

When God created humans in His image, notice He did not say, "I am creating humans in My image and I like hazel eyes so hazel eyes are to be preferred over any other eye color and people who have brown skin tones are to be preferred over any other skin tones and people with long hair are to be preferred over people with short hair but make sure your hair does not grow past your shoulder blades and you must keep it curly. " And God did not say, "I only prefer people who live in the Eastern hemisphere over people who live in the Western hemisphere and do not ever wear anything with the color orange, even though I created that color, I just do not want you to wear that color." Even in writing this how silly it sounded, but have you ever heard similar things, or have you even said or thought similar things? I believe God gave us our free will and we can have preferences and likes but those are not to define us nor define others. For instance, I decided I wanted my husband to have green eyes. God put it on my heart to list characteristics I wanted in my husband as well as physical attributes and then He wanted me to trust that He was able to provide, which He did. When I first made my list of what I wanted in a husband, the first things I listed were all about him loving God, loving Jesus, loving God's Word, and living like He did. After I had listed all these things, it was God Who told me it was okay to have physical attributes that I liked because He was the One Who created me and my husband. So, I add green eyes as the final attribute on my list but that does not mean people with green eyes are better than everyone else. Nor does it mean, God prefers green eyes over any other eye color and considers those with green eyes to be superior over others who have different eye colors. See, when I look into my husband's eyes, I am reminded that there is nothing that is impossible for my God, that He keeps His promises, and He is more than able to give me His best in every area of my life so it makes me not want to compromise or accept anything less than God's ways and His best. And because this is how He dealt with me I do not expect Him to deal with others in the same manner unless He puts the same thing on their heart. I just know I am created in God's image, so it is His image that is to be most important to me and anyone else who is His child. Being God's child is not determined on marital status, age, gender, geographical location, nor outward appearance because He defines who we are and how He created us. What is important to Him should be important to us and what is not important to Him should not be important to us. And if it is not important to Him, it should not be important to us. We are God's children because God, Who is the I Am (the self-sufficient, self-sustaining God, Who was, Who is, and Who will be), created us in His image and no one else's. This is how we are to see people and this is how we are to treat people. Imagine if everyone got a hold of this realization and began to put this into practice. I have not always known this and have not always lived with this revelation myself. I did not grasp this understanding growing up and made decisions accordingly. I made decisions trying to fit other images and other expectations of myself sometimes making what people thought factor into my decisions. However, when we do gain this understanding and begin to put this into practice in our daily life it changes how we think and act. It changes how we think and act about ourselves and others. I remember finally understanding this and being okay with being single over just marrying anyone even over other's opinions or doing so would make me feel like I was accepted by others. Who better to know me, Who better to know what and who is best for me, and what I like than the One Who created me in His image? Who better to trust than God Who created me in His image and created my husband in His image? Who better to get acceptance and love from than the One Who created me? Who better to define me than God? No one except God, Himself.

People can sometimes respond to others based completely on outward appearances. How many times have you walked into a room and looked for people who looked like you or how many times have you noticed people doing the same thing? Do you get ready to go somewhere and think about how to look based on where you are going? And do you look to socialize with only people who are dressed like you or have the same income bracket as you or even the same skin tone? I remember going on mission trips and when people found out I lived in Texas they asked me if I had a horse because they had an image of people living in Texas having horses. Although I responded that I did not have a horse, I do recall having horses when I lived in Florida and Alabama. How many people associate horses with Florida or Alabama? And what images do you have of those states and people who live in those states? We can have images for all types of things and then draw conclusions based on those images and often put people into categories and make generalizations based on those images. But we were not made according to a list of preferences people may have or how people may try to categorize or make generalizations about us so their opinions and preferences should not define us. Only God Himself should be the One we look to as to Who defines us. It should be firmly settled within us to where we are never moved from knowing our identity comes from the One Who created us in His image.

One of my favorite scriptures in the Bible is found in 1 Samuel 16:7 NKJV: ***"But the Lord said to Samuel, "Do not look at his appearance or at his physical stature, because I have refused him. For the Lord does not see as man sees; for man looks at the outward appearance, but the Lord looks at the heart."*** It reminds me of how God sees people and how He sees people is much better than how people often see each other. God always sees our heart, He sees the core of our being, and He always understands us. We may can hide our true self and nature and what is going on deep inside of us, our self- talk, but we cannot ever hide from God. I have been in situations where I drew comfort knowing God knew my heart and my intentions, even though there have been times I knew I was being wrongly judged and treated accordingly, even within church circles. I knew if I needed any correction or needed to make any changes God would lovingly show me. If I did not need correction, even though man would sometimes be wanting to bring the correction, God still knew me and He still accepted me because I only needed to please Him. He knew my sincerity when I did mess up and knew I wanted to not make the same mistake and wanted to make the necessary correction. He knows me even though I have my fair share of mistakes because I am still learning and am nowhere close to perfection, He still knows my heart to want to do what is right in His eyes. I realize my identity is in Him and not in the mistakes because I understand I am created in His image so my reliance is on Him and how He created me, even if there are times He is the only One in Whom I am able to rely on. I had started to allow my identity to be formed in and through Him, though it was a process and remains an ongoing process, as I am continually being transformed into His image by changing how I think about myself into how He thinks about me. I had come to know the love of God and how He operates in love, even if correction is involved. I have heard others tell of how God sternly deals with them and they would make Him appear like He always harshly corrected them. And this has never set well with me for each time I hear such an example I always think and sometimes even said out loud that is not how He deals with me. For anytime God has corrected me, I have always known His love and how much He loves me and He has always spoken to me in love. God is love and God is good so correction from Him is love and is good. For He tells us in Hebrews 12:6-7 NLT: ***"For the Lord disciplines those He loves, and He punishes each one He accepts as His child. As you endure this divine discipline, remember that***

***God is treating you as His own children. Who ever heard of a child who is never disciplined by its father?*"** Because I had already accepted God as my Father and had begun to understand it was His image I had been created, any discipline from Him I also willingly accepted. Because I was created in His image and He is love, I realized He loved me and a part of Him loving me was to bring discipline when needed. And that He was looking at my heart just like He is looking at everyone else's heart. He sees differently and far better than man can until man begins to see as He sees. Even then, God truly is the only One Who can see into a person and see that person's heart, see what is going on within that person, to see the person's intentions. Knowing that has helped me to stay out of judgment because I truly will never know what all has happened to someone, what all someone has gone through, how the person has been taught (even about God) and regardless of what I may see in a person standing before me, only God can truly look within that person and He truly knows how that person thinks about Him and His Son, Jesus. And He truly knows what that person really thinks about himself and how he thinks about others. Discipline is not about punishment but it is about teaching. Whatever brought the correction, God wants us to make the change to follow His Word and His ways. We have Holy Spirit to help teach us what corrections need to be made so we are not continually making the same errors. He can help us see how Jesus would handle the situation and how He would respond so we can then line up how we would do the same.

In 1 Samuel 16:7, God was referring to Saul who had stopped listening to God and had stopped following God's commands, so God was going to appoint another king. Even though God had appointed Saul as king and Saul looked the part of a king, Saul no longer looked the part of a king on the inside and God could tell. God was not looking at the outward stature of a person to determine who the next king would be rather He was looking at the heart, looking on the inside of the next person to be king. And this person, David, would not outwardly look the part but would inwardly because God knew David loved Him and would follow Him. Saul had begun to seek after man and had begun valuing what man said and thought over God. He had begun looking at the one who was created above the One Who was the Creator. He had forgotten Whose image he was made in and Who had appointed him king and Who he was to follow even though he was ruling over others. In Saul's heart, the opinions of man overruled God's commands. God made His reasons to Saul clear in 1 Samuel 13:14 NKJV: ***"But now your kingdom shall not continue. The Lord has sought for Himself a man after His own heart, and the Lord has commanded him to be commander over His people, because you have not kept what the Lord commanded you."*** When we know Whose image we were created, we can better follow His commands rather than follow man's. If man's commands are ever against God's, we know God wins out each time no matter what and God stands behind His commands and behind His people. God is good and we were created in the image of good. God is love and we were created in the image of love. God is good and His commands are good. God is love and His commands are love. Following God's commands is following love and good.

Prior to Saul, there were two people who forgot Whose image they were created in and forgot Who God was and that was Adam and Eve. We find these two people for the first time did not keep God's command and it cost them greatly and cost every one of us since then. God Who created Adam and Eve, created Saul, created David, created us and He knows what is best for us thus the reason He gives us His commands. He knows without

Him man will mess up because Adam and Eve did and this set up the fall of man where man makes wrong decisions without God. He knows in creating us in His image what we need and do not need and what commands we need. God wants you and He wants me to follow Him and to do so with our whole heart, including following His commands, following His side of the story. God gave Adam a command after He placed him in the Garden of Eden in Genesis 2:15-17 NLT: ***"The Lord God placed the man in the Garden of Eden to tend and watch over it. But the Lord God warned him, 'You may freely eat the fruit of every tree in the garden – except the tree of the knowledge of good and evil. If you eat its fruit, you are sure to die."*** Here God was clearly giving Adam a command by telling him what he could and could not eat and the outcome of what would happen if he ate from what he was told not to eat. Adam had free reign over the Garden of Eden and could eat all the fruit and as much of the fruit he wanted except from the tree God told him not to eat from. And this was what was expected of Eve as well. There was more than enough food for Adam and Eve and plenty of trees to eat fruit. God had provided all they needed in the Garden. And their enemy was watching and listening. Their enemy, our enemy, satan, can be clever in his approach and how he spins things, how he can make things sound and look, all to create destruction in our lives while making it look the opposite. And he can use others and often does, to do his bidding for him, to do his work, being sly, subtle, working behind the scenes so he can deceive, destroy, and steal. This is what he did to Adam and Eve and this is what he is still doing today. We see Adam and Eve clearly being deceived in Genesis 3:1-7 NLT: ***"The serpent was the shrewdest of all wild animals the Lord God had made. One day he asked the woman, 'Did God really say you must not eat the fruit from any of the tress in the garden? Of course we may eat fruit from the trees in the garden,' the***

woman replied. 'It is only the fruit from the tree in the middle of the garden that we are not allowed to eat. God said, you must not eat it or even touch it; if you do, you will die.' 'You will not die!' the serpent replied to the woman. God knows that your eyes will be opened as soon as you eat it, and you will be like God, knowing both good and evil.' The woman was convinced. She saw that the tree was beautiful, and its fruit looked delicious, and she wanted the wisdom it would give her. So, she took some of the fruit and ate it. Then she gave some to her husband, who was with her, and he ate it, too. At that moment their eyes were opened, and they suddenly felt shame at their nakedness. So, they sewed fig leaves together to cover themselves." The first command of God to be broken and the outcome was shame that was now felt by man. Adam and Eve knew no shame before satan, who had appeared as the serpent, tricked them. Now shame, which was never meant for them or us, was now mudding how they saw themselves. *Shame* as defined in the Merriam-Webster Dictionary is a painful emotion caused by the consciousness of guilt, shortcoming, or impropriety and the susceptibility to such emotion; a condition of humiliating disgrace or disrepute; something that brings censure or reproach or a cause of feeling shame. Shame did not nor does it come from God rather it comes from not following God and following His commands. Because not following the commands of the One, Whose image you were created in, there is a consequence and one that can be felt. Prior to this, there was no shame as seen in Genesis 2:35 NLT: ***"Now the man and his wife, were both naked, but they felt no shame."*** God had created them to feel no shame which they did not feel as long as they remained connected to God. Once tricked into being disconnected to God, the first thing they felt was shame. Something that was not a part of the image they were created in. And something that is not a part of the image we are created in.

I have learned to not question God and realize God knows what is best. He is good with me asking Him questions and creating a dialogue with Him. He wants to fellowship with me and talking is a part of fellowship. However, I know God created me so I know to simply trust what He commands, no verification needed other than knowing God said it so I will follow what He said, follow His side of the story. Unfortunately, I have not always done that or understood Who God is and that He always has my best interest at heart, even when He has a command for me to not do something. I felt my share of shame because I have not always followed God, followed His Word, followed His ways. I would often still be the why kid but as an adult. I would think something sounded good, others were doing it, and I wanted too as well. So, why not? How can something look good, sound good, and even feel good be bad, especially if others are doing it and deem it acceptable? Thankfully, I no longer ask why or look to confer with man regarding what is right and what is wrong. I no longer go by how I feel or how I think about what may be okay or not okay. Rather, I have learned to allow Holy Spirit to help me because He will always ensure what I do is right in God's eyes. I now look to follow God's commands, His Word, Jesus and His ways with the help of Holy Spirit. I now look to follow God's side of the story even if His side is less popular and no one else is following His side. Thanks to Jesus I am now able to do this because Jesus came to restore fellowship with God and us that was broken with Adam and Eve. Jesus did follow God and His commands to perfection because Jesus knew Who He was and Whose image He was created in and He did not listen to the lies of satan because He knew and listened to God's Truth. Jesus always chose to follow God's side of the story each and every time. And now we can do as He did. Regardless of how clever satan tries to be or how misleading he can be, we can follow God's commands and Jesus' ways. Even if it involves trying to tamper with our image, we can hold firm in knowing God and it is in His image we were created in.

When God first began creating, He had an order and way of creating. He was specific and He spoke accordingly, whatever He spoke happened (see Genesis 1). This included Him creating male and female in His image and God made it clear how he created male and how he created female. He tells us he formed man first in Genesis 2:7 NLT: ***"Then the Lord God formed the man from the dust of the ground. He breathed the breath of life into the man's nostrils, and the man became a living person."*** Think about how extraordinary a Creator God is because He took some dust and made a man and then He breathed life into the man. Have you ever driven down a dirt road and afterwards your vehicle was covered in dust, and you were not able to tell the color of your vehicle because of the dust covering it? God did not take dirt to make man but just the dust was enough for Him. And then it was His breathe He breathed into man and when He did that man became a living human. There is no man who can re-create like God, let alone actually create like God, nor will there ever be. Regardless of all the technology or any advancements of mankind, it will never compare to God, the Creator. How much more should I want to know Him, how much more should I want to know His side of the story and follow Him, follow His side? Not only did He take the dust from the ground to create Adam, God took the dust from dirt that was not a part of the Garden of Eden. God had not made the Garden before He made man. Genesis 2:8 NLT tells us: ***"Then the Lord God planted a garden in Eden in the east, and there He placed the man He had made."*** God can take anything that is not good and make it into something good. When He touches something, it is being touched with His love and His goodness. And after God created man, He realized man needed someone as we see in Genesis 2:18 NKJV: ***"And the Lord God said, "It is not good that man should be alone; I will make him a helper comparable to him."*** Notice, God did not say I will make a woman who is less than or not as good as a man. God Who creates good also created a woman who is good just like He created a man who is good. And He said the woman would be comparable to the man. Genesis 2:18 in YLT98 says: ***"make to him an helper – as his counterpart."*** For one to be comparable to another, one is of equivalent quality, worthy of comparison, or is likened to another. For one to be a counterpart to another, one is identical to or closely resembling another or one of the two parts complement or correspond to each other. Then God made the woman as seen in Genesis 2:21-25 NKJV: ***"And the Lord God caused a deep sleep to fall on Adam, and he slept; and He took one of his ribs and closed up the flesh in its place. Then the rib which the Lord God had taken from man He made into a woman, and He brought her to the man. And Adam said: 'This is now bone of my bones and flesh of my flesh; She shall be called Woman, because she was taken out of Man. Therefore, a man shall leave his father and mother and be joined to his wife, and they shall become one flesh."*** If a man is to be joined to a woman and the two flesh becomes one, the woman is to be the man's wife and if she is not a man's wife the two are not to be joined together as one flesh because this is God's side of the story according to His standards. God did not say a man and woman are to become one flesh and they can do so outside of marriage. Nor did He say two men can become one flesh or two women can become one flesh. God established His way of doing things when He created male and female and how they were to be together in marriage. He has not changed His way of doing things nor has He changed His side of the story, nor will He. God was specific in how He created a male and He was specific in how He created a female so God created a male to be a male and He created a female to be a female. God did not create male and female so that they could change how He had created them. God knew what He was doing and He was more precise in creating male and female not only because He created them in His image but how He went about creating them. He did not just speak and they were created but He formed them which meant He actually used His hand or hands. He used His personal touch in creating a man and in creating a woman. And He used His breathe to bring a man to life. Mankind first came alive through God's breathe, God was up close and personal with man from the very beginning which includes the woman even though He made her afterwards. He made her to be a helper, not less than, because both were still made with His personal touch and both made in His image. Sound familiar? God gave us Holy Spirit as our Helper. God gave the woman to man as his helper. God thinks no less of Himself in providing His Spirit and referring to Him as our Helper no more than He thinks less of woman in creating her and call her man's helper. God began creation by speaking but He ended creation with His touch, more intimate. And because He made you and made me to be like Him, He wants you and He wants me to touch the world for Him, to help the world know and see Him intimately. One way is for you and for me to understand Who we were made after and to live that out unapologetically with no regard for any other stories or reports or news other than our knowing intimately and living out boldly our intimacy for the One Who made us. For His side is good and how He creates is good so following Him, following His side of the story is also good. Because in Genesis 1:31 NLT it says: ***"Then God looked over all He had made, and He saw that it was very good!"*** Even Jesus believed God's side of the story and He spoke it in Matthew 19:46 NKJV: "***And He answered and said to them, "Have you not read that He who made them at the begin-***

ning 'made them male and female and said, 'For this reason a man shall leave his father and mother and be joined to his wife, and the two shall become one flesh'?" So then, they are no longer two but one flesh. Therefore, what God has joined together, let not man separate." Jesus knew God's side of the story and how He created male and female and that it was good and He was willing to retell God's side of the story. Jesus retold how God sees a man and a woman are to be together in marriage because He referred to the woman as a wife. And Jesus retold how God approves of marriage because He sees them as being joined by Him and He sees man not being able to separate them. He wants a marriage to be between a man and a woman as He designed it to be because He is the One Who created man and woman to begin with. He is good, and how He creates and designs is good. He created marriage to be good. And like anything else, we have an enemy who has been able to taint, to destroy, to mock, to mess up marriage because that is his nature. I had no idea what a marriage was to be or look like according to God. I remember when my husband and I were still dating wondering if we would marry though we both did want that. We had more than one discussion on not having had any good examples growing up and who were any examples we knew of at that time, including in the church. I recall seeing some marriages that seemed more like a business arrangement. And others I thought may not make it if they ever did not have a ministry or something else to focus on. I recall seeing at one point that the divorce rate in the church was higher than in the world. And remember thinking that is not God's best nor is it showing Him and how good He is. I believe knowing who we are in Him is the most important and we should have a firm grip on our identity as He sees us prior to entering marriage. And that you should both enter the marriage with that understanding that you both are God's children and from there everything else flows, including marriage. I recall listening to another pastor preach and he talked about getting this revelation. He had gotten upset at his wife and had actually hurt her feelings. He said she remained in love during that situation even though he had blatantly stepped out of love. He recalled how God immediately informed him that his wife was His [God's] child and that he had just talked to His [God's] child that way. This provided the revelation he needed to make the correction in his marriage and he began to see and treat his wife like the child of God she was and how a child of God should be treated.

Prior to becoming serious about and committing my life to Christ Jesus and as I like to say being born again for real, I saw someone as attractive and I went the world's way. I may think are they a Christian, meaning are they going to heaven and not hell, and may have some standards of what I thought was good and bad and how I wanted to be treated but I gave no thought to their relationship and fellowship with God. I gave no thought to them having Holy Spirit as their Helper and following Jesus and His ways. I have had discussions with youth who have been interested in someone and I have asked do they know Jesus. And each time they have told me they do not know. It has been an opportunity to teach them God's side of the story and His way. 2 Corinthians 6:14 NLT says: ***"Do not team up with those who are unbelievers. How can righteousness be a partner with wickedness? How can light live with darkness?"*** It matters who you marry, who you allow to influence you, who you spend time with on a regular basis. I do want to make a disclaimer that God never wants us in harms way or to be hurt. He is love and He is good and neither of those lead to harm or hurt. Sometimes we can make a mistake and sometimes people can fake good. And we can only account for our actions and beliefs. We cannot control if someone else decides to run after a lie of satan. And if anyone is in a bad situation bringing them harm, I believe God's love, His mercy, and His grace is sufficient to get out of a bad situation and away from anyone bringing harm and hurt, especially if the person is set on not changing. With that said, I was never told how a marriage was to look according to God and though He actually tells us in His Word, I had not read it myself nor been given any revelation about it. Yet, God tells us in Ephesians 5:21-33 NLT: ***"And further, submit to one another out of reverence for Christ. For wives, this means submit to your husbands as to the Lord. For a husband is the head of his wife as Christ is the head of the church. As the church submits to Christ, so you wives should submit to your husbands in everything. For husbands, this means love your wives, just as Christ loved the church. He gave up His life for her to make her holy and clean, washed by the cleansing of God's Word. He did this to present her to Himself as a glorious church without a spot or wrinkle or any other blemish. Instead, she will be holy and without fault. In the same way, husbands ought to love their wives as they love their own bodies. For a man who loves his wife actually shows love for himself. No on hates his own body but feeds and cares for it, just as Christ cares for the church. And we are members of his body. As the Scriptures say, 'A man leaves his father and mother and is joined to his wife, and the two are united into one.' This is a great mystery, but it is an illustration of the way Christ and the church are one. So, again I say, each man must love his wife as He loves himself, and the wife must respect her husband."*** And when I was single, I was thankful I realized how Jesus was my husband. He was the One I could count on, He was always there for me just like He is for His church. Do I think that to be silly or think how silly it may seem to others or do I think only as to how it looks to God and go with what He says? I choose to go with God and how He sees things, especially about me. Because God says in

Isaiah 43:7 NKJV: ***"Everyone who is called by My name, Whom I have created for My glory, I have formed him, yes, I have made him."*** If God formed us, which He did, and God made us, which He did, we can believe and follow His Word, His side of the story regardless. He can always be counted on, He will never leave me, He keeps His promises and I am His child.

The Oxford Languages Dictionary defines *image* as a representation of the external form of a person or the general impression that a person presents to the public. As being created in God's image, we should be His representation on earth. Everyone we come in contact with should get the general impression that we belong to God. Our words, actions, thoughts, and beliefs should line up with God and His image, with God and His Word, with God and His Son Jesus, with God and His Holy Spirit, and with God and how He sees. People should see us and know we know who we are as God's children and it should compel others to want to become God's children. And for those who are already God's children, it should compel them to want to be better children or it should compel them to want to understand who they are and how they are to live as God's children. Not that I have arrived but I want too. I want to go further in who I am in God and living more and more like the child of God I am. Holy Spirit remains here helping us. God always makes a way for us we just have to recognize the way as it is shown to us and then walk in the way. I can be driving and notice my turn and keep going. Or I can notice my turn and think there is another turn I can take that I think is a better way of getting to where I am going. God always shows the way we are to go as His children and Holy Spirit always helps by pointing out the way. 2 Corinthians 3:5 AMPC tells us: ***"Not that we are fit (qualified and sufficient in ability) of ourselves to form personal judgments or to claim or count anything as coming from us, but***

our power and ability and sufficiency are from God." Our power and ability and sufficiency are from God, Whose image, we were created in and Who gave us the power and ability and sufficiency to be His representatives on earth with Holy Spirit's help. 1 Corinthians 2:12 NKV tells us: ***"Now we have received, not the spirit of the world, but the Spirit Who is from God, that we might know the things that have been freely given to us by God."*** Jesus came to help reestablish and reaffirm our image is in God and be the bridge reconnecting us to God and providing our sonship. Holy Spirit came to be our seal, joining us together with God, keeping us connected and established in Him, so we are not alone here on earth, rather we are empowered by God to live as His children, to live as a part of His family. Genesis 5:1-2 TPT reaffirms: ***"When God created human beings, He made them in the likeness of God and created them as male and female. After He created them, He lovingly blessed them and named them 'humanity.'"*** Notice, there was no separation or segregation or any difference made other than male and female. Cambridge Dictionary defines *humanity* as all people in the world as a whole, or the qualities characteristic of people and understanding and kindness toward other people. We are to see as God sees and when we first see ourselves as He sees us, it aligns our eyesight with His enabling us to see others as He does. Enabling us to see people as He created humanity rather than how they may be seeing themselves and acting in ways other than how He created them to act. Rather than seeing people as our enemy because they are acting on lies provided by our enemy, satan, we can be praying they be restored back to God. We can see the fruit of being God's children and want the same for them. We can be God's examples so they can see what it means to be God's children.

CHAPTER 5

Your Mirror is God's Good News

GOD'S SIDE OF THE STORY can be seen from Genesis 1:1 to Revelation 22:21 and it is all Good News, it is all from God, it is all about Jesus, it is all for you, and it is all for me. It is the best self-help book, the best advice, the best stories about life, and how to live your best life and it is all found in God's Word. No other influence should rank above His Word because no other influence will outlast God's Word and only God's Word is divine. 1 Peter 1:24-25 in AMPC makes it clear: ***"For all flesh (mankind) is like grass, and all its glory (honor) like [the] flower of grass. The grass withers and the flower drops off, but the Word of the Lord (divine instruction, the Gospel) endures forever. And this Word is the Good News which was preached to you."*** God gives us clear instructions of what we are to do with His Word in Joshua 1:8-9 NLT: ***"Study this Book of Instruction continually. Meditate on it day and night so you will be sure to obey everything written in it. Only then will you prosper and succeed in all you do. This is My command – be strong and courageous! Do not be afraid or discouraged. For the Lord your God is with you wherever you go."*** How many hours have people spent studying what man has said, what man has developed, what curriculum man has come up with in school, including college? I worked at the library when I was in college and it was full of words written by man. I spent countless hours in the library researching and studying on top of working. And when I went on to get my master's degree, I found myself back at the library pouring over man's work, man's words, studying even more, writing even more about something man wanted me to write about and all so I could get a degree established by man. And not one moment was attributed to God's Word nor any importance given to how God sees things, how God provides help to those in need, or how God's Word will help make the necessary changes in a person's life. Even though I was getting both of my degrees in social work because I wanted to help people, I only realized afterwards how important and far more life changing is God's Word. And I realized with all the help, education, and resources of man, it is God and His Word that people need. God's Word is where we find our image of how God created us and where we find our identity and how God sees us and how we are to see ourselves. The key is we must get to the place where we will not believe anything that goes against God's Word, especially about ourselves or others. And we get to the place where we believe God's Word regardless of how many people may not believe God's Word. Even if we have to study for something like our job, we will not let what we are having to learn override God's Word nor will we compromise God's Word for a job. We will know God as our source and God will always provide for us because we have learned how by getting in His Word and allowing Him to show us. No matter how much education I have gotten from man, it does not compare to God and how He has educated me, especially about who I am and who I am to Him.

I remember a time in my life when I was searching for answers, searching for relief from a deep ache, trying to find a place to fit in, for a sense of belonging, looking for happy stories and special quotes that would make things better, looking to man for answers and coming away with even more questions, and yearning for something beyond what I could see because I knew there had to be more all the while coming up empty. Yet, I did not realize I had at my fingertips the answers I was needing and there would be nothing ever written that would compare or replace God's Word and nothing would be able to transform and make the needed changes in my life other than God's Word. Changes that would continue and develop as I continued and developed in and through God's Word. Because God's Word is powerful, God's Word has always been with Him, God's Word was brought to earth in the form of Jesus, God's Word remains here with us as our guide, our navigation tool to Him, and how God created us. God's Word is powerful and alive as we see in Hebrews 4:12 in AMPC: ***"For the Word that God speaks is alive and full of power [making it active, operative, energizing, and effective]; it's sharper than any two-edged sword, penetrating to the dividing line of the breath of life (soul) and [the immortal] spirit, and of joints and marrow [of the deepest parts of our nature], exposing and sifting and analyzing and judging the very thoughts and purposes of the heart."*** The very Word of God can penetrate deep within us transforming us into the very image of how God originally created mankind and revealing to us our identity and how we are to live out our identity according to God's side of the story and no one else's.

God, in His goodness, in His love, has given us a way we are to see ourselves and how we can line up with that way and not line up with any other way or any other story except His. In the story of Snow White, a mirror is used to ask a question of who is the fairest of them all and the mirror provides the answer. However, as the question keeps being asked, the mirror's response changes, and this evokes anger in the queen who has been doing the asking. The mirror had been telling the queen she was the fairest of them all and now it was telling her Snow White was the fairest of them all. How many mirrors are in the world where people are looking for answers and then wholeheartedly digesting the answers given not knowing they are seeking the wrong mirrors and obtaining the wrong answers? How many are looking to others for how they are to act, how they are to look, and how they are to think? How many are looking to others for who is the fairest and defining what is fairest? Thankfully, God has given us His own mirror by giving us His Word, which does not, nor will it ever change no matter who is doing the asking, no matter the questions being asked, no matter who it is regarding, and no matter the topic. God's Word remains consistent, steady, truthful, and infallible. And He does not compare us to others like the world and like the mirror in Snow White. We can embark on our own journey toward what is fair as God sees fairness by following in the ways of Jesus. God sent His purest, His fairest when He sent Jesus. Jesus Who is our good news came to demonstrate God's Word for us. Unlike the movie's depiction of fairest, mainly being about one's outward appearance, God was wanting to make an inward change that would be impactful now and for all of eternity. Jesus was not about His own interest's but He was about God's.

Jesus was about God's love and God's ways regarding how we are to think, speak, and live, including our identity. The Merriam-Webster Dictionary defines a *mirror* as something that gives a true representation or is an exemplary model. God's Word gives us a true representation and provides us with an exemplary model of Who He is, Who Jesus is, Who Holy Spirit is, and who we are. No matter when we look at the Word, no matter the season, no matter how we may even view ourselves or others right now, God's side of the story remains the same because God's Word remains the same. And how we see ourselves and others, how we are to respond to others, how we let others respond to us, and our reaction to how others respond to us, is always according to God's Word and according to how He tells us to respond. How we respond to other stories and news is always to be according to God's Word and how He wants us to respond. God's Word does not go on a feeling nor was birthed from emotions or intellectual thought. His Word does not go by popular opinion or polls nor according to what news is being reported. His Word does not change with the times, with a new discovery, a new method, or according to politics. God's Word is without any error and will always be so and will always be here. God does not need so many people to view His Word or give their reviews because His Word came from Him, the I Am Who has always been here and Who is the Creator of this world and mankind. There will never be enough self-help books that will compare to God's Word and be able to provide the help found in His Word. How much more should we value and want to know God's Word over any other word printed or spoken by mankind? God's Word should always be valued more because His Word is the most valuable. I am forever grateful that I gained the understanding of how valuable God's Word is and how valuable His Word has become to me. I am forever thankful that I have established deep within me to not deviate from God's Word, to take the time to get in His Word for myself on a daily basis, not from a place of some religious duty, but because of the life I found in His Word, the life that is His Word. And I am forever grateful I have Holy Spirit to help bring me the revelation and understanding of God's Word because His Word has changed my life and continues to make changes, changes that are for my benefit and good. And these changes are and will always be for my good. And God's Word will do the same for anyone and everyone who looks to God's Word and allows His Word to be their mirror. For 2 Timothy 3:16-17 NLT tells us: ***"All Scripture is inspired by God and is useful to teach us what is true and to make us realize what is wrong in our lives. It corrects us when we are wrong and teaches us to do what is right."*** And TPT says: ***"God has transmitted His very substance into every Scripture, for it is God-breathed. It will empower you by its instruction and correction, giving you the strength to take the right direction and lead you deeper into the path of godliness. Then you will be God's servant, fully mature and perfectly prepared to fulfill any assignment God gives you."*** God not only used His breath to breathe life into man He used it to breathe life into His Word. God's Word tells us what is right in His eyes and empowers us to see and do what is right accordingly. He has given us what is true, what is accurate, what is honest, and what is correct, so we will not be fooled or deceived by anything that is false even if presented as true. He has given us a way to make the needed corrections in our lives by holding our lives up to what requires correction. He has provided us with ongoing instructions that will not be updated or ever become outdated because there is only one model, one brand, One Word of God because God's Word holds true through all times. We have to hold it up, we have to look into it, we have to follow, and live out what it says. God's Word has to be our mirror we continually look in for our answers and how we are to see as God's sees about ourselves and everything else. No one can do it for us. We have to look in the Word ourselves. Someone can tell me what I look like but I will only truly know when I look into the mirror myself. Someone may describe me as looking a certain way but when I look into the mirror of God's Word, I realize how I actually look because I can see myself as God sees me and how He created me to look. Each time I look into God's Word I must realize God is talking back to me with all His love and goodness and with all His love and goodness He has for me. I can make any adjustments needed, especially if there is another voice trying to tell me something different than God. God's Word is personal and was specifically created for us. We must receive His Word in the same way as being personal and specifically created for us.

Have you ever gotten influenced by the majority and did something because it was popular or did not do something because it was unpopular? Have you wanted to do something that you knew God wanted you to do but then allowed yourself to get talked out of it? Have you ever felt like you did not fit in with what was considered the norm so you try to fit in somewhere that is outside the norm? Have you ever just wanted to be accepted? I can recall times when I did and recall how it never worked out. I was not holding up God's Word as my example but looking to others and other means to determine how I was to look and how I was to act. Yet, all I needed was to know what God's Word said and to let His Word be my example. Because God's Word provides us with all the answers regarding what is to be our norm, what is to be popular and unpopular, how and where we fit, how we are accepted and by Whom (God), and how we are to follow what God says. God makes everything clear in His Word because He does not operate in confusion or half-truths. Whenever God says something, we can know with confidence He will not change what He says. His Word is true and will always be true. God is a keeper of His promises, a keeper of His Word, a keeper of covenants. When He tells us something, He means it and He will always stand by what He says. This holds true when God told the Israelites that He was giving them the land of Canaan. He said it so He meant it. He wanted them to trust Him and know He was going to give them what He had promised. They just needed to believe Him, follow His instructions, and continue to obediently trust Him to see the plan unfold, to see themselves as He saw them. God told Moses in Numbers 13:1-2 NLT: ***"The Lord now said to Moses, 'Send out men to explore the land of Canaan, the land I am giving to the Israelites. Send one leader from each of the twelve ancestral tribes.'"*** Notice, God's instructions to Moses was to "send out the men to explore" and He told him which land and which men to send, and He told him that He, God, was giving this land to them. Sometimes we can take what God said, even in His Word, and want to add to or take away from what God said but God is always clear in what He says, especially in His Word. If something is in God's Word, it has purpose and meaning and it is never to be adjusted to fit what we or others think or want or according to how we feel or how others may feel. God knows Who He is and He knows what He says to be true. He wants us to know Who He is and know what He says to be true and follow accordingly. We see Moses following God's instructions in Numbers 13:3 NLT: ***"So Moses did as the Lord commanded him. He sent out twelve men, all tribal leaders of Israel, from their camp in the wilderness of Paran."*** It was a command for Moses to do what God told him to do, and it was a command for the tribal leaders to do what God told them to do through Moses being God's messenger. But notice in Numbers 13:17-20 NLT: ***"Moses gave the men these instructions as he sent them out to explore the***

land: 'Go north through the Negev into the hill country. See what the land is like and find out whether the people living there are strong or weak, few or many. See what kind of land they live in. Is it good or bad? Do their towns have walls, or are there many trees? Do your best to bring back samples of the crops you see,' (It happened to be the season for harvesting the first ripe grapes)." What would have happened had Moses said to the men: "God wants you to go and explore the land of Canaan, the land He is giving you so go and do as God said." When you go to explore land, you go to that land to learn and familiarize yourself with the land, you go looking for what resources the land has to offer. Would it have been a different outcome had Moses simply gave the instructions as God had given rather than add his own? The twelve leaders went and explored the land for forty days and returned to give their report as seen in Numbers 13:27-28 NLT: ***"This was their report they gave to Moses: 'We entered the land you sent us to explore, and it is indeed a bountiful country – a land flowing with milk and honey. Here is the kind of fruit it produces. But the people living there are powerful, and their towns are large and fortified. We even saw giants there, the descendants of Anak!'"*** The men reported how good the land was with all its resources but then they began talking about how the people there were superior to them. Of the twelve, one man tried to speak up and give a different report. This man was not concerned with popular opinion or what things may look like in the natural, but he was concerned with Who God was and what God had promised them. We see his report in Numbers 13:30 NLT: ***"But Caleb tried to quiet the people as they stood before Moses. 'Let's go at once to take the land,' he said. 'We can certainly conquer it!'"*** Caleb saw exactly the same things the others saw but his report was completely contrary to their report. His report lined up with God's. God told them He had given them the land and that is all

Caleb needed. He trusted God, He trusted what God said and that settled it for him. He was not going by what he saw and he was not going by what others were reporting but he was going by God's news, God's side of the story and what God had said. His mirror was reflecting what God was seeing and what God was saying. At any moment, someone else could have stepped up beside Caleb and believed God's report over the other report being told. Caleb was willing to voice what God had said over what others were saying. Twelve went in but only one, Caleb, was standing up for God's news, His side of the story and was willing to tell God's side above everyone else's side. And we see how the others responded in Numbers 13:31 NLT: ***"But the other men who had explored the land with him disagreed. 'We cannot go up against them! They are stronger than we are!' So, they spread this bad report about the land among the Israelites: 'This land we traveled through and explored will devour anyone who goes to live there. All the people we saw were huge. We even saw giants there, the descendants of Anak. Next to them we felt like grasshoppers, and that is what they thought too!'"*** Notice, there was never any mention of them talking to anyone when they went into the land. Instead, they were reporting what they observed about the land but also about the people. God's instructions never involved them going into the land to explore the people or report anything about the people. Their focus was never to be on the people and yet, that is where their focus was. They were also reporting how they felt and how they thought the people saw them. Rather than standing firm on how God saw them as going into the land and possessing it, they were reporting how they thought the people viewed them solely from the vantage point of that is how they saw themselves. They were the ones reporting they felt like grasshoppers and they were the ones drawing the conclusion that the people thought the same about them. No one had come up to them and referred to them as being like grasshoppers. God had a good plan for them. He wanted them to believe Him and believe His plan He had for them. God knew who lived there but He also knew His promise to them was that they would go in and possess it. He wanted them to trust Him with all the details as how that was going to occur by them going as He commanded. God saw them going in and possessing the land and He wanted them to see themselves going into the land possessing the land, He wanted them to see as He was seeing. He saw them as being His people, who He was giving them a land to go in and occupy. He was the One sending them so He was the One Who would equip them with all they needed to live in the land. Instead of seeing themselves as He did and seeing themselves going into the land and possessing it like He did, they saw themselves by how they felt and how they thought others saw them. We should never see ourselves by how we feel or how we think others see us. We should always see ourselves as God sees us and we should always do what He tells us to do because we see ourselves doing exactly as He tells us. Because when He tells us to do something, He sees us as doing it. We need to see ourselves as doing the same knowing He will equip us as we step out and follow His lead, as we step out and follow His commands. God saw the Israelites as being worthy of having a land to call their own, a land that was good and bountiful, a land that would benefit them. The Israelites saw themselves as being much smaller, weaker and less than the people living in the land God was giving them. They felt and thought of themselves as such yet God wanted them to go in as His people, as His children, and take what He was giving them. And in doing so, they would be showing Who He is and Who they are to Him and Who they are in Him. This is still God's plan for us, for His children, as He wants us to see ourselves as worthy of possessing this land, this world for Him, for His glory because we see ourselves as He does.

And it only took ten people, ten leaders, to sway a whole nation against God and against doing what He said rather than going with God and doing what He said. At any time, the people could have chosen to go with the one person (Caleb), the one leader, and believe him. They could have seen themselves as he saw himself in the eyes of God. One person, one leader (Joshua) did choose to stand with Caleb. And the others could have as well. Even the other leaders could have had a change of heart, a change in how they felt and saw themselves. They could have allowed themselves to be encouraged by Caleb and Joshua because they both were standing with God. They could have remembered what God had already done for them and encouraged themselves with how He always comes through for His people, for His children. God showed how capable He is when He delivered them out of Egypt and did so with them taking all the riches of Egypt with them, they left rich. And everyone was healthy and strong when they left. God was already showing them how He will take care of and provide for them. Even if the leaders were not reporting correctly as God was reporting, anyone could have spoken up and believed God and remembered what He had already done for them. Anyone could have remembered all He had done for them since they left Egypt. How different would it have been had they come back and reported what they observed about the land? How different would it have been had anyone reported what God had already done for them? How different would it have been had they saw themselves going in as God had told them? How different would it had been had they saw themselves as God saw them? It may have sounded something like this: "Look what God has already done for us, He delivered us from being captive in Egypt, we left with all their money and possessions, our clothes and shoes have not even worn out since we left, no one was or has been sick, we have had plenty to eat and drink, we are strong because God has made us so even after having to work so hard and in such poor conditions, God made sure we have not suffered physically. He led us through the Red Sea, caused it to open right up, and then caused it to close right back up on the Egyptians so we got away free. They have no hold on us and will never bother us again. God has been with us in the pillar of fire when it is dark and He has been with us during the day with a cloud of smoke. He has made Himself known to us and is here with us now. Let's go, He is with us and will remain with us, He will give us this land because He said He would, He knows how He is going to do it so all we have to do is go when He tells us and do as He says when we go. Whatever strength and resources we need, He will give it to us because He has done so before." However, the people responded to the report that went against God's report, even after Caleb was reporting God's side. Even though the people had not gone into the land to observe firsthand themselves, they had still observed all God had already done for them personally and collectively. They shared the testimony of God's deliverance, protection, and provision. God saw them as being His people. They could have relied on Who He is and Who He was saying they were. We can see how they responded in Numbers 14:1-3 NLT: ***"Then the whole community began weeping aloud, and they cried all night. Their voices rose in a great chorus of protest against Moses and Aaron. 'If only we had died in Egypt, or even here in the wilderness!' they complained. 'Why is the Lord taking us to this country only to have us die in battle? Our wives and our little ones will be carried off as plunder! Would not it be better for us to return to Egypt?'"*** Now that makes no sense, does it? Why would a person or community of people want to go back to a place where they were enslaved, where they lived in poor and harsh conditions, where they were not properly cared for, and could not move around freely? Where they were not seen nor treated like the people they were and how they were created? Yet, this is exactly what they wanted over what God was saying, over what God had already done for them, and over what God was wanting to give them. He had His best ahead for them but they were not able to see it and respond in a manner where they could receive what God was wanting to give them. God was not going to bring them through all He had to see them destroyed nor will God regarding us. Once delivered, always delivered in God's eyes. Moving forward into His best for us is always what He has for us.

After the people's response, we see Caleb still conveying God's truth, still conveying God's side of the story and what He said He would do and Joshua, who was one of the twelve who went into the land to observe, is standing with Caleb. Even though the majority have now joined in with the ten leaders, we see two, who are remaining firm in believing God and see how He sees their situation. We see how they respond in Numbers 14:6-9 NLT: ***"Two of the men who had explored the land, Joshua, son of Nun and Caleb, son of Jephunneh, tore their clothing. They said to all the people of Israel, 'The land we traveled through and explored is a wonderful land! And if the Lord is pleased with us, He will bring us safely into that land and give it to us. It is a rich land flowing with milk and honey. Do not rebel against the Lord, and do not be afraid of the people of the land. They are only helpless prey to us! They have no protection, but the Lord is with us! Do not be afraid of them!'"*** Caleb and Joshua knew Who God was and they knew who they were in God. They knew they were stronger than their enemy, they knew the Lord would do as He said, they knew not to get in fear, and they knew God was with them. And they were ready to go as God was leading without hesitation.

Sometimes other people may see us how God sees us before we are able to see ourselves as He does. Only Joshua and Caleb saw themselves as capable of going in and possessing the land God had told them they would possess and they saw the other Israelites as doing the same. They tried to convince everyone else by remaining strong in their conviction that God would do what He said He would do. Even though the people continued to not believe God, Joshua and Caleb faithfully believed God. Two against a multitude and they still believed God's side of the story and they still saw themselves and their situation as God did. Their trust remained firmly in God and His promises. They were making God's side of the story their story. Because the rest of the people would not believe and follow God, they all ended up having to die before God could give them the land. And through all that time of waiting, Joshua and Caleb remained strong in their belief of Who God is and who they are in Him. Joshua and Caleb were also going to see what their enemy thought about them. Joshua was now the leader because Moses had died and all those who had walked in unbelief toward God's promises had died. Now Joshua was sending in spies to scout out the same land he and Caleb had. This time there were only two sent and this time we see them interacting with someone in the land. Joshua 2:8-11 NLT reveal to us: ***"Before the spies went to sleep that night, Rahab went up on the roof to talk with them. 'I know the Lord has given you this land,' she told them. 'We are all afraid of you. Everyone in the land is living in terror. For we have heard how the Lord made a dry path for you through the Red Sea when you left Egypt. And we know what you did to Sihon and Og, the two Amorite kings east of the Jordon River, whose people you completely destroyed. No wonder our hearts have melted in fear! No one has the courage to fight after hearing such things. For the Lord your God is the supreme God of the heavens above and the earth below.'"*** These are the same people that were described as being stronger than the Israelites and were described as saying they saw the Israelites as grasshoppers compared to them. All said by ten Israelite leaders but now we see how the Israelites were truly seen and how this lined up with how God saw them and how God wanted them to see themselves. Because how God sees, is the truth to how we are to see. And He gives us His Word as our mirror so we can see how He sees. He gives us His truth to look at, to look into, providing us with the image of how we are to see as He sees. When we look into God's Word, His Word (Jesus made flesh Who was with Him in the beginning and will always be here forever) is staring back at us. We see ourselves not as we looked before looking at God's Word rather, we see ourselves as we look after we have looked at God's Word. His Word reflects back to us how we are to see and His Word will always reflect back how God sees. The two who believed God and had remained strong in their beliefs and their identity in God were now going to lead new generations of Israelites into God's promised land. They valued God's Word and God valued them. Proverbs 13:13 TPT tells us: ***"Despise the Word, will you? Then you will pay the price and it will not be pretty! But the one who honors the Father's holy instructions will be rewarded."*** The MSG says: ***"Ignore the Word and suffer; honor God's commands and grow rich."*** The land was plentiful and filled with everything the Israelites needed and they were going to get to experience it. When God's Word is honored, rewards follow. His children get to experience His best. The only cost is to be fervent in believing and trusting God's Word even when unpopular and met by resistance. Adhering to how He sees and how He sees us while remaining steadfast in allowing God's Word to be our mirror and only mirror. Because our enemy, satan, holds up other mirrors as distractions and deceptions trying to trick people into not believing God's Word. Calab and Joshua were not tricked because they allowed what God said to hold true above what everyone else was saying. They looked at what He said and kept what He said before them. We can do the same regarding any situation, regarding any news or stories being told, regarding any emotions or thoughts from ourselves or others, when we continually look at God's Word for our guidance and how we are to see everything. Which will always enable us to see as God sees, including ourselves. When we see ourselves according to God's Word, we can operate in the strength and courage that comes with being God's children.

A mirror serves no purpose when it goes unused. It remains a mirror and the purpose it was created does not change. More so with God's Word. His Word is His Word regardless if we look at His Word. His Word remains unchanged even though we may choose to not let His Word be our mirror for how we are to see ourselves, see others, and see God. I remember not having an understanding of the importance and value of God's Word growing up. I like to read and read a lot. Unfortunately, God's Word was not on my reading list nor was it on any reading list at any school I attended. We had Bibles at home but I do not recall anyone reading one. I do recall you were to take a Bible to church but then you put it back where you had gotten it before church. I do remember there being a focus on devotionals and pamphlets that were church approved. However, I do not recall the emphasis being placed on God's Word and how I needed to get into His Word myself. Perhaps, it was explained somewhere along the way and it just did not click with me as important. I am willing to admit that but no one really stands out as having really lived or talked about God's Word for the real value His Word is. I remember hearing more of what you were not supposed to do. I was told you were not to cuss but I heard people cussing anyway. And I heard some who had changed the words to something else. So, I guess that was okay? Yet, what does God's Word say regarding how I am to talk? Is there a problem, what does God's Word say? They called you a what, what does God's Word say? They do not like you, what does God's Word say? You are confused about something, what does God's Word say? Are you tempted, what does God's Word say? Everyone else is doing it, what does God's Word say? I think I was born this way, what does God's Word say? It feels good so it has to be okay, what does God's Word say? We were just having some fun, what does God's Word say? Everybody who is somebody will be there, what does God's Word say? Who am I, what does God's Word say? We have the answers in God's Word and we need to look in His Word ourselves for those answers. I got into God's Word for myself regarding cussing and found where Colossians 3:8 NKJV says: ***"But now you yourselves are to put off all these: anger, wrath, malice, blasphemy, filthy language out of your mouth."*** And Ephesians 5:4 GNT which says: ***"Nor is it fitting for you to use language which is obscene, profane, or vulgar. Rather you should give thanks to God."*** Not only did I find in God's Word how not to talk I found in God's Word how to talk. It is fitting for me to give thanks to God. His Word provides us with a firm foundation. A firm foundation that can be built upon so we can live in this world according to God's Word.

Joshua and Caleb had remained confident in God and who they were in Him. Now, Joshua would be leading the people into the promise of God. The people were believing God along with Caleb and Joshua. They were going to discover God has no timeline or time limit for His promises, for His Word. He told them they would go in and possess the land, they believed Him and now it was happening. God being a keeper of His promise made another promise with Joshua as seen in Joshua 1:5-6 GNT: ***"Josh-***

ua, no one will be able to defeat you as long as you live. I will be with you as I was with Moses. I will always be with you. Be determined and confident, for you will be the leader of these people as they occupy this land which I promised their ancestors." God was letting Joshua know that He was with him so Joshua could be bold, focused on God and His promises, while not allowing anyone to prevent him from walking in all God had promised. Joshua did not give up on God and God was not going to give up on Joshua. God wants us to not give up on Him because He will not give up on us. His promises remain the same and are for everyone who will believe in and trust His promises by believing in and trusting His Word and trusting Him. God first gave man this land, the world, by giving Adam and Eve the Garden of Eden. God's plan was for them to spread the Garden of Eden, to spread His ways, His Word throughout the whole earth. They believed the report of our enemy, satan, over God's report, over how God saw them and over how God created them. They were to occupy this land, this world, for God because He had given this land, this world, to them. Yet, they were tricked by satan into handing over the land, this world, to him. This is still satan, the god of this world's, plan. However, God's plan remains the same. He has given His children this land, this world. It is up to us, as His children, to believe Him, as Joshua and Caleb did, and go into this world, into this land, and possess it. It is up to us to believe in who we are in Him and what we can do through Him, through Jesus Christ, with Holy Spirit's help. Knowing and continually looking into God's Word helps enable us to possess and occupy this world for God's Kingdom.

CHAPTER 6

Your Identity as God's Child

IDENTITY AS DEFINED by Dictionary.com is the state or fact of remaining the same one or ones, as under varying aspects or conditions; the condition of being oneself and not another; condition or character as to who a person is; the state or fact of being the same one as described. Do you have a firm understanding of your identity or does it vacillate according to circumstances? Are you able to remain the same under pressure? Do you act differently when someone is around verses when you are alone? Would you be described as having good character or flawed character? If I were to ask ten people about you, would they all say similar things or would I get ten different answers? Regardless of how we may answer these questions, God has an answer for us. And His answer begins with Jesus, His First Son Who made a way for us to also become God's son, God's daughter. Jesus fully grasped His identity in being God's Son and He never wavered. Hebrews 13:8 NLT informs us: *"Jesus Christ*

is the same yesterday, today and forever. Jesus was the embodiment of consistency in knowing Himself as God's Son and all that entailed. Jesus saw Himself through God's eyes and He wants us to do the same. He wants us to live our life according to God's side of the story, to live our life according to how God sees us. Jesus had a firm understanding of His identity as being God's Son and it did not vacillate according to circumstances. Jesus remained the same under pressure and He acted the same when alone or around others. Jesus' character was good and He knew His Father's character was good. Regardless of how many people you asked about Jesus, Jesus remained Jesus because He knew Himself as God's Son. Some recognized Him as God's Son while others did not. Yet, Jesus never wavered in how He saw Himself as God's Son and how He presented Himself as God's Son. Jesus did not allow His surroundings, His culture, where He grew up, or where He lived define Him. Jesus was not moved by what people said about Him, how they identified Him, or by anyone's influence. Nor was He moved by people's perceptions, beliefs, opinions, or customs. Jesus did not allow governments, political affairs, religious leaders, religious establishments, or family define Him. Jesus allowed God and only God to define Him and establish His identity. Jesus was focused and He set the example for us to be able to do the same. Jesus knew His assignment while He was here and He completed it to the full measure required of Him. Jesus was focused on what He needed to do for us. He knew He was the way, He was the door, leading us to God. John 10:9 AMP says: ***"I am the Door; anyone who enters through Me will be saved [and will live forever], and will go in and out [freely], and find pasture (spiritual security)."*** Jesus was here to provide our freedom from sin and death and establish a secure life with God that would last for eternity. Hebrews 12:2 NKJV tells us: ***"Looking unto Jesus, the author and finisher of our faith, Who for the joy***

that was set before Him endured the cross. He counted it all joy, including going to the cross." Jesus was going to the cross and He knew He would have to endure what He did leading to the cross and then once He was at the cross. And He counted it all joy, every moment of it was joy to Him. He was that focused on knowing what He was going to do no matter how horrible, painful, and ugly it was it would mean the door would open for us to become God's children having our identity firmly established in Him. No matter what they said about Him and how loudly people cheered for Him to be crucified, Jesus was counting it as joy because He knew the reward would be we could become God's children. He knew the value of being God's Son and He wanted the same for us. He knew once we were God's children and we saw ourselves as His children we could live in this world as victorious as He did. He knew we could focus on Him and maintain our focus to live as successfully for God as He did. Hebrews 12:2-3 TPT says: ***"We look away from the natural realm and we focus our attention and expectation onto Jesus Who birthed faith within us and Who leads us forward into faith's perfection. His example is this: Because His heart was focused on the joy of knowing that you would be His, He endured the agony of the cross and conquered its humiliation, and now sits exalted at the right hand of the throne of God! So, consider carefully how Jesus faced such intense opposition from sinners who opposed their own souls, so that you will not become worn down and cave in under life's pressures."*** Jesus remained faithful to God and to God's Word, He remained faithful to God's side of the story. He remained faithful as being God's Son and showing others He was God's Son. And we can do the same. Jesus fully understood and lived James 1:2 NLT as our example: ***"Dear brothers and sisters when troubles of any kind come your way, consider it an opportunity for great joy. For you know that when your faith is tested, your endurance has a chance to***

grow. So let it grow, for when your endurance is fully developed, you will be patient and complete, needing nothing." Jesus was establishing for us a new way of life that would be transformational for all of eternity. And it would be a life that would begin when we receive Jesus and we receive the life He provided. It is a life that we must see as Jesus saw and live our life unapologetically as Jesus lived. Living our life being fully persuaded we are God's children so we not only see as God sees but we see as Jesus sees. We live our life to the full measure of God's Word just as Jesus did because we live in the full measure as God's children just as Jesus did.

Jesus lived His life in faith. He had total confidence in and completely trusted God's Word and all the promises contained within. He was fully persuaded that God would standby His Word and His Word would always come to pass. Jesus knew if God said something it was true and it would always be true. Jesus knew He could always count on God's Word to override any circumstance, any situation, any other story or news, or anything that could be seen in the natural. Jesus knew He was going to beat death for us, Jesus knew He was going to pay the price of sin for us, and He knew God was going to raise Him up from the dead. Jesus knew for the first time in His life He was going to have to experience being separated from God and He was still willing to do this for us. He knew He would have to go to hell and take back our authority that Adam and Eve had lost to satan and He went for us. He wanted us to rule and reign in this world as God's children, to rule and reign here on earth as if we were in heaven. He knew what He had to do and He did it all for us. Jesus birthed in us our faith, the same faith as He had, the same faith as God. A faith that He wants us to grow and develop in and we can as we continue in God's Word and developing in our understanding of who we are as God's children. We can then not be swayed by any other stories or any other news vying for our attention. Rather, we can solidify our identity in being God's child. Romans 10:17 WEB tells us: ***"So faith comes by hearing, and hearing by the Word of God."*** The NLT says: ***"hearing the Good News about Christ."*** Not only do we need to keep hearing, and hearing, and hearing God's Word but as we do, we are hearing, and hearing, and hearing about Jesus Christ, Jesus the Anointed One and His Anointing, Who, is our Good News. He is Good News to us and for us and He shows us our identity through God's eyes and through His eyes. As we continue to hear, and hear, and hear God's Word we are hearing, and hearing, and hearing about who we are as God's children. We are hearing, and hearing, and hearing, how we are to believe and live in this world as God's children. We are hearing, and hearing, and hearing, God's voice louder and above all other voices.

Jesus was so focused on His assignment and so focused on the unseen realm that He was able to walk through a mob unnoticed. A mob that was filled with people Jesus knew from His home town and identified Him as being Joseph's Son. A mob that started as a group of people meeting in a synagogue where Jesus read God's Word. And though their reactions vacillated and escalated into violence, Jesus remained fully persuaded as to Who He was and how He identified Himself as God's Son. He remained fully persuaded that this was not His appointed time to die and God was going to see Him safely though this situation. And He remained focused, consistent, constant, and never wavering in knowing, believing, and speaking God's side of the story, speaking God's Word. Jesus spoke what He heard His Father tell Him to speak. Jesus first read God's Word to the people in Luke 4:18. Then Luke 4:22 TPT lets us know how they responded: ***"Everyone was impressed by how well Jesus spoke, in awe of the beautiful words of grace that came from His lips. But they said among themselves,***

'Who does He think He is? Is not He Joseph's son, Who, grew up here in Nazareth?" They knew Who Jesus was in the natural and they were only able to recognize Him in the natural. As a result, they were only able to hear what He said in the natural which limited how they received to the natural. They were not able to recognize Him in the supernatural, in the unseen realm where God lives, because they were not able to see Him through the eyes of faith. They could not see Jesus as God did, as being God's Son and being able to fulfill what God had called Him to fulfill. However, Jesus fully knew Who He was and He was not moved by what they said or did. He was not moved by how they identified Him. Jesus felt the pressure but He did not allow the pressure to distract nor define Him. He was not moved by their emotions, by their reactions. He did not bend to the pressure or compromise because Jesus fully knew Who He was, His identity was already established well before people got mad at Him and His credentials because of what He was teaching and how He was preaching. Jesus remained in faith. Again, Jesus spoke but this time the people responded differently as seen in Luke 4:28-30 TPT: ***"When everyone present heard Jesus' Words, they erupted with furious rage. They mobbed Jesus and threw Him out of the city, dragging Him to the edge of the cliff on the hill on which the city had been built, ready to hurl Him off. But He walked right through the crowd, leaving them all stunned."*** Jesus taught and preached according to Who He was in God and not Who the people thought He was or even wanted Him to be. Jesus did not change how He taught or preached according to people's reactions or responses or what they wanted to hear. Jesus knew Who He was, the reason He was here, and He did not lose focus. Even when people reacted in a rage and made a threat toward His life, Jesus still trusted God and trusted God would do what He says. Jesus knew He was God's Son and He knew He was about His Father's business. Jesus only looked to please His Father by telling His Father's side of the story and telling others about His Father and His Father's Kingdom.

Jesus even had an understanding of Who He was at an early age. Luke 2:40 TPT tells us: ***"The Child grew more powerful in grace, for He was being filled with wisdom, and the favor of God was upon Him."*** Jesus was growing in His understanding of seeing things God's way, seeing God's side of the story, seeing Himself through God's eyes, and understanding the reason He was on the earth. Proverbs 2:6 NKJV informs us: ***"For the Lord gives wisdom, from His mouth come knowledge and understanding."*** God was giving Jesus the wisdom He was needing while Jesus was growing up. And God will give us the wisdom we need any time we need it because He says so in James 1:5 NKJV: ***"If any of you lacks wisdom, let him ask of God, Who, gives to all liberally and without reproach, and it will be given to him."*** Not only does God give us wisdom but He gives us above and beyond what we need. If you need an answer for something, ask God and God will not only give you the answer but He will give you above what you asked for. God knew we would need wisdom so He gave us Jesus because He lets us know in 1 Corinthians 1:30 NKJV: ***"But of Him you are in Christ Jesus, Who, became for us wisdom from God – and righteousness and sanctification and redemption."*** Jesus came to give us God's wisdom and then He gave us even more by giving us righteousness, sanctification, and redemption. We needed wisdom and God said I am giving you that and much, much, much more. Proverbs 8:11-14 GNT describes wisdom as: ***"I am Wisdom, I am better than jewels; nothing you want can compare with Me I am Wisdom, and I have insight; I have knowledge and sound judgment. To honor the Lord is to hate evil; I hate pride and arrogance, evil ways and false words. I make plans and carry them out. I have understanding, and I am strong."*** Notice, how Wisdom is identified in first-person. Jesus became for us wisdom from God so we can read it like this: "Jesus is Wisdom and He is better than jewels; nothing anyone would ever want will ever compare to Him; Jesus is Wisdom and He has insight, Jesus has knowledge and sound judgment. Jesus honors the Lord and hates evil; Jesus hates pride and arrogance, evil ways and false words. Jesus makes plans and carries them out. Jesus has understanding and He is strong." Jesus wants this for us and has provided the way for us to have and do what is spoken of in God's Word, including the wisdom of how to walk in God's Word ourselves. When we realize our identity was first established in Jesus, God's first Son, we can gain a better understanding of who we are and how we are to live.

Even though Jesus was growing up with His parents, we saw where Jesus was growing in God as a Child. Now at the age of twelve, we can see Jesus was gaining more wisdom and beginning to see the plan God had for Him. His parents did not fully understand the plan but that did not deter Jesus as He remained focused. Luke2:41-52 NLT reveals to us: ***"Every year Jesus' parents went to Jerusalem for the Passover festival. When Jesus was twelve years old, they attended the festival as usual. After the celebration was over, they started home to Nazareth, but Jesus stayed behind in Jerusalem. His parents did not miss Him at first, because they assumed He was among the other travelers. But when He did not show up that evening, they started looking for Him among their relatives and friends. When they could not find Him, they went back to Jerusalem to search for Him there. Three days later they finally discovered Him in the Temple, sitting among the religious teachers, listening to them and asking questions. All who heard Him were amazed at His understanding and His answers. His parents did not know what to think. 'Son,' His mother***

said to Him, 'why have you done this to us? Your father and I have been frantic, searching for You everywhere.' 'But why did you need to search?' He asked. 'Did you not know that I must be in My Father's house?' But they did not understand what He meant. Then He returned to Nazareth with them and was obedient to them. And His mother stored all these things in her heart. Jesus grew in wisdom and in stature and in favor with God and all the people." We know Jesus was apart from His parents for at least five days. They traveled a day before they realized He was gone so it would take them another day to travel back. Then it took them three days to find Him once they had returned. Yet, Jesus was fully content being in God's house and being in God's Word and it did not appear as if Jesus had missed His parents. There is no mention that He was even aware that they had left until they found Him in the Temple, which Jesus referred to as His Father's house. How had He eaten or where had He stayed during these days when He was not with His parents? He was twelve years old but He had already found contentment in being God's Son, being in God's house, and being in God's Word. Perhaps, He drew strength from this and even nourishment in the natural. We do not know because it does not tell us in God's Word. But had Jesus already gained an understanding of the very Word of God that He would later speak to satan? After all, He was Wisdom Himself, He was the Word made flesh. Deuteronomy 8:3 NKJV says: ***"So, He humbled you, allowed you to hunger, and fed you with manna which you did not know nor did your fathers know, that He might make you know that man shall not live by bread alone; but man lives by every Word that proceeds from the mouth of the Lord."*** Jesus knew this passage of God's Word because He spoke it to satan as previously mentioned. Was He already living this passage of God's Word? Had God's Word given Him the sustenance He needed while He was away from His parents for those five days?

Jesus knew there was more to life than the natural, more to life than what you eat and drink. Was this preparation for going into the wilderness for forty days without food? Jesus knew His Father God could be trusted. Matthew 6:25 NKJV tells us: ***"Therefore, I say to you, do not worry about your life, what you will eat or what you will drink; nor about your body what you will put on. Is not life more than food and the body more than clothing?"*** Was Jesus already demonstrating this passage of scripture while He was in His Father's house and away from his parents? Regardless, Jesus wants us to be aware of how important God's Word is to us, how important God's side of the story is, how important it is that we know who we are as God's children and that we see ourselves as His children as firmly and unwaveringly as Jesus did, not allowing anyone else define us except God. Jesus understood that God's Word and every Word spoken by God can fully sustain you. He knew there was a spiritual side to things and God's Word was a part of this. And He wants us to know this as well.

God's Word makes it clear, where the world would say otherwise, that we are to live and function through our identity in Jesus (see Acts 17:28 TPT). Jesus opened up the unseen realm to us, He opened up heaven for us, all so heaven can come to earth and God's Kingdom can be established through God's sons and daughters here on earth. Jesus established our identity and He meant for us to live in our identity because it is a part of our inheritance from Him. Even though we are born in the natural, Jesus was making away for us to be born again, a birth that is more powerful and has a spiritual side. A spiritual side that supersedes the natural just as the spiritual side superseded the natural through Holy Spirit touching Mary's womb. The supernatural led to Jesus' birth now the supernatural is leading to our new birth through Jesus. Ephesians 2:10 NLT tells us: ***"For we are***

God's masterpiece. He has created us anew in Christ Jesus, so we can do the good things He planned for us long ago." God always planned for us to have complete dominion on this earth and for us to operate in His Kingdom. He provided the way through Jesus and satan cannot undo or outdo what Jesus has done. Spinning lies, creating deception, causing bad things to happen all over the world, creating divisions, causing destruction and all other manners of evil is how he operates to get God's people to cooperate with his lies rather than cooperating with God's Truth, rather than cooperating with God's Word and living out their identity in Jesus as God's children. There is a growth process, a sanctification process where we learn who we are in Jesus Christ, where we grow in revelation of God's Word, and where we learn how to be led and helped through Holy Spirit. It is imperative that we stay on this journey of actively learning who we are in Christ and who we are as God's children all the while keeping God's Word before us and leaning on Holy Spirit for His help. We are God's masterpiece and we are to see ourselves as His masterpiece, as His greatest work, as His greatest achievement. All crafted thanks to Jesus and His precious blood.

God wants us to know what Colossians 3:10 TPT reveals: ***"For you have acquired new creation life which is continually being renewed into the likeness of the One Who created you, giving you the full revelation of God."*** The NLT says: ***"Put on your new nature, and be renewed as you learn your Creator and become like Him."*** God has made it obtainable, our new creation life thanks to Jesus. Receiving this new life is as easy as getting dressed each day. We make a choice. We can wear what the world tells us or we can wear what God tells us through His Word, through His ways and through Jesus' ways. Holy Spirit helps us to dress in our new nature every day and He helps us understand how we are to properly walk around in our new nature all for God's glory and all so we can be seen as the children of God we are. And as we daily walk in our new nature, it becomes more and more natural, making it our new norm. We learn each day more than we did the day before how our new nature functions and how we are to function in our new nature. All while, Holy Spirit is with us and in us helping us. And God's Word is our mirror letting us know how we are to look and act in our new nature. 2 Corinthians 5:17 NLT tells us: ***"This means that anyone who belongs to Christ has become a new person. The old life is gone; a new life has begun!"*** Our old life gets replaced with our new life when we are born again. We have to line up our thoughts, our words, our actions to walking in this new birth. We grow up in it just as we grow up in the natural. We learn how to walk in this new birth and we get more and more proficient in it as we grow. We can get to the point where our new birth becomes more real to us than our natural birth. We can get to the point where we identify more with our new birth just as Jesus identified God being His Father when He was twelve and was found in the temple by his parents and He knew He was to be about His Father's business because He was His Father's Son. John 1:12-13 NKJV lets us know: "***But as many as received Him, to them He gave the right to become children of God, to those who believe in His name: who were born, not of blood, nor of the will of the flesh, nor of the will of man, but of God.***" When you receive Jesus as your Savior and Lord, you become God's child, your identity changes. Yes, we still belong to our natural family and honor them but we should relate to being God's child in how we are to believe, think, talk, and act. When I got married, my identity changed from being single to married, my last name changed from Billings (my madden name) to Lopez (my married name). On occasion, I will get mail addressed to Billings and my husband will say this person no longer exists, or if someone refers to me by my madden name my husband will also say this person no longer exists. I have had to learn to identify and function as someone who is now married rather than as someone who was single. I am no longer just my own but now I am joined with my husband. My new identity is in being Lopez and not Billings. We are joined to Jesus Christ which now makes us God's children and we are to learn to identify and function as His children. We have to remind ourselves and others that we are God's children and we have the identity He has given us so that old person no longer exists. And this is something we grow into through changing how we think and see ourselves by thinking about and seeing ourselves as God does.

Jesus made a way for us to be close to God, no longer separated from Him, but able to draw near to Him. He made a way for us to run to God at any time we want completely uninhibited or restricted. Ephesians 2:13 NLT tells us: ***"But now you have been untied with Christ Jesus. Once you were far away from God, but now you have been brought near to Him through the blood of Christ."*** When Jesus was so focused that He went to the cross, completely emptying His body of His blood, He knew the price it would pay, He knew the power in His blood. He knew His blood would establish our new bloodline in us being able to become God's children. He knew this was a gift He was giving us, a gift we would be able to easily receive. And we could by receiving Jesus for Who He is, God's Son, Who God raised from the dead. God wants us to see Jesus through His eyes, to see Him as the gift He is to us, and all we are able to have and do thanks to Jesus. As we do, we use our faith, a faith given to us by Jesus where we can see and operate beyond this natural realm because we can see and operate in the supernatural realm just as Jesus when He was on earth. Ephesians 2:8-11 NKJV tells us: ***"For by grace you have***

been saved through faith, and that not of yourselves; it is the gift of God, not of works, lest anyone should boast. For we are His workmanship, created in Christ Jesus for good works, which God prepared beforehand that we should walk in them." We have the faith to receive Jesus as our Lord and Savior and receive all He provided for us, a faith that helps us see as Jesus sees, a faith that helps us see as God sees. When we operate in our faith, we are believing and trusting God and only in what He says, what we can do as His children, and what His Word tells us. We believe and trust in Who Jesus is and all He has done and that we can walk in His ways. We believe and trust in Holy Spirit and Who He is and all He does to help us in our faith walk, help us as we need, help us see as God and Jesus sees and helps us walk as Jesus walked. Because God stands by His Word. He says what He means and He means what He says. God tells us we are His children because we are His children. He tells us how we become His children. We can always believe in and rely on what He tells us. He will never take it back or change His mind. He lets us know in 2 Corinthians 6:18 NLT: ***"And I will be your Father, and you will be My sons and daughters, says the Lord Almighty."*** And God reaffirms we are His children in 1 John 3:1 NLT: ***"See how very much our Father loves us, for He calls us His children, and that is what we are! But the people who belong to this world do not recognize that we are God's children because they do not know Him."*** It is imperative that we recognize we are His children because the world will not because the world does not recognize Jesus for Who He is. We must go by God's definition of us, how He sees us, and we do not allow the world to define us. Thanks to Jesus we are made new, a newness we can receive by faith and receive the full understanding of all that entails. We just have to belong to Jesus and not this world, we have to follow Him and not this world, we have to follow God's side of the story and not the worlds.

Jesus grew in grace as He grew up and we can grow in grace as we grow up as God's children. And as we grow, we mature and we can recognize more and more how God's sees things. We can see stories and news reports and see them how God sees them. We can respond how God would have us respond. We can see how satan is using these platforms to spin his lies to create a web of discord, dysfunction, division, and deception. We can see as God sees and not get pulled into his trap as Adam and Eve did. We can remain firmly grounded in our identity as God's children just as Jesus did. Jesus had nothing to prove to satan nor do we. Jesus played by God's rules and so can we. We can recognize stories that do not line up with God's Word and His ways so we do not line up with those stories but remain strong in God's Word and His ways like Jesus did. Regardless of who may be telling the story or even doing the teaching, we still grow in our understanding of God and His Word and who we are as His children so we are not deceived. Ephesians 4:14-15 NLT says: ***"Then we will no longer be immature like little children. We will not be tossed and blown about by every wind of new teaching. We will not be influenced when people try to trick us with lies so clever they sound like the truth. Instead, we will speak the truth in love, growing in every way more and more like Christ, Who, is the head of His body, the church."*** As God's children, when we realize who we are in Him, we can believe His side of the story and we can become His mature children. We can look and sound like Him so we can make an impact on this earth for Him, just like Jesus did. We can follow in His plan for His Kingdom to come on this earth. We can know His Word so we can tell people His Word, we can show people His Word because we are living in His Word and we can do so with and in His love. We can stand firm and not be moved to follow other stories or news but follow God's Good News. We can look and sound like Jesus and not look and sound like the world.

We can be set apart as the children of God with a bold belief in God's side of the story, in God's Word, in who we are thanks to Jesus. 1 John 3:3-6 GW says: ***"So all people who have this confidence in Christ keep themselves pure, as Christ is pure. Those who live sinful lives are disobeying God. Sin is disobedience. You know that Christ appeared in order to take away our sins. He is not sinful. Those who live in Christ do not go on sinning. Those who go on sinning have not seen or known Christ."*** As we know Christ, we can live a pure life as Christ lived and we can live in obedience to God and His Word as Christ lived. We can live our lives as an ongoing testimony of God's goodness and love and show the world what is means to be God's children.

CHAPTER 7

It is Your Birthright

IMAGINE YOU WERE BORN into the wealthiest family and you were the first born. As the first born, it was custom that you would inherit everything belonging to your father and you enjoy thinking about what will one day be fully yours. You know you have the favor of your father over your younger sibling. Your tastes differ greatly and you consider yourself superior to your sibling. One day you decide to embark on an adventure which takes longer than you planned and you run out of your provisions quickly. Your adventure did not turn out like you thought it would and you find yourself disappointed, exhausted, and famished. You keep thinking about what you want to eat and how you should have planned better. As you approach your home, you begin to smell the most delicious aromas which only intensifies as you enter your home. You realize the depths of your hunger as your body responds in kind. Your annoying younger sibling walks in from the kitchen and asks you if you want something to eat. You know the meal will taste even more scrumptious as the smell because your sibling is a great cook. This makes him more annoying because you have to admit he is good at something. To your surprise, he says he will share his meal with you. But then you are no longer surprised because it comes with some conditions and this sound more like your brother. The price to share this meal is that you have to hand over your birthright as the firstborn to your brother. This would mean you would be left with nothing and he would get everything. You laugh at him because of how absurd this sounds but he remains serious about his proposition. It is then the full complexity of your hunger kicks in and you yield to your body's current need and throw out all logic and reason and agree to take the deal. You think you will get what you currently want while your brother will go on about his affairs leaving you alone. Yet, you did not fully understand how powerful are your words and how binding of an agreement you just entered, even though it was merely verbal and you did it only so you could eat. After all, you are still the firstborn and he remains your younger brother who you still consider as being inferior to you. So, you hastily eat the meal which satisfies your temporary hunger but you have yet to grasp the entirety of what you just agreed to.

You find this actual story in Genesis 25:29-34 and it is about two brothers, Esau, the firstborn, and Jacob, the second born. Genesis 25:33-34 NLT tells us: ***"But Jacob said, 'First you must swear that your birthright is mine.' So, Esau swore an oath, thereby selling all his rights as the firstborn to his brother, Jacob. Then Jacob gave Esau some bread and lentil stew. Esau ate the meal, then got up and left. He showed contempt for his rights as the firstborn."*** NKJV says: ***"Esau despised his birthright."*** AMPC says: ***"Esau scorned his birthright as beneath his notice."*** TPT says:

"Esau cared nothing about his own birthright." Esau took a bowl of meatless soup and bread in his own house where he was the firstborn, with all the rights of the firstborn and valued that one simple meal over a lifetime of inheritance and blessings that he was entitled to. Esau failed to see the importance of his birthright. He did not place the proper value it truly represented nor the value it was supposed to represent in his life. As a result, he would not be able to enjoy the fullness of all his birthright could afford him nor the blessings that came with his birthright. Esau did not understand God's side of the story. He took a temporary situation where his flesh was hungry and he yielded to his bodily appetite and it caused him to forfeit something greater and more powerful that would reach beyond his current circumstance of being hungry. Genesis 25:31 NLT says: ***"'Look, I am dying of starvation!' said Esau. 'What good is my birthright to me now?'"*** Not only did Esau allow himself to be robbed of his birthright, he took his current situation and embellished it to the point he convinced himself that his birthright had no value. It is important that you not only understand your birthrights as God's child but you understand the value of those birthrights. And you make certain to never despise those birthrights regardless of how you may feel, how someone may try to make you feel about yourself, or how someone may actually feel about you. Jesus did not waiver or go by His feelings when tempted by satan. And Jesus had gone a lot longer without eating any food than Esau. Jesus valued His birthrights and He valued us because He knew we would inherit His birthrights. Jesus knew if He withstood being tempted then it would make a way for us to be able to withstand being tempted. 1 Corinthians 10:13 NLT says: ***"The temptations in your life are no different from what others experience. And God is faithful. He will not allow the temptation to be more than you can stand. When you are tempted, He will show you a way out so that you***

can endure. When Jesus spoke God's Word back to satan, satan left, he stopped tempting Jesus. God's Word was greater and God's Word is still greater. When we speak God's Word, it provides a way out for us. God is faithful to His Word, He is faithful to us. Just as He showed Jesus what to say, what to do when satan was tempting Him, God will do the same for us when we are tempted. We just have to listen for His voice and then follow His voice and Holy Spirit is our Helper.

See in that moment, Esau identified himself as hungry, so much so, that he was willing to give up his birthright. And to do so to his younger brother who was not entitled to the same rights. Esau let his natural body override all reason and sensibility and made a rash choice that would last a life time for something that was temporary and only lasted for as long as he was eating. I believe as the oldest sibling, Esau may have even had certain rights within the household and could have even told Jacob that he did not have to agree to anything and that Jacob, being younger, had to serve him the food. And he could have just taken some bread. There is no way that Jacob had full reign over the kitchen and all that was in the kitchen. Bread can be quite filling and even eating bread could have curbed Esau's appetite for him to cook his own meal or even get someone else in the household to cook for him. Or just fill up on bread. He could have sustained his hunger long enough to realize he was about to make a big mistake or he could have chosen to not yield to his hunger and enter into such a costly agreement. He could have realized his temporary hunger was not as important as his long term inheritance. But Esau took the quick easy line of sight to fulfill a natural need. He had a lapse in judgment over his identity that ultimately cost him all that this identity held for him or would hold for him. Esau not only allowed his hunger to define him but his younger brother.

Jacob was in essence saying to Esau I do not think you deserve this birthright and all the blessings but I do and I am going to deceive you into giving up those rights to me and I am going to use your current weakened state against you. Jacob was looking to steal from Esau what was rightfully Esau's by birth. He was jealous of Esau just like satan is jealous of God and God's children. Jacob did not go to Esau when Esau was not hungry but he waited till he saw Esau having a weak moment. 1 Peter 5:8 NLT tells us: ***"Stay alert! Watch out for your great enemy, the devil. He prowls around like a roaring lion, looking for someone to devour."*** Notice, it says he roams around like a roaring lion because he is a deceiver, he wants people to think he has the power of a lion, that he has power over them so they will buy into his lies just like Adam and Eve. A lion has power and knows his power as does those around him. However, someone like a lion does not have the same power as a lion but is trying to make others think he does. See Jacob could not take Esau's birthright but he tricked Esau into giving up his birthright. Esau made an agreement with Jacob because Esau yielded to something that was physical, was occurring in the natural, was temporary, and had less value than his birthright. Adam and Eve did not properly value their birthright because they believed the lie satan told them over the truth God told them. No one picked the fruit for them and no one feed them the fruit. It was something they choose to do themselves by believing satan's side of the story over God's. And people are still giving up their birthrights today by not knowing, not listening to, and not believing God's side of the story. Some people are believing the lies told by satan, even though he may cleverly disguise those lies through social constructs and other means, people are choosing those lies and aligning themselves with other identities. These other identities rob them of their true birthrights just like it did for Esau, just like it did for Adam and Eve.

Unlike Esau and unlike Adam and Eve, Jesus was not tricked. And because Jesus was not tricked by satan, He made away for anyone who would believe in Him, to become His younger siblings. And by becoming His younger siblings, we can also not be tricked by satan or anyone influenced by him. We can follow in Jesus' footsteps, follow His example, follow God's Word, follow God's side of the story just as Jesus did. Jesus knew we were to live beyond our natural senses and to live beyond the natural realm because He did. Jesus was full of God's Word and God's Spirit and we can be full of God's Word and God's Spirit. We then can live in such a way that we fully live in our birthrights and not give up those rights under any persuasion even if it is a story or news that sounds good or may appear to fill a need. God understands the cost of when we miss the mark by not following His side of the story, by not understanding we have birthrights. He understands we can live through Jesus and His ways and not give up our birthrights just as Jesus did not give up His birthrights. We can live in and live out of our birthrights just like Jesus. God tells us in Hebrews 12:16 NLT: ***"Make sure that no one is immoral or godless like Esau, who traded his birthright as the firstborn son for a single meal."*** And the MSG says: ***"Watch out for the Esau syndrome: trading away God's lifelong gift in order to satisfy a short-term appetite."*** God is letting us know there will be times when we have a choice and satan will make sure there is some type of influence to try and persuade us to give up our birthrights. There will be something presented that will appear significant and important at the time, especially to our natural self, and it is meant to trick us like Esau was tricked. When we do fall under pressure like Esau did, God is telling us we become immoral and godless. We become short-sighted because we chose to not look beyond a current need to see how much God has already provided us with a lifelong supply of all we need or will need. And this lifelong supply was provided for us through Jesus. When Jesus was in the wilderness and was hungry, He did not yield to His hunger because He knew God would supply whatever He needed. Jesus did not yield to satan and his lies. Matthew 4:8-11 NLT shows us: ***"Next the devil took Him to the peak of a very high mountain and showed Him all the kingdoms of the world and their glory. 'I will give it all to You,' he said, 'if You will kneel down and worship me.' 'Get out of here, satan,' Jesus told him. 'For the Scriptures say, 'You must worship the Lord your God and serve only Him.' Then the devil went away, and angels came and took care of Jesus."*** Jesus did not buy into satan's story, He was not persuaded to give up His birthrights. He withstood the temptations even though He had not eaten anything in forty days and He was in the wilderness. Right after satan left, God fulfilled Jesus needs by sending angels to care for Him. God intervened in the natural through the supernatural. Angels were able to physically care for Jesus. There had been no mention of them prior to this but now they were with Jesus taking care of Him. And God will provide for us when we are in need. Even if God has to send angels, He will. God was Jesus' source and He is our source. Philippians 4:19 NKJV tells us: ***"My God shall supply all your needs according to His riches in glory by Christ Jesus."*** NLT says: ***"And this same God Who takes care of me will supply all your needs from His glorious riches, which have been given to us in Christ Jesus."*** And AMPC says: ***"And my God will liberally supply (fill to the full) your every need according to His riches in glory in Christ Jesus."*** We experience all God has for us through Jesus and what He has done for us. Jesus opened the way for us to experience all our birthrights afford us because we now have access to all we need thanks to Him.

Dictionary.com defines *birthright* as any right or privilege to which a person is entitled by birth. As God's child, we are entitled by birth to rights and privileges and God wants us to have and live in those every day of our lives. God knew to become His child, He would have to first give us His first Child, Jesus, and by receiving Jesus, we could obtain what is rightfully ours as God's children. John 3:16-17 AMPC informs us: ***"For God so greatly loved and dearly prized the world that He [even] gave up His only begotten (unique) Son, so that whoever believes in (trusts in, clings to, relies on) Him shall not perish (come to destruction, be lost) but have eternal (everlasting) life."*** And that eternal everlasting life starts now, on earth, whenever we receive Jesus and all of the life more abundant, He provided for us. This is a part of our birthrights, a part of God's side of the story to us and about us. James 1:18 NLT lets us know: ***"He chose to give birth to us by giving us His true Word. And we, out of all creation, became His prized possession."*** Jesus (God's Word in the flesh) is God's true Word given to us for our birth as God's children. We must only do our part and believe God's part, believe God sent Jesus to save us, believe Jesus is God's Son, believe in what Jesus did for us, and receive Jesus and all He did for us. 1 John 5:1,4-5 ESV says: ***"Everyone who believes that Jesus is the Christ has been born of God, and everyone who loves the Father loves whoever has been born of Him. For everyone who has been born of God overcomes the world. And this is the victory that has overcome the world—our faith. Who is it that overcomes the world except the one who believes that Jesus is the Son of God?"*** God not only gave us His Son so we could become His sons, His daughters but He also provided us with the means to become victorious over this world, to be victorious over satan (the god of this world). We just have to believe God's side of the story, believe His Word, believe what He says over what anyone else says. By becoming God's children, by being born again, we are able to see God and His Kingdom as He sees, we are able to see beyond this world and its kingdoms, we are able to see beyond this natural realm. Jesus was not tempted when satan showed Him all the kingdoms of this world and we cannot be tempted by this world and all the kingdoms of this world. Jesus knew God's Kingdom was greater and He had access to God's Kingdom because He was God's Son. We can see ourselves as Jesus saw Himself and we can see God's Kingdom as Jesus saw God's Kingdom. Jesus tells us in John 3:3 NLT: ***"I tell you the truth, unless you are born again, you cannot see the Kingdom of God."*** Thanks to being born again, we can see God's Kingdom and experience His Kingdom on earth. Ephesians 4:5-6 NKJV says: ***"[There is] one Lord, one faith, one baptism, one God and Father of all, Who, is over all, in all, and living through all."*** By faith, we can strongly believe and trust in God and His side of the story by making His story our story and not believe or trust any other story regardless of how it may look, sound, or feel. We will remain firm in seeing how God sees.

We can believe Colossians 1:15-22 NLT: ***"Christ is the visible image of the invisible God. He existed before anything was created and is supreme over all creation, for through Him God created everything in the heavenly realms and on earth. He made the things we can see and the things we cannot see – such as thrones, kingdoms, rulers, and authorities in the unseen world. Everything was created through Him and for Him. He existed before anything else, and He holds all creation together. Christ is also the head of the church, which is His body. He is the beginning, supreme over all who rise from the dead. So, He is first in everything. For God in all His fullness was pleased to live in Christ, and through Him God reconciled everything to Himself. He made peace with everything in heaven and on earth by means of Christ's blood on the cross. This includes you who were once far away from God. You were His enemies, separated from Him by***

your evil thoughts and actions. Yet now He has reconciled you to Himself through the death of Christ in His physical body. As a result, He has brought you into His own presence, and you are holy and blameless as you stand before Him without a single fault." This is God's side of the story about us, about Jesus and Who He is and about what He has done for us. Jesus restored everything that was lost through Adam and Eve back to us. All they lost as been fully restored and more because we are God's children thanks to Jesus. What happened prior has been replaced by Jesus' precious blood. Our slate was not whipped clean but we were given a new one so we can start brand new in Jesus, we can start our new birth in Him. We are in good standing with God, He holds nothing against us when we receive Jesus. We have nothing to do or prove except receive Jesus and the new life He provided for us. When He looks at us, He looks at us with the same love and admiration He has for Jesus. When He looked at Jesus as being His beloved Son Who He was well pleased with, He looks at us as being His beloved children who He is well pleased with. We can enter His presence any time we want and spend time with Him because He wants to spend time with us. He is not holding our past against us and He does not want us to hold our past against ourselves or against others. Romans 5:10 AMPC informs us: ***"For if while we were enemies we were reconciled to God through the death of His Son, it is much more [certain], we are reconciled, that we shall be saved (daily delivered from sin's dominion) through His [resurrection] life."*** We can walk daily in all the benefits of our birthright which includes walking daily free of sin. We can walk daily in all the benefits of our birthright which includes walking in right standing with God in fellowship with Him. We can be fully persuaded through our faith that this is our birthright thanks to Jesus and not be deceived otherwise.

God informs us in Romans 6:4-8 NKJV: ***"Therefore, we were buried with Him through baptism into death, that just as Christ was raised from the dead by the glory of the Father, even so we also should walk in newness of life. For if we have been united together in the likeness of His death, certainly we also shall be in the likeness of His resurrection, knowing this, that our old man was crucified with Him, that the body of sin might be done away with, that we should no longer be slaves of sin. For he who has died has been freed from sin. Now if we died with Christ, we believe that we shall also live with Him."*** When Jesus died, our old sinful self, died with Him. Because Jesus had not sinned, He took our sin with Him to the cross, loosing sins hold on us. When He was raised again from the dead, we were raised again to our new life in Him. By faith, we receive this new life in Him just like walking through a door. Jesus is the door to our new life, the door to us being in right standing with God, the door allowing us to boldly approach God as His children. I see my old sinful self, standing at a door. I see myself walking through the door Who is Jesus, His precious blood covering me, and when I walk to the other side, I am a completely new person. I was dead in sin but now I am alive in Christ Jesus. My old sinful self remains behind the door of Jesus, dead and useless to me. I no longer identify with my dead and useless me because that is no longer me. I now identify with my new life in Christ Jesus because that is who I am. This was a part of God's plan for us, a part of our future He had for us. Our future, which is our present, started the day we received Jesus Christ and walked through His door. Romans 8:29-30 NLT tells us: ***"For God knew His people in advance, and He chose them to become like His Son, so that His Son would be the firstborn among many brothers and sisters. And having chosen them, He called them to come to Him. And having called them, He gave them right standing with Himself. And having given them right standing, He gave***

them His glory. Because we are in right standing with God, we get the benefit of experiencing His glory right now on earth. We get the benefit of experiencing His presence and getting the benefit of experiencing His goodness, His holiness, and His power in our lives. All for us and all for God's glory so others can experience Him as being the real, loving, good, and all-powerful God that He is. Hebrews 8:12 NLT tells us: ***"And I will forgive their wickedness, and I will never again remember their sins."*** A part of our birthright is God chooses to never remember our sins and He chooses to not hold our sins against us. God sees us in our new nature, in our newness of life in Christ Jesus and this is how He wants us to see ourselves. Esau gave up his birthrights because he allowed himself to be influenced by what he was feeling in the natural. He allowed himself to be talked into giving up his birthright by looking at something that was temporary. He let how he was feeling override his thinking and stopped thinking like the firstborn who had all the rights of the firstborn. Jesus was the firstborn Who gave up His life so we could be second born and share His birthrights. Unlike the world's ways, God's and Jesus' ways are higher. The world, through satan's influence, would want to trick us like Jacob tricked Esau. But Jesus being the firstborn Who knew Who He was and was walking in God's ways, shared His birthrights with us. He gave us what He had by first giving up His life for us on the cross. How much more should we steward what He gave us and honor Him through living our life like God's children?

Ephesians 2:6 TPT says: ***"He raised us up with Christ the exalted One, and we ascended with Him into the glorious perfection and authority of the heavenly realm, for we are now co-seated as one with Christ!"*** Jesus has provided us with all authority in the heavenly realm. We must see through God eyes by seeing ourselves sitting as one with Christ Jesus in the heavenly realm and being able to fully operate from the heavenly realm while we remain in our physical form here on earth. As a part of our birthrights, we can live in this world but not of this world and instead, live in this world while living like heaven, while living like God's Kingdom. We can live as One with Jesus just as He lived as One with God when He was on earth. God remained in heaven and all He had was given to Jesus. Now Jesus is in heaven and we are co-seated with Him and all He was given is now given to us. Jesus Himself told us in John 17:21-23 NKJV: ***"'That they all may be one, as You, Father, are in Me, and I in You; that they also may be one in Us, that the world may believe that You sent Me. And the glory which You gave Me I have given them, that they may be one just as We are One I in them, and You in Me; that they may be made perfect in one, and that the world may know that You have sent Me, and have loved them as You have loved Me."*** God loves us the same as He loves Jesus. We have been made perfect in Jesus and we are joined together as One with Him. We can live beyond the natural and live in all our birthrights affords us and not forgo or give up our birthrights. We can live in a manner where others can see and know Jesus was sent by God for each and every one who will believe in Him and receive all He has provided for them. We can live in the fullness of our birthrights as God's children through our faith. We can see through the eyes of our faith who we are and how we are to operate here on earth. Seeing through our eyes of faith is seeing as God sees. We take what God has for us, including our being saved (see Ephesians 2:8), by our faith. Everything we need to live as God's children here on earth, including Holy Spirit and God's Word, and everything Jesus did and provided for us is obtainable through our faith. Through our faith, we see what is unseen as real as picking up a title to a vehicle. The vehicle is mine, it has been paid for, and my name is on the title. I believe I have the vehicle and all I have to do is take the title so I can go get my vehicle. I am not able to see the vehicle but it has already been promised to me. I see the title and see myself taking the title. Once I have the title, I go get my vehicle and start driving it. I see what God has for me and I take it by faith. Once I take what God has for me (all of my birthrights), I then walk in what God has for me. I see myself as God's child and I take my identity as God's child and then I begin walking like the child of God I am. Esau could have chosen to not walk by what he was seeing, how he was currently feeling hungry. Jesus did make a different choice and He walked by His faith while here on earth showing us, we can do the same. 2 Corinthians 5:7 NKJV tells us: ***"For we walk by faith, not by sight."*** Through faith, we believe and trust what God tells us over what anyone else tells us, including how we may be feeling or how something may appear. We are to always go by our spiritual eyesight of faith over our natural eyesight.

Through our faith eyesight, what we are not able to currently see with our natural eyesight does not move us. Instead, we continue to look through our spiritual eyesight, while remaining hopefully expectant, because we know it is in the spiritual realm, and we know it will soon arrive in the natural realm. While waiting, we keep looking through our spiritual eyesight, and remain confident that it will come into view and become a reality in the natural realm because we know it is already a reality in the spiritual realm. And we have our faith eyesight, our spiritual eyesight, as apart of our birthright and new born nature. Hebrews 11:1-3 TPT says: ***"Now faith brings our hopes into reality and becomes the foundation needed to acquire the things we long for. It is all the evidence required to prove what is still unseen. This testimony of faith is what previous generations were commended for. Faith***

empowers us to see that the universe was created and beautifully coordinated by the power of God's words! He spoke and the invisible realm gave birth to all that is seen." The AMPC says: ***"Now faith is the assurance (the confirmation, the title deed) of the things [we] hope for, being the proof of things [we] do not see and the conviction of their reality [faith perceiving as real fact what is not revealed to the senses]."*** Esau could have trusted in his birthright but he trusted in how he was feeling hungry. Jesus trusted in His birthright over his hunger feeling and we can trust in our birthright independent of how we feel. For, we have our new nature and our new eyesight. God spoke and the world existed. God spoke and we existed. God is God and there is no Other like Him. God's Word is true and God's side of the story is always true over any other side or story. Romans 10:17 NKJV lets us know how we grow in our faith: ***"So then faith comes by hearing, and hearing by the Word of God."*** We must hear God's Word and keep on hearing His Word on an ongoing basis. Faith comes by hearing, and hearing, and hearing who God's Word says we are. Faith comes by hearing, and hearing, and hearing how God's Word tells us we are to live. Faith comes by hearing, and hearing, and hearing God's Word is my Truth. Faith comes from hearing, and hearing, and hearing about my birthrights found in God's Word. Hebrews 4:12-13 NLT tells us: ***"For the word of God is alive and powerful. It is sharper than the sharpest two-edged sword, cutting between soul and spirit, between joint and marrow. It exposes our innermost thoughts and desires. Nothing in all creation is hidden from God. Everything is naked and exposed before His eyes, and He is the one to Whom we are accountable."*** And AMPC says: ***"For the Word that God speaks is alive and full of power [making it active, operative, energizing, and effective]; it is sharper than any two-edged sword, penetrating to the dividing line of the breath of life (soul) and [immortal] spirit, and of joints and marrow [of the***

deepest parts of our nature], exposing and sifting and analyzing and judging the very thoughts and purposes of the heart." God's Word exposes what needs to be exposed so what needs to be corrected can be corrected. It is a good exposure and a good correction because God is good and His Word is good. God does not expose us like the world would. He does not make an announcement saying look Michelle messed up, she has this problem in her life, here I made copies for everyone to see. Now watch how I am going to discipline her so she knows I am the boss and she will know her place. I want her to feel bad about what she has done. God is good and He wants to reveal anything and everything that is in our lives that can get in the way of us receiving all the good He has for us. He wants to reveal anything and everything that is in our lives that can hinder us living like His children and seeing ourselves as His children. He wants to remove those things and replace them with His Word so we will see ourselves as His children like He sees us and we will operate in this earth like He sees us operating. God's Word is powerful enough to make those needed changes. 2 Timothy 3:16-17 TPT informs us: ***"God has transmitted His very substance into every Scripture, for it is God-breathed. It will empower you by Its instruction and correction, giving you the strength to take the right direction and lead you deeper into the path of godliness. Then you will be God's servant, fully mature and perfectly prepared to fulfill any assignment God gives you."*** God's Word will change us into the very image of God as we grow in our faith through His Word. When we get into God's Word, God breathes His life into us changing us into His image. The more we get into God's Word the more of His image we are changed into. The more we are then empowered to go forth as God's children because we will look and sound more like His kids. We are positioned to hear God and follow His leading all with Holy Spirit's help. We can go as He says go and stay as He says stay. We speak and do as He tells us just like Jesus. We live by faith. Romans 1:17 NLT says: ***"This Good News tell us how God makes us right in His sight. This is accomplished from start to finish by faith. As the Scriptures say, 'It is through faith that a righteous person has life.'"*** And TPT says: ***"This Gospel unveils a continual revelation of God's righteousness – a perfect righteousness given to us when we believe. And it moves us from receiving life through faith, to the power of living by faith. This is what the Scriptures means when it says: 'We are right with God through life-giving-faith!'"*** God's Word lets us know we can receive our right standing with God through our faith. Holy Spirit can help us gain revelation of God's Word, including how we are right with God solely based on what Jesus did. Our faith empowers us to receive and live in our birthrights.

God wants us to live beyond this temporary world, beyond our natural senses. He wants us to see things as He does and then live our life accordingly. God wants us to understand we are a spirit, just like He is a Spirit, and we can make decisions influenced by our spirit rather than our body or soul. 1 Thessalonians 5:23-24 TPT says: ***"Now, may the God of peace and harmony set you apart, making you completely holy. And may your entire being – spirit, soul, body – be kept completely flawless in the appearing of our Lord Jesus, the Anointed One. The One Who calls you by name is trustworthy and will thoroughly complete His work in you."*** My entire being is made up of three parts: spirit, soul, and body. And I can be set apart just like Jesus was set apart and live by my spirit just like Jesus. When we get born again, our spirit is then made alive. Our faith empowers us to live by our spirit and to live with the help of God's Spirit (Holy Spirit) just like Jesus. We walk by faith knowing we are a spirit, we live in a body (our flesh) and we have a soul (our mind, our emotions and our will). Esau made a decision based on his body being hungry. Adam and Eve made a decision based on their mind reasoning it was okay to eat what God told them not to eat. They yielded to a story that was not God's. Jesus walked by His Spirit because He knew Who He was as God's Son and nothing else moved Him. Gaining this understanding was revolutionary for me. Growing up, I had no idea that when I got born again, my spirit was alive and made right in God. I had not heard any teaching on this and thought you got born again so you did not have to go to hell. Then you lived your life the best way you could by keeping a set of rules while you allowed your soul to govern your life. Not only was I living based on my emotions but also based on my intellect. And if I was not living from being influenced by my soul, I was living by yielding to my body. There was no understanding that there was a world that could not be seen, activity going on beyond what your natural senses could detect. It seems so simple now that I have an understanding of how I am created and what it really means to be born again. I can choose to live by my spirit rather than my soul and flesh. I am thankful that I gained the knowledge that I am a spirit and I can live by my spirit and not live how I had been living. I do not have to be controlled by my soul or flesh. I can feed my spirit on God's Word so my spirit gets stronger and I can yield more and more to my spirit. I can fill up on God's Spirit (Holy Spirit) and allow Him to help me because He is in me and with me always. I can spend time with God obtaining the refreshment I need anytime I need it all while growing in my fellowship with Him. Romans 8:9 GNT says: ***"But you do not live as your human nature tells you to; instead, you live as the Spirit tells you to – if, in fact, God's Spirit lives in you. Whoever does not have the Spirit of Christ does not belong to Him."*** We obtain the Spirit of Christ (God's anointing and the anointed One) when we get born again and we can live as the Spirit tells us. God, in His goodness, did not leave us to perish, to self-destruct, or to live in darkness. He provided a way out and it is through Jesus. He is the way where we can live free from darkness or any other type of destruction and we can do so for the rest of our lives. Ephesians 5:8-11 TPT tells us: ***"Once your life was full of sin's darkness, but now you have the very light of our Lord shinning through you because of your union with Him. Your mission is to live as children flooded with His revelation! Then you will learn to choose what is beautiful to our Lord. And do not even associate with the servants of darkness because they have no fruit in them; instead, reveal truth to them."*** And NKJV says: ***"For you were once darkness but now you are light (for the fruit of the Spirit is in all goodness, righteousness and truth), finding out what is acceptable to the Lord. And have no fellowship with the unfruitful works of darkness, but rather expose them."*** God has given us Holy Spirit to help us know what pleases Him, to help us recognize darkness, and to help us shine His Light on the darkness. When we shine His Light on the darkness, those trapped in darkness and the lies can know there is a way out. They can know there is God's Light that leads to Truth, that leads to Him, that leads them into a life full of God's love, that leads them to Jesus and leads them out of their darkness into God's marvelous Light. As God's children, we are to show others Jesus' ways by how we live in His ways, by how we live in His Light, by how we live in His love. I can talk about Him all day long, which is good and has its place, but when I am living as God's child, showing in my everyday life Who He is and Who He is to me, says a lot more. When I identify as God's child and others can see that I am His child, it will speak louder and greater. I can tell you I am married, I can show you my marriage license and talk about being married; however, when you see me around my husband and you can observe how we interact with each other and see the fruit of our marriage you will get even more of an understanding of my being married. We are joined together with Christ as One. People need to see our union with Him in how we talk, in how we act, how we interact with others, how we interact with those who are trapped in darkness, how we respond to news and reports told by man, and how we live each and every day. People need to see we do not change with the times or how things may be looking at the time. People need to see our trust in the One true God Who can be trusted. People need to see we believe and know Who Jesus is and our knowing Him is reflected in our lives because He is our ultimate influencer. People need to see Holy Spirit is our Helper because He is our source. People need to see God's Word in operation in our lives because His Word is our mirror. People need to see we are God's children because we are living out our birthrights and identity found in Him. People need to see we are connected to Jesus because He is our big Brother who established our new genealogy. Jesus tells us in John 15:5 NLT: ***"Yes, I am the vine; you are the branches. Those who remain in Me, and I in them, will produce much fruit. For apart from Me you can do nothing."*** We are connected to Jesus just like branches are connected to a vine. The branches only produce fruit because of their connection to the vine. The fruit is what gets picked and enjoyed. We only produce fruit that is good for us and others when we stay connected to Jesus. When I go to pick grapes, I am not looking for the grapes but I am looking for the whole grapevine. I am looking for what is holding the grapes. Once I see what is holding the grapes, I can then see the grapes and pick what grapes I am needing. I am not looking for the branches because I know they can not produce or maintain grapes if they are not still attached to the grapevine. When I was growing up, one of the places we lived had some grapevines in the yard. I remember when I was going to pick the grapes, I was going to the grapevines to pick. The grapevines in our yard held the grapes I was wanting.

I knew where to find the grapes because I knew where the grapevines were and the grapevines identified where the grapes were. If someone asked me where are the grapes, I would have said on the grapevines feel free to go pick for yourself. As God's children, we are to be so connected to Jesus people can see God's fruit in our lives. Our lives should look good to them, our lives should look like Jesus to them. We will not be able to produce fruit without Jesus being first in our lives. God was first in Jesus' life. He knew He could do nothing without His connection to God and God's Spirit was His Helper. We can do nothing without Jesus and God's Spirit as our Helper. Whatever we do without Him, will not be fruitful and will not lead people to God and His Light, will not lead people to Jesus and His Life. As God's children, we are to be producing good results that are beneficial and profitable for His Kingdom on earth. We do this by remaining connected with Jesus, by being joined with Him. 1 Corinthians 6:17 NLT tells us: ***"But the person who is joined to the Lord is one spirit with Him."*** We are one with Jesus and we can live as one with Him on earth producing much fruit. We do this by yielding our will to His and living in His Ways. We realize our life belongs to Him just like I realize my life as being married now belongs to my husband. I can still choose to do what I want as being married. And in my choices, I can consider my husband and how I am joined with him in marriage. I can make choices that will produce fruit in our marriage and reflect my love and commitment to him. People can see my devotion to him and my love for him. They can see how I honor him and our marriage. Or I cannot consider my husband and our marriage in my choices. I can make choices to live like I am not married and just do whatever I want whenever I want. People can then look at me and see someone who looks single rather than married. And if they find out I am married, my life choices and how my life looks would not make marriage attractive or be a good advertisement for marriage. It is the same with our lives in being God's children. We can use our faith and live our lives like we are joined as one spirit with Jesus, which we are, or we can live our lives like we are not joined as one spirit with Jesus. One produces much fruit that is good and pleasing and can be shared with others and one does not.

John 6:63 NKJV tells us: ***"It is the Spirit who gives life; the flesh profits nothing. The words that I speak to you are spirit, and they are life."*** Apart from Jesus, apart from God, apart from Holy Spirit, and apart from God's Word, our lives are not profitable. The world and its ways would tell us otherwise. The world has its ways of wanting to define us, and with satan's help, get us to want to do things on our own terms, gets us to want to do things that sounds good to our flesh, that sounds good to our soul, that sounds good to the world. We have to be willing to listen to what God says and follow His Ways, follow Jesus Ways. We have to make the choices to uphold and maintain our connection with Jesus. I have to uphold and maintain my connection to my husband. I can go around upholding and maintaining other connections and make those top priority or I can make my connection with my husband top priority. Our top priority as God's children is maintaining and upholding our connection with Jesus. When we do, our other connections with people, including spouses, will be much better, will be more healthy, will be more fruitful. When we yield to our spirit, and our Helper Holy Spirit Who is in us, we are fruitful. Galatians 6:8 NLJV tells us: ***"For he who sows to his flesh will of the flesh reap corruption, but he who sows to the Spirit will of the Spirit reap everlasting life."*** The NLT says: ***"Those who live only to satisfy their own sinful nature will harvest decay and death from that sinful nature. But those who live to please the Spirit will harvest everlasting life from the***

Spirit." Not only will sowing into our flesh not profit us it leads to corruption. There is a life beyond what we see today, it is an eternal life. We can live life for what we see today, according to the world's standards, according to our own fleshly wants which will only lead to corruption and not make an eternal difference. Or we can live life by not what we see today, but rather how we see ourselves as God's children and how we are to live for His Kingdom on earth. We can live a life that is fruitful for us and others when we live sowing into our spirit over our flesh. We can do this by allowing Holy Spirit to help us and we can benefit from His fruitfulness just like Jesus. Galatians 5:22-23 AMPC: ***"But the fruit of the [Holy] Spirit [the work which His presence within accomplishes] is love, joy (gladness), peace, patience, (an even temper, forbearance), kindness, goodness (benevolence), faithfulness, gentleness (meekness, humility), self-control (self-restraint, continence). Against such things there is no law [that can bring a charge]."*** And TPT says: ***"But the fruit produced by the Holy Spirit within you is divine love in all its varied expressions: joy that overflows, peace that subdues, patience that endures, kindness in action, a life full of virtue, faith that prevails, gentleness of heart, and strength of spirit. Never set the law above these qualities, for they are meant to be limitless."*** When we allow Holy Spirit His proper place in our lives, we can have an unlimited supply of His Fruit. We get an unlimited supply of: His love (which is God's love that will never end), His joy (that overflows and is our strength), His peace (which passes all understanding), His kindness (which is only how we truly can be kind to others), His goodness (because God is good and only good comes from Him), His faithfulness (remaining steadfast in living like Jesus), His gentleness (we speak and operate in God's love), and His self-control (yielding to Him and our spirit). Because we are children of God, we can have all the fruit of Holy Spirit and reap all the benefits of His fruit. A grape maintains itself as a grape because it is a part of the grapevine. Without the grapevine, there would be no grape, there would be no fruit. We have all Holy Spirit has because we first have Jesus and all He has and it is a part of our birthrights.

As God's children, we can know His voice over any other voices. We can follow His voice over any other voices. When a baby is born, the baby starts recognizing his parents' voices. He heard them when he was in his mother's womb. After he is born, he can tell which voices are his parents over other voices in a room. The more he hears his parents voices the more quickly he recognizes them. As he grows up hearing their voices, he can automatically pick out their voices among a crowd. He knows how they discipline, he knows how they expect him to live, he knows how to honor them, he knows what pleases them, and he knows he is their son. He knows because he has heard their voices over and over tell him these things about himself. He has learned to believe these things told by them over anything else told by others. Jesus recognized His Father's voice over all others. He recognized when Holy Spirit was helping Him and guiding Him over all others. And we can do the same. And we can know Jesus' voice above all others. He tells us we can in John 10:27-29 NKJV: ***"My sheep hear My voice, and I know them, and they follow Me. And I give them eternal life, and they shall never perish: neither shall anyone snatch them out of My hand. My Father, Who, has given them to Me, is greater than all; and no one is able to snatch them out of My Father's hand. I and My Father are One."*** A shepherd by trade takes care of his sheep by tending to their needs which includes feeding them, protecting them from predators, guiding them to good pastures, overall making sure they are safe, and caring for their overall well-being. The sheep can trust their shepherd. And they have learned his voice over all other voices. Even if another shepherd came into their fold, they would know he was not their shepherd and that they did not belong to him. He could give them commands but they would only be listening for the commands to come from their shepherd, the voice they followed. We can know His voice and not follow any other voices. We can know how Jesus lived, we can know His ways, we can know God's Word and what God says, we can spend time fellowshipping with God, we can know Holy Spirit and how He leads us and when someone tries to tell us something different, we can know not to listen. Even if that someone is called a pastor, who says something different than my Shepherd says, I can know my Shepherd's voice and follow what He says. My Shepherd will always lead me by what God says. Jesus was listening to God and His voice over satan when satan was tempting Him. Jesus was listening to God and His voice over those who were doubting and saying He was not God's Son. Jesus was listening to God and His voice when He went to the cross and was not listening to how He was mocked and to all the hate that was being spoken. He kept His focus on God's voice and on what He was saying. No matter how good something may sound, we can listen to Jesus' voice and Holy Spirit helps us. His voice is always the voice to be trusted. Adam and Eve listened to the wrong voice when they listened to satan. God had already told them what to eat and not eat. When they did not listen to God, and acted on what satan said, they handed over their rightful birthrights. No one took their rights; they forfeited them. It was like they handed over their birth certificate to satan and he gave them a counterfeit one. Now they identified with the counterfeit birth certificate because they identified with this world and satan is the god of this world. It was like his name had gotten written down as being their father. And when they took the counterfeit birth certificate, they fell under all the rights of satan, which leads to death and away from Life, which leads to darkness and away from Light. They got a package deal full of lies and all that comes with those lies. Their ears became more in tune to want to hear lies over the Truth, God's Word. No one snatched Esau's birthrights from him but he handed them over to his brother by listening to his brother's voice and the deception he spoke. Esau could have used his voice to tell his brother to go away and leave him alone. Adam and Eve could have used their voices to tell satan to go away and leave them alone. Jesus used His voice to tell satan to go and he did. And He tells us we can do the same in James 4:7 NKJV: ***"Submit yourselves therefore to God. Resist the devil, and he will run away from you."*** The RIV says: ***"It is imperative that you make the decisions to properly align yourselves under the authority of God – in a submitted position that actually gives you the ability to defy, oppose, stand steadfastly against, and withstand the accusing, slanderous, trap-setting behavior of the devil. In fact, he will be so terrified of you that he will move his feet as fast as he can to get away from you. Not only will he flee from you, he will run like a criminal terrified of prosecution – so scared that he will want to do all he can to put as much space between him and you as possible."*** Notice, who does the running away, the devil (satan) does. We do our part by being God's sheep who are under the leading and guiding of their Shepherd and Whose voice they will only heed and follow. We align ourselves with God and His Word and put ourselves under His authority. When we do, we have all the authority He has and all the backing and support He provides just like Jesus had with Holy Spirit's help. Literally, it becomes four against one. And when we resist satan's lies trying to convince us we are criminals still snared by sin, he actually runs away knowing he is guilty of slander and can be prosecuted for his slander. He is so scared of our resisting him; he cannot run away from us fast enough. It is important Whose voice we listen to and Whose voice we follow. If satan has set a trap through the world's news or any other means, we must resist and only listen and respond like Jesus. When God told me not to drink coffee, I listened. No matter who may have made fun of me, who may have still offered me coffee, no matter who may still be drinking coffee, or if I missed drinking coffee I listened to Him. As I listen to Him, I know what is sin and what is not sin, I know what love is and what love is not, I know what marriage is and what marriage is not, I know what gender means and what gender does not mean, I know what is good and what is not good, I know how I am to see others and how I am not to see them, and I know who I am and who I am not. God knows the cost of when I do not listen to Him and He knows the benefit of when I do listen to Him. And satan knows. It is imperative that I know and I listen to God and learn His voice myself because I am His child. No one else was standing with Jesus when satan appeared. Jesus knew Whose voice to listen to and the voice He was not to listen to ran from Him. We will get the same result as Jesus when we do the same as He did. Not listening to God causes us to miss the mark, to miss what God has for us. He already has it and it is right there available for us to pick it up any time we want. We can use the gift He has given us if we pick it up and use it. When I listen to the wrong voice or voices, it is like my navigational system is leading me to the wrong house for pick up. I have the address where I am to go get my gift from God, I put in that address but then my navigational system leads me to a different address. My gift is still mine, is still waiting for me at the same address I was given but I am listening to the wrong navigational voice of how to get to the right address. Holy Spirit is my navigational voice Who is in me and He will always lead me to the right address, He will always lead me how God leads. Holy Spirit will lead me to where my gift from God is each and every time. Another voice tries to interfere, I know Whose voice to listen to and tell the other voice to go. There is something on the news or social media that is saying something that goes against what God says, I do not listen. Those news and media sources are trying to get me to believe or respond to what they are saying and it goes against how I am to believe and respond I do not listen to them. God always has His side and how I am to respond and His side is the side I go by.

1 John 3:4 NLT says: ***"Everyone who sins is breaking God's law, for all sin is contrary to the law of God."*** When we sin, we break God's law which is always greater than any law of man. Some laws of man line up with God's like we are not to murder anyone. Some laws of God can be seen as morally wrong within some social cultures and norms like not having an affair. God's law, through Jesus, will say we are not to even look at anyone and think about having an affair. How many laws of man talk about our thoughts? God says if you have already lusted in your heart, then you have already sinned. We are not to put anything or anyone above God. How many can search their hearts and say they are not putting anything or anyone above God? If God tells us to do something and we do not, have we just put what He told us to do above Him because we are not following what He is telling us? I ask that question as much for my benefit and to search my heart for how I would answer. Cambridge English Dictionary defines *idolatry* as having a very great admiration or respect for someone or something, often too great. I really liked coffee but not more than my admiration, respect, and like for God. Something may seem small and insignificant so we think it is not important and God would understand after all coffee is just coffee, right? I can still drink coffee and really like coffee and I can still really, really like and love God because He knows how long I have been drinking it and He knows how much I truly love Him, right? If I do something that annoys my husband and I keep doing it when he

tells me not to and I know it annoys him, am I really honoring him? If you are drinking coffee, again, please continue and enjoy it. The key, the focus, is if I am submitting all of myself, my entire life, including what I like and do not like, to God. I remember liking sin, certain sins, before I fully submitted my life to God. I can like a sin and somebody else not like that sin. But then that person like a sin that I not like. But we are both still in sin. Only man, with satan's influence, will grade sin, or number sin like one is greater than another. We have to see sin as God sees and we have to respond to sin as God responds. And we have to see all sin is covered by Jesus' precious blood and we have been washed completely free from all sin as if we had never sinned. This is how we are to live and we can as God's children. This is a part of our birthrights.

God is so loving that He has even made a way for us when we do find ourselves messing up. He understands we are learning how to daily walk in our newness of life in Jesus. And if we do miss the mark and sin, we can easily get right back on track by repenting. God is a good God, He is a giving God, and He has given us the gift of repentance. Acts 3:19 NLT says: ***"Now repent of your sins and turn to God, so that your sins may be wiped away."*** The TPT says: ***"And now you must repent and turn back to God so that your sins will be removed, and so that times of refreshing will stream from the Lord's presence."*** God does not become some I am mad at you, you deserve what you get, you should have known better God when we sin. The world would say that and would want us to respond the same about ourselves and others. No, God says, "I know you missed it and I still love you, that has nor will never change, so repent and let Me give you a big hug because you are still My child. The price Jesus paid for your sin still applies, His precious blood still washed you clean and you remain clean. Now look at your mistake as I do so you will not make the same mistake. So rather than do what you did, here is what you do instead. Think about how much I love you and think about what I showed you rather than the mistake you made. Remember what your big Brother did for you and He is still your biggest fan cheering you on. I hear Him going on and on about you all the time and how good of a sibling you are." Jesus removed sins hold on our lives and He set us free and we remain free. When we mess up, we do not allow ourselves to buy any lie telling us we are to identify with our mess up. We believe the Truth about ourselves that we are free and remain free and we buy into our identity as being God's children. And with our identity as God's children, we have the birthright of repentance. Before being born again, we did not have this birthright. After being born again, we do. When we sin as God's children, it removes us from God and His presence. When we repent, it moves us back to God and back to His presence. God did not go anywhere, we just stepped away from Him to go sin. When we repent, we step back to Him except we have now exchanged how we thought about the sin for how He thinks about the sin. We now think like Him and line up our actions with our thinking like God which keeps us in His presence. For illustration purposes, let's say eating an orange is a sin. One day I am sitting at the table with God, I am having fellowship with Him, and really enjoying His company. Suddenly, I think about an orange and start thinking about how I used to like oranges and how I would really like an orange. Before I got born again, I could eat orange after orange and they were so good. I do not see how something that was so good to me could be so bad. Has God ever eaten an orange? I think I can take just one bite. It's not like I am eating the whole orange. God said eating an orange is a sin, so what is one bite? He did not say it was a sin to not take a bite of an orange. While I am fellowshipping with God, I decide to take a break and go find an orange. Once I find the orange, I take a bite. After I have taken the bite, I realize I messed up and sinned. I now know taking one bite is the same as eating an orange in God's eyes. And I realize my thinking about the orange led me this far and even thinking about it was sin in God's eyes. I realize thinking about it was a sin because it caused my actions to line up with my thoughts. I have such a strong conviction that comes over me I realize how I have messed up in God's eyes and I no longer want to eat an orange. I ask God to forgive me but now I see eating an orange the same as He does so I change how I see the orange to how He sees the orange. I change how I think about the orange to how He thinks about the orange. I choose to think about how God loves me and how Jesus freed me from sin, so not only do I not have to take a bite of an orange, I can choose to not even think about it and I no longer want to do either, think about or take a bite of an orange. Suddenly, I realize I no longer have any desire for oranges but am flooded with my desire for God and to be in His presence. I then remember I was fellowshipping with God and I run back to the table where we were. I find God still sitting there. We pick up our conversation and fellowship where we left off as if I had not ever left the table. God knew where I went but He is not holding that against me and chooses to not remember or think about how I had just sinned. He received my repentance and when He looks at me He stills sees me as if I had always been sitting at the table. He sees me free from sin because Jesus freed me. He sees the power of Jesus' precious blood. I choose to see and respond to myself the same way as God. Now back at the table with Him, I am back in His presence able to fully enjoy His fellowship and presence because I am fully free from sin. That is the gift of repentance. That is my birthright.

Hebrews 13:20-21 ESV says: ***"Now may the God of peace Who*** *brought again from the dead our Lord Jesus, the Great Shepherd of the sheep, by the blood of the eternal covenant, equip you with everything good that you may do His will, working in us that which is pleasing in His sight, through Jesus Christ, to Whom be glory forever and ever. Amen."* Through Jesus we are equipped with everything we need, everything we need is good and it enables us to do God's will, which includes us living free from sin and living in fellowship with God enjoying His presence. James 1:17 RIV tells us: *"I want you to know that everything given by God is always good, beneficial, and profitable. Make no mistake – that is what God always habitually and perpetually gives. Even more, absolutely everything bestowed on us by Him never subtracts from our lives rather, what He gives adds to our lives, it advances us, completes us, matures us, and perfects us. This is categorically what comes from Heaven – and it comes pouring down from the life-giving Father, Whose, specialty is light that dispels death and darkens. I want you to know that if you draw near to Him, you will discover that with Him, there is absolutely no inconsistency on the question of what He gives and what He never gives. For on this issue, He never changes. God is not like the shadow on a sundial that is constantly changing because the sun's position is always changing and moving. On the contrary, on the question of what God gives and what He never gives, His position is so fixed that it never even budges."* God remains consistent; His yes remains a yes and His no remains a no. He will not change His mind for anyone especially about us, His children. Sin is sin to Him. Being set free from sin is being set free from sin to Him. Repentance is repentance to Him. Forgiveness is forgiveness to Him. What He says, He always stands by and He never changes what He says. His side of the story is His side and He will not change it for anyone nor does He want us to. God is our Father and we go by what He says because we follow His voice.

When we do, we stay on mark, we stay on course for fulfilling His will for our lives which contain our birthrights as His children. 1 John 5:18-21 NLT says: "***We know that God's children do not make a practice of sinning, for God's Son holds them securely, and the evil one cannot touch them. We know that we are children of God and that the world around us is under the control of the evil one. And we know that the Son of God has come, and He has given us understanding so that we can know the true God. And now we live in fellowship with the true God because we live in fellowship with His Son, Jesus Christ. He is the only true God, and He is eternal life. Dear children, keep away from anything that might take God's place in your hearts.***" It is imperative that we make God first in our life, that we make Him top priority by also making what He says top priority. We then take it a step further and make doing what He says a top priority and follow Him like Jesus did. One of the best things I have learned to do is to include God in all of my decisions regardless of how small or big the decision may be. In doing so, I have not only benefited in making better decisions all the way around but I have benefited in growing more intimate in my fellowship with Him. As I have taken the time to fully include Him in my life, the more I do, the more of Him I make accessible to me. The more I include Him, the more I live my life like Jesus and follow in His ways.

CHAPTER 8

Your Thoughts & Words Matter

NOTHING GOD DOES or says is by happenstance, including His thoughts. God tells us in Jeremiah 29:11 NKJV: ***"For I know the thoughts that I think toward you, says the Lord, thoughts of peace and not of evil, to give you a future and a hope."*** The NLT says: ***"For I know the plans I have for you, says the Lord. They are plans for good and not for disaster, to give you a future and a hope."*** And AMPC says: ***"For I know the thoughts and plans that I have for you, says the Lord, thoughts and plans for welfare and peace and not for evil, to give you hope in your final outcome."*** God was already thinking and talking about us favorably even though our actions were less than favorable. And He already had a favorable and good plan for us that lined up with how He was thinking and talking about us. Thankfully, God thinks, talks, and plans differently than man, but just like everything else, God wants us to think and talk like Him so we can walk in the plans He has for us.

Thankfully, He has shared all of this with us by sharing His Good News, His Word with us. Thankfully, God's plans for us are filled with His love and His goodness and line up with how He thinks and talks about us. God is good so His thoughts and words are good. God is love so His thoughts and words are love. And from those, His plans are filled with His goodness and love and are designed specifically for us, His children. His thoughts and plans for us are full of His goodness and love He has for us which lines up with how He talks about us. How we think and talk play a role in how we live out God's plan for us. God was even thinking about us before He even created the heavens and the earth. Before He ever made anything, including us, He was thinking about us. Ephesians 1:4-6 TPT it tells us: ***"And in love He chose us before He laid the foundation of the universe! Because of His great love, He ordained us, so that we would be seen as holy in His eyes with an unstained innocence. For it was always in His perfect plan to adopt us as His delightful children, through our union with Jesus, the Anointed One, so that His tremendous love that cascades over us would glorify His grace – for the same love He has for the Beloved, Jesus, He has for us. And this unfolding plan brings Him great pleasure!"*** The NKJV says: ***"Just as He chose us in Him before the foundation of the world, that we should be holy and without blame before Him in love, having predestined us to adoption as sons by Jesus Christ to Himself, according to the good pleasure of His will, to the praise of the glory of His grace, by which He made us accepted in the Beloved."*** His plan for us, to give us a future and a hope, He had the plan already in place to carry out before Genesis 1:1 NLT: ***"In the beginning God created the heavens and the earth."*** There was another in the beginning and it started with God's good thoughts and plan for us. His thoughts and plan of love and acceptance, of making us His beloved children, without any spot, blemish, stain, or sign of sin. And this thought and plan greatly pleased Him.

Adam and Eve did not line up their thoughts and words with God's. God had already shared His plan with them regarding what trees they could eat from and not eat from. Yet, satan used his words to convince them to go against what God had said. They came into agreement with satan over God. They did not consider or think about what God had said over what satan was saying. They used their free will to go against their Creator, going against the very nature of how He had created them. Had either of them spoken up and repeated what God had told them, had either of them been thinking about what God had told them, and had either of them believed what God had said, over satan, the outcome would have been different. Silence sometimes is speaking because our thoughts can still be telling us something. And if we are not speaking what God says when others are speaking against what God says, what are we thinking? And what are we thinking about regarding what they are saying? Are we agreeing or not agreeing with them in our thoughts? Do we need to speak up or not speak up? Thankfully, we have God's Word and we have God's Spirit (Holy Spirit) to help us know how to think and how to speak and to help us know when to speak and how to speak. And He is far greater in every way than satan. Holy Spirit has all the wisdom of God, knows God's Word better than satan thinks he does, knows Jesus intimately as He knows God, He fully understands the magnitude of what Jesus has done on the cross, He was there with Jesus every step of the way (even when satan tempted Him), and He was the One Who raised Jesus from the dead when God said it is time. And He is the One Who lives in us. He was a part of God's plan when God said He had a plan for our good and it would give us a hope and a future. Holy Spirit was as much a part of God's plan for us as Jesus. Jesus provided our birth into God's family and showed us how to live in God's family and Holy Spirit goes with us hand in Hand enabling us to live in God's family as His children are to live.

Holy Spirit can help us keep our thoughts and words lined up with God because He is well versed and familiar with God's thoughts and words. We have an advantage over Adam and Eve because they had God with them, and we do to, but now we have God in us because we have His Spirit (Holy Spirit) in us. The father of lies, satan, can cast a lie so it appears as a thought to think on, to make it look appealing, and not like a lie. One play he plays over and over because he has had a long time to practice. Yet, we have the advantage still because we have One Who can forewarn and tells us what to believe and reveal any lies to us. The fallen angels (demons), who followed satan over God and were cast out of heaven with him, now carry out satan's plans and still have no authority over us because we have the Greater One in us helping us. We have the Greater One in us reminding us of who we are, reminding us we are God's children, and reminding us of how we need to think, speak, and act like Jesus. Jesus thought of Himself as God thought of Him and He spoke of Himself as God spoke of Him. He did not allow anything or anyone to influence Him to change how He thought and spoke, especially satan. We previously saw where He had been in His Father's house at the age of twelve learning about His Father's Word, He had already been speaking His Father's Word to others, and He had been growing in His Father's Wisdom. When Jesus responded to satan, He did not just start quoting Scriptures to him. Jesus spoke the Word of God back to satan because Jesus was listening to God tell Him what to say with the help of Holy Spirit. Jesus had already been in the habit of thinking and talking like God before He was tempted. Jesus did not allow Himself to think about what satan was saying when He was being tempted nor did He delay in responding to satan. Jesus did not try to reason with satan nor was He worried about what He was going to say. Jesus knew God's Word and He had already been thinking about and speaking God's Word. Luke 12:11-12 NLT tells us: ***"And when you are brought to trial in the synagogues and before rulers and authorities, do not worry about how to defend yourself or what to say, for the Holy Spirit will teach you at that time what needs to be said."*** He is our Helper for what we need to say whenever we need to speak regardless of our audience, which can include satan or any of his demons. We just need to ask Him, listen to Him, and speak what He says. He led Jesus into the wilderness and He led Jesus to say what He needed to say when tempted by satan. Holy Spirit will always know what God says because He is God's Spirit. He cannot say anything against Himself anymore than God can say anything against Himself. He may lead us to just say one word. He may give us a Rhema Word (Word that is timely and what we need for that right now moment) to say. It may be from His Word or it may be something new directly from Him to us. If it is a Rhema Word, it will always line up with His written Word. In Luke 4 when Jesus was tempted three times, He responded the first two times with it is written and the third time He responded by saying it has been said. I believe God was showing us how Holy Spirit will sometimes give God's Word to speak because that is what is needed and sometimes He will give us God's Rhema Word because that is what we need to speak.

There was a time when Paul and Silas wanted to go to Asia to preach but Holy Spirit led them to not go. Acts 16:6-8 NLT says: ***"Next Paul and Silas traveled through the area of Phrygia and Galatia, because the Holy Spirit had prevented them from preaching the word in the province of Asia at that time. Then***

coming to the boarders of Mysia, they headed north for the province of Bithynia, but again the Spirit of Jesus did not allow them to go there. So instead, they went to Mysia to the seaport of Troas." Paul and Silas could have dismissed Holy Spirit's leading because they thought it was better to go to Asia because he knew they needed to hear God's Word and God had called them to preach. However, both yielded to Holy Spirit and did not go to Asia. And as they continued their journey of going and preaching, we see Holy Spirit again leading them to not go somewhere though they were headed there. And again, both men yielded to Holy Spirit's leading. They could have chosen differently and went on thinking it was a good idea after all they were going to preach God's Word. When we decide to go somewhere, there are thoughts that proceed. We do not just get into our vehicle and find ourselves stopping at a store. We thought about what we were needing or wanting and then where to go and get it before we went to the actual store. Even if it was a last-minute decision, there were still thoughts involved. Paul and Silas had given some thought as to where they were going because they had already started in that direction when Holy Spirit prompted them to not go. We may be heading somewhere when Holy Spirit prompts us to not go. We must always listen to Holy Spirit rather than our own thoughts and go anyway. I could have thought it better to just keep going through that flashing yellow light rather than yielding to God's leading through Holy Spirit. I could have yielded to thoughts of how tired I was and wanting to just go home without any further delays. Paul and Silas could have thought they knew better and went on to where they wanted to go anyway. Holy Spirit never provided any explanation to Paul and Silas He just led them not to go because He was leading them how God was showing Him. Notice, Holy Spirit was referred to as Spirit of Jesus. Same Spirit helping Jesus is same Spirit helping us. Thanks to Jesus, He can now help us because Jesus sent Him to us when He went back to heaven. Thanks to Holy Spirit, we can always know what to think and what to say.

When we have a thought, it is from God, it is from ourselves, or it is from satan. There are no random thoughts, because when we believe there are, we just believed a thought that generated from satan. There is nothing that would please him more than to lull us into thinking we have no control over our thoughts and we just allow a ticker tape of thoughts to continually scroll through our mind. Never once trying to line up our thoughts with God and His Word especially regarding our identity as being His children and how He sees us. Never once do we speak up because we think this is normal. We think this is how it has always been and no one knows our thoughts but us so does it really matter? God says it does so it should matter to us. God was clear when He said He knew the thoughts He was thinking toward us. Before people do something, there usually has been a series of thoughts that preceded their actions. How often have you heard of someone killing themselves and they left a note? There were some thoughts that happened prior to the action that led to suicide. Have you ever gone to do something and you just froze and then you heard someone yell, "do not think about it just do it?"Have you ever over thought and ended up not doing something because you over loaded your mind with too much thinking? Have you ever done something without much thought, perhaps because someone else was wanting you to, and then later thought how that was not such a good idea? Has God ever told you to do something and you talked yourself out of doing it? Holy Spirit is here to help us sort through our thoughts and to know which are from God, which are from us, and which are from satan. I can line up my thoughts with Gods and Holy Spirit can help me. Paul and Silas could have thought it was better to go onto Asia. Someone could have sent for them and been waiting for them. What would he think if they did not show up? They could have heard how much the people needed God's Word and thought it was important enough for them to go on. They could have been given any number of thoughts by satan to go on because satan knew they would be in danger by going on. When they thought it was good to go, they could have heard the thoughts: "you know there is not anyone else who can go, what are the people going to do if you do not go, and you do not want to disappoint God?" We do not know how they were thinking because God's Word did not tell us. However, we do know they listened to Holy Spirit and did not go. And any number of those scenarios I just spoke of can very well play out at any time in our own lives if we do not realize how important our thoughts are and how we can line up how we think with how God thinks. I can not just think God will protect me, find a scripture that says He will protect me, and then go out and do something for Him because I think that is what He wants. It all sounds good because I have God's Word and I am going to do something for Him. I have to ask Him what He wants me to do, where He wants me to go, what Word of His I need to be speaking over my situation, and then follow how Holy Spirit is leading me.

We can have God's thoughts when we get into His Word and line up our thinking according to how He thinks and how He thinks is revealed in His Word. Holy Spirit helps reveal God's Word to us. If I think I am unworthy or start thinking badly about myself, I can go to God's Word and change those thoughts to line up with what God's Word says about me. There is nowhere in God's Word that says I am unworthy or that I am bad and should be thinking about myself that way. I can immediately realize those thoughts are either coming from me or satan or a combination of both but know they are not coming from God. I can even look at Jeremiah 29:11 and begin talking and thinking about Jeremiah 29:11. I can start saying and thinking like this: "God thinks good of me so I think good of me. God has good plans for me and I trust Him and His plans for me. He is providing me with a future so I know my future will be good and it starts now because God is good and whatever He does is good. God gives me a hope, He gives me an expectation, which comes with a desire that something good will happen in my future, and I look forward to all the days that follow today. And I am thankful for today because today is a part of my future that is filled with God's goodness. God created me and what He creates is good so I am good. Now thoughts that are not wanting to line up with God and how He sees me and how He thinks about me, you go right now in the name of Jesus. I refuse to think like this any longer because I am good just like God is good and I am good just like Jesus is good. No, thought I told you to go and you have to listen. I am not going to think this way. I am going to think like God and I can and will think like God. I am good and God is good. Holy Spirit I am thankful for You and Your help." The more of God's Word I know and the more I lean on Holy Spirit, I can know what to say and what I say can replace those thoughts that do not line up with God's thoughts. The more I practice this the easier it gets. I realize I cannot just let my guard down but actively take control of my thoughts.

We must examine every thought to see if it lines up with God's Word. If it does not, we get rid of it; we slap it away and keep slapping it away until it is gone. And we do so with a force that takes the authority we have been given through Jesus. The more we know who we are and accept who we are in Jesus and being God's children the more we will want to slap away any thought that does not line up with what God says, especially about us. We can visually see our hand in our mind slapping that thought and seeing that thought leave. If it tries to come back, we will again slap it away. Have you ever gone to reach for something and had someone slap your hand? And they did it with such force your hand just flew out of the way and you almost went with your hand? More so, we can slap that thought and that thought has to go. We then replace that thought with what God says and immediately start thinking what God says. We remind ourselves in our thoughts and do this by thinking about what He told us over what thought is trying to tell us differently. And we can speak it out loud. 2 Corinthians 10:5 TPT informs us: ***"We can demolish every deceptive fantasy that opposes God and break through every arrogant attitude that is raised up in defiance of the true knowledge of God. We capture, like prisoners of war, every thought and insist that it bow in obedience to the Anointed One."*** The MSG says: ***"We use our powerful God-tools for smashing warped philosophies, tearing down barriers erected against the truth of God, fitting every loose thought and emotion and impulse into the structure of life shaped by Christ."*** The GNT tells us: ***"We pull down every proud obstacle that is raised against the knowledge of God; we take every thought captive and make it obey Christ."*** We are the ones who control our own thoughts and we can. We can close the door in the face of any thought that enters our mind that is not from God and how He thinks. Those thoughts are trespassing because we belong to God. And we can open the door to God's thoughts by thinking about His thoughts and speaking His thoughts out loud. We can go around every day and all day thinking the good, God thoughts about ourselves and even others.

We have to be looking at God's Word over anything else for how we are to think and talk. We cannot be looking at the news or reports from man and be thinking about those all the time thinking it does not matter. Riots do not start because people were thinking happy thoughts. People are not murdered because someone was thinking about happy thoughts. People become serial killers because of how they have been thinking and their actions line up. Have you ever gone to do something and thought right before you did that you should not be doing that? Once you start that pattern of thinking it can and often does get easier and easier to do what God does not want you to do. When I gave the example of sin being like an orange, a series of thoughts were involved before the action to sin occurred. A series of thoughts are usually involved before sin takes place. Our thoughts matter just like our words matter. They both are usually closely connected. However, we can be successful in our thoughts and our words thanks to God's Word and His thoughts He has shared with us in His Word. Joshua 1:8 NLT tells us: ***"Study this Book of Instruction continually. Meditate on it day and night so you will be sure to obey everything written in it. Only then will you prosper and succeed in all you do."*** The GW says: ***"Never stop reciting these teachings. You must think about them night and day so that you will faithfully do everything written in them. Only then will you prosper and succeed."*** The GNT says: ***"Be sure that the book of the Law is always read in your worship. Study it day and night, and make sure that you obey everything written in it. Then you will be prosperous and successful."*** And TPT says: ***"Recite this scroll of the law constantly. Contemplate it day and night and be careful to follow every word it contains; then you will enjoy incredible prosperity and success."*** Notice the common thread, we are to be thinking about God's Word, day and night. We do not just have a set time to get into God's Word each day. We take something God's Word says and we deeply think about it. We ponder what it says and we think about how it applies to us and our life. We think about how God's Word shows us Who God is. We think about God's Word and think about God's Word throughout our day and night. We also speak God's Word as we think about God's Word. As we start saying what God's Word says, we start to be more aware of Holy Spirit being in us as our Helper. We begin to ask Him about what God's Word is saying and listen for what He may want to reveal. Our recipe for our life is found in God's Word. How many times have we cooked something because we knew the recipe. We had seen the recipe and we followed the recipe. Any time we wanted to cook the same thing we followed the same recipe and we got the same results. Each time we cooked, it got easier and we became more proficient and comfortable. Yet, we still stuck with the recipe. God's Word is what we are to follow over and over never deviating. Each time we do we get more proficient and comfortable because we have been thinking about and talking about God's Word, day and night. And if some other recipe has tried to come to get us to think about it, we slap it away and say no we have the right recipe and we begin thinking about it, God's Word, His recipe that is the right recipe for our life.

When we look at God's Word, we change how we think and start thinking like God. The more we get into God's Word, the more we change how we think to think like God thinks. The more we get into God's Word, the less we will think like the world thinks. Romans 12:2 NLT tells us: ***"Do not copy the behavior and customs of this world, but let God transform you into a new person by changing the way you think. Then you will learn to know God's will for you, which is good and pleasing and perfect."*** And TPT says: ***"Stop imitating the ideals and opinions of the culture around you but be inwardly transformed by the Holy Spirit through a total reformation of how you think. This will empower you to discern God's will as you live a beautiful life, satisfying*** *and perfect in His eyes."* The AMPC says: ***"Do not be conformed to this world (this age), [fashioned after and adapted to its external, superficial customs], but be transformed (changed) by the [entire] renewal of your mind [by its new ideals and its new attitude], so that you may prove [for yourselves] what is the good and acceptable and perfect will of God, even the thing which is good and acceptable and perfect [in His sight for you]."*** We can have a complete over haul on how we think through God's Word. We can copy Him, copy Jesus and not this world, not satan, with changing how we think. God's Word makes the necessary transformation in changing our thoughts so our words and our actions line up with God and line up with Jesus. Holy Spirit is our inward guide helping along the way in our transformation, helping us achieve this transformation. Notice, the first change happens in how we think because how we think will determine if we live out God's good and pleasing and perfect will. Jesus did because He thought like God and like God's Word. We can when we think like Jesus by thinking like God's Word. If we want to walk in all God has for us, we must line up our thoughts with His and line up our whole life with Him and with His Word over this world and its influences. As Romans 12:1-2 MSG tells us: ***"So here is what I want you to do, God helping you: Take your everyday, ordinary life – your sleeping, eating, going-to-work, and walking-around life – and place it before God as an offering. Embracing what God does for you is the best thing you can do for Him. Do not become so well-adjusted to your culture that you fit into it without even thinking. Instead, fix your attention on God. You will be changed from the inside out. Readily recognize what He wants from you, and quickly respond to it. Unlike the culture around you, always dragging you down to its level of immaturity, God brings the best out of you, develops well-formed maturity in you."***

We do not belong to this world because Jesus did not belong to this world. Jesus did not come to this world to tell the world about its self. Jesus came to this world to talk about God and His Kingdom so God and His Kingdom could change this world. Jesus tells us in John 17:16-17 NLT: ***"They do not belong to this world any more than I do. Make them holy by Your truth; teach them Your Word, which is truth."*** The AMPC says: ***"They are not of the world (worldly, belonging to the world), [just] as I am not of the world. Sanctify them [purify them for Yourself, make them holy] by the Truth; Your Word is Truth."*** Because we are changed into our new life thanks to Jesus, we are to change how we think and no longer think like the world or satan thinks. We are purified and made holy through God's Word and this includes our thoughts and how we think. We are set a part from this world and this includes our thoughts and how we think. Colossians 3:1-3 NKJV says: ***"If then you were raised with Christ, seek those things which are above, where Christ is, sitting at the right hand of God. Set your mind on things above, not on things on the earth. For you died, and your life is hidden with Christ in God."*** And TPT says: ***"Christ's resurrection is your resurrection too. This is why we are to yearn for all that is above, for that is where Christ sits enthroned at the place of all power, honor, and authority! Yes, feast on all the treasures of the heavenly realm and fill your thoughts with heavenly realities, and not with the distractions of the natural realm."*** God is emphasizing the importance of our thoughts and our thoughts should be on things in heaven, where He and Jesus are, where His Kingdom is. We are the ones who fills our own thoughts with God's Word and the things of God over the things of this world. We can know God's thoughts because He has made His thoughts available and accessible to us just as He did for Jesus. We obtain His thoughts just like Jesus did by choosing to think like God and His Word. And we can because with our new life God provided through Jesus came a new mind. 1 Corinthians 2:16 NLT tells us: ***"For, who can know the Lord's thoughts? Who knows enough to teach Him? But we understand these things, for we have the mind of Christ."*** And the AMPC tells us: ***"For who has known or understood the mind (the counsels and purposes) of the Lord so as to guide and instruct Him and give Him knowledge? But we have the mind of Christ (the Messiah) and do hold the thoughts (feelings and purposes) of His heart."*** Just as we were raised up with Christ, we were given His mind to think like Him, to think like God and according to His Kingdom, to think according to God's side of the story. God anointed our mind to think like Jesus so we can live like Jesus. Holy Spirit helps remind us how we are to think by reminding us we can think like Jesus because we have the mind of Christ to think with. When we think with our Christ mind, peace always follows and we can keep our thoughts and mind filled with God's peace. It is a peace that passes all understanding and we do not have to understand it because we have His peace instead. Isaiah 26:3 NLT says: ***"You will keep in perfect peace all who trust in You, all whose thoughts are fixed on you!"*** Fixing our thoughts on God comes with His peace. When we fix our thoughts on God and His Kingdom, we gain confidence in knowing God will take care of His children and we can experience His fruit of peace. Matthew 6:31-33 NLT tells us: ***"So do not worry about these things, saying, 'What will we eat? What will we drink? What will we wear?' These things dominate the thoughts of unbelievers, but your heavenly Father already knows all your needs. Seek the Kingdom of God above all else, and live righteously, and He will give you everything you need."*** We can live free of worry and free of thoughts filled with worry. We can keep our thoughts on God and His Kingdom rather than the world and its kingdom. We can keep our thoughts fixed on God and His Good News rather than this world and its news. When we worry, we are allowing our thoughts to dwell on a difficulty or trouble. Instead, we can allow our thoughts to dwell and think on God and His Promises and His Promises will see us through each and every time. When we are seeking something, we are searching, inquiring, endeavoring to find, or discovering something. We can allow our thoughts to be seeking God and His Kingdom over any problems. We think about God's Promise which rule and reign over any problem. When our thoughts are in line with God's, our reliance is also on God taking care of us and our every need over looking to the world. And the by product is our soul and body will reap the benefit of God's peace and how we are thinking like Him. Romans 8:5-6 NKJV tells us: ***"For those who live according to the flesh set their minds on the things of the flesh, but those who live according to the Spirit, the things of the Spirit. For to be carnally minded is death, but to be spiritually minded is life and peace."*** Dictionary.com defines *carnal* as pertaining to or characterized by the flesh or the body, its passions and appetites. By living according to the Spirit and being spiritually minded, by thinking according to the Spirit, we obtain and live in all the fruits of Holy Spirit. It is like there is a fruit bowl filled with all of Holy Spirit's fruit and it always remains full. The bowl is always right there within my reach. I need peace, I keep my thoughts on peace by thinking like God and His Word and I immediately reach into the bowl and get peace. And I immediately begin to experience peace. I need love, I keep my thoughts on love by thinking like God and His Word and I immediately reach into the bowl and get love. And I immediately begin to experience love. And on and on it can go so as my thoughts go on and on as they are to go with God and His Word.

I have not always had this revelation, this understanding, and am thankful I now do. I always thought whatever thoughts came to my mind I was literally at their mercy. And I did my best to not follow whatever thoughts popped into my head. There were rules to follow so I did my best to not break any of those if a thought came to mind that thought otherwise. Thinking about my job helped me to not do many things but it did not help with a lot of other things. My flesh took over at times which added to the complexity and torment of my thought life which led to me sometimes going the way of my thoughts. My soul would often get in the way as well and I would find myself yielding to those soulish thoughts. Past hurt would cloud my thoughts. Around and around the merry go round my thoughts would go because I did not know there was an off switch, I did not know I could stop the merry go round. I was not thinking God's thoughts because I did not have an understanding of how He thought. I did not have an understanding of how I could exchange all of my thoughts for His thoughts. And I did not realize how life changing it would be when I did. Thankfully, God was still thinking God thoughts about me and He had let me know in His Word. His thoughts were there waiting on me. This exchange also included any thoughts that were attached or associated with fear. 2 Timothy 1:7 NKJV tells us: ***"For God has not given us a spirit of fear, but of power and of love and of a sound mind."*** And the TPT says: ***"For God will never give you the spirit of fear, but Holy Spirit Who gives you mighty power, love, and self-control."*** When we have a sound mind, our mind is unimpaired by anything. God is telling us He has given us a mind that is unimpaired by anything, including this world and the world's way of thinking, including our own thoughts and any thoughts from satan. We have the power, with the help of Holy Spirit, to think soundly, to think with the self-control that is a fruit of Holy Spirit, which we have complete access to. We exchange any thought that is attached or associated with fear with God's thoughts, which are filled with His power, His love, and Christ's mind. We can then begin and continue to think like Philippians 4:8 in AMP tells us: ***"Finally, believers, whatever is true, whatever is honorable and worthy of respect, whatever is right and confirmed by God's Word, whatever is pure and wholesome, whatever is lovely and brings peace, whatever is admirable and of good repute; if there is any excellence, if there is anything worthy of praise, think continually on these things [center your mind on them, and implant them in your heart]."*** And the TPT says: ***"Keep your thoughts continually fixed on all that is authentic and real, honorable and admirable, beautiful and respectful, pure and holy, merciful and kind. And fasten your thoughts on every glorious work of God, praising Him always."***

Thoughts and words often go hand in hand followed by actions. Psalms 103:2-3 NLT reveals to us: ***"Let all that I am praise the Lord; may I never forget the good things He does for me."*** By praising God, it helps remind us of how good He is and keeps our focus on His goodness. It helps us recall the times when He has helped us rather than our thoughts wanting to think differently and focus on the negative. When we are praising, we are using our words to express God's goodness to us and then our thoughts get in line and help by recalling how good He has been to us. It becomes a lifestyle because I make my whole life an active praise to God. I yield my life, my will to His so my life becomes an ongoing expression of His character, His goodness, and His love and how He cares for His children. When God began creating the heavens and the earth, He began speaking. He had already been thinking good about us and speaking good now He was going to begin putting His plan in motion and it began with His Word. He spoke precisely what He wanted and it happened. Even though Genesis 1:2 NKJV says: ***"The earth was without form, and void; and darkness was on the face of the deep."*** God spoke in Genesis 1:3 NKJV and said: ***"Let there be light, and there was light."*** Then God saw His words take action in Genesis 1:4 NKJV: ***"And God saw the light, that it was good."*** Not only did God speak and then see what He spoke come to pass, what He spoke created something good. He saw His very essence begin through His goodness and glory coming forth as Light and it was all through His words. Light, His Light shown first into the darkness of this world because He knew we would need His Light. He knew we would be able to receive His Light for ourselves and break free from darkness because He was going to be sending us His Light through Jesus. He knew there was more than the natural realm going into motion because there was already a spiritual realm. And as He spoke the spiritual realm gave birth to the natural realm. Throughout His creation as He spoke and what He spoke came to be, it was always good. God spoke, it happened, and it was good. God's words lined up with Him and His goodness. Proverbs 18:21 TPT tells us: "***Your words are so powerful that they will kill or give life.***" And NKJV says: ***"Death and life are in the power of the tongue."*** Notice, it is one or the other when we speak. God was speaking life into the world, His life, and He wants us to be doing the same even over ourselves. When we speak, we are speaking words that give life or we are speaking words that kill and bring death. There is no in between or gray area. It does not matter what topic we are speaking about or the tone we use. Nor does it matter if the conversation is formal or casual, who we are speaking to, or the number of people listening. If we are speaking seriously or jokingly, we are speaking death or life. Thankfully, God is letting us know we have a choice and the consequence of each choice. And He had already set the example when He created. Our words make a difference when we speak just as God's did. God's words created life and it was a good life. When we speak, God wants us to be speaking life, a good life, into every situation because our words possess creative power.

In Genesis 25, when Esau handed over his birthrights, it was a verbal exchange. Jacob crafted his words to steal from Esau and Esau used his words to agree with the theft. Words put into motion the outcome of Esau losing his rightful birthrights. Esau gave into how he was feeling through his words. He placed more value on his temporary circumstances over his longstanding birthrights all through his words. Nothing was put in writing but the value of words that create life or death are still as powerful. Let's look again at this exchange in Genesis 25:32-34 MSG, with the focus this time being on words: ***"Esau said, 'I am starving! What good is a birthright if I am dead?' Jacob said, 'First, swear to me.' And he did it. On oath Esau traded away his rights as the firstborn. Jacob gave him bread and stew of lentils. He ate and drank, got up and left. That is how Esau shrugged off his rights as the firstborn."*** Esau shrugged off the value of his birthrights with how he used his words. He used his words to depict his birthrights as being unimportant and insignificant and something that is easily disregarded. We may believe we only said something and it held no meaning because it was not written down. However, what we spoke held either life or death and the outcome produced whichever one we spoke. We may believe what we spoke had no long-lasting impact because we did not really take seriously what we were saying. We may believe how serious we are when we say something has more meaning than the words we say. There is even a correlation between how we think about words and how we speak because how we believe may be tied to how we are thinking. I may think something has no meaning when it actually does. Thoughts and words usually line up to become beliefs and beliefs usually end up being expressed through our thoughts and words. God was precise with His Words when creating. He did not speak something and then say He had changed His mind and then speak something else. He knew what He wanted to say because He knew what He wanted to create so He spoke it exactly how He wanted it. And it came to pass the exact way He had spoken. God wants us to speak like Him as well as think like Him and as His children we can. His Word helps us to know how to do both as well as Holy Spirit being our Helper.

One of the ways we walk in faith is through our words being filled with faith. We are to believe and trust God and His Word by also believing and trusting Him and His Word with our words. We believe and trust and then we talk like we believe and trust. We believe and trust and we think thoughts like we believe and trust. We must get to the point in our lives that we know, that we know, that we know God and His Word can always be trusted and trusted in our own lives no matter what. We must get to the point in our lives that we know, that we know, that we know, we are His children no matter what. We must get to the point in our lives that we know, that we know, that we know what Jesus did was for us and we can live in the life He provided for us. Times will test, the world will test, satan himself will test, if we truly believe and are holding fast to what we know through our faith, through our faith-filled words, our faith-filled thoughts, and our faith-filled actions. And we will know if we are walking by our faith as God's children. In Luke 1, two people found out about their faith walk. God sent one of His angels to deliver two different messages to two different people. One message given to a priest who was serving God and had prayed for a child. The other was given to a young lady who God saw as worthy and was engaged to be married. Both responded with a question, both using their words, but only one was filled with faith and was operating beyond the natural perspective. Luke 1:8-18 NLT tells us the first response: ***"One*** *day Zechariah was serving God in the Temple, for his order was on duty that week. As was custom of the priests, he was chosen by lot to enter the sanctuary of the Lord and burn incense. While the incense was being burned, a great crowd stood outside, praying. While Zechariah was in the sanctuary, an angel of the Lord appeared to him, standing to the right of the incense altar. Zechariah was shaken and overwhelmed with fear when he saw him. But the angel said, 'Do not be afraid, Zechariah! God has heard your prayer. Your wife, Elizabeth, will give you a son, and you are to name him John. You will have great joy and gladness, and many will rejoice at his birth, for he will be great in the eyes of the Lord. He must never touch wine or other alcoholic drinks. He will be filled with the Holy Spirit, even before his birth. And he will turn many Israelites to the Lord their God. He will be a man with the spirit and power of Elijah. He will prepare the people for the coming of the Lord. He will turn the hearts of the fathers to their children, and he will cause those who are rebellious to accept the wisdom of the godly. Zechariah said to the angel, 'How can I be sure this will happen? I am an old man now, and my wife is also well along in years.' Then the angel said, 'I am Gabriel! I stand in the very presence of God. It was He who sent me to bring you this good news! But now, since you did not believe what I said, you will be silent and unable to speak until the child is born. For my words will certainly be fulfilled at the proper time.'"* Zechariah was asking for confirmation or evidence to establish with certainty that Elizabeth was going to get pregnant. He was questioning the validity of what the angel was telling him because he was not able to see past the natural state of things. He could only see himself and his wife as being old and not being able to have children. He was walking by his sight. He was leaning on His own understanding. He was not following God and the message He was providing that was guiding him along the path God wanted him to go. He did not recognize the message was an answer to his prayer and he was not positioning himself to receive the answer. God had not sent just any angel but one who had spent time in His presence. It was as if God was saying I have a message I am delivering to you and along with the message I am sending My presence. And the message was full of all the details and plans God had for John, the baby, He was giving Zachariah and his wife. John in Hebrew is *Yohanan*, which means God (*Yhwh* or *Yahweh* which is God's name in Hebrew) has been gracious. Zachariah was a priest who was in God's sanctuary serving Him the day His angel appeared to him. He told him all his child was going to do for God, God Himself had even named him and his very name would be a continual reminder of God's grace, He was going to give him His Spirit even before his birth, His Spirit would continually be with him helping him serve God, and he was going to do mighty things for God. But Zachariah did not appear to have heard any of those things. He could have latched onto any one of those things and shouted for joy to God. Yet, he spoke, I believe what he had been thinking, what was truly in his heart, that he and his wife were too old to have children. He could have been thinking about all the things Gabriel was telling him until his thoughts exploded into rejoicing and his words lined up with God's message. Because God had a plan and He still had chosen them to be John's parents, Zachariah was not going to be able to use his words until God's plan could be first birthed. God knew the power of words and since Zachariah had not used his words to glorify and exemplify God and His plan, He did not want anything else to be spoken to bring death to His plan. Two choices when we speak, life or death, and Zachariah had chosen to not speak life when He heard God's message. Luke 1:26-34 NLT tells us the second response: ***"In the sixth month of Elizabeth's pregnancy, God sent the angel Gabriel to Nazareth, a village in Gali-***

lee, to a virgin named Mary. She was engaged to be married to a man name Joseph, a descendant of King David. Gabriel appeared to her and said, 'Greetings, favored woman! The Lord is with you! Confused and disturbed, Mary tried to think what the angel could mean. Do not be afraid, Mary,' the angel told her, 'For you have found favor with God! You will conceive and give birth to a son, and you will name Him Jesus. He will be very great and will be called the Son of the Most High. The Lord God will give Him the throne of His ancestor David. And He will reign over Israel forever; His Kingdom will never end! Mary asked the angel, 'But how can this happen? I am a virgin.' The angel replied, 'The Holy Spirit will come upon you, and the power of the Most High will overshadow you. So the baby to be born will be holy, and He will be called the Son of God. What is more, your relative Elizabeth has become pregnant in her old age! People used to say she was barren, but she has conceived a son and is now in her sixth month. For the Word of God will never fail.' Mary responded, 'I am the Lord's servant. May everything you have said about me come true.' And then the angel left her." Mary was asking for the mechanics of how she was going to get pregnant. Mary was asking the angel how this was going to happen because she knew there was something beyond what she could see or even think was going to be involved. She knew it was going to happen she just did not know the details as to how it was going to happen. Mary was walking by faith. She was not leaning on her own understanding. Rather, she was wanting to gain God's understanding as to how He was going to see to it that she became pregnant since she had not participated in the natural way of getting pregnant. She was wanting to know what were the steps to take as she went down the path God had for her. She was putting into action Proverbs 3:5-6 NKJV: ***"Trust in the Lord with all your heart, and lean not on your own understanding; in all your ways acknowledge Him,***

and he shall direct your paths.*"** And she was putting into action 2 Corinthians 5:7 NKJV: ***"For we walk by faith, not by sight." Mary considered herself God's servant even though she was not a priest who regularly served God in His sanctuary. She used her words to come into agreement with God's message and plan rather than blurt out just any words she was thinking about while Gabriel was speaking. She knew in the natural how someone got pregnant. She knew she was following the system that was customary during her time for how one got married and this system honored God. She knew she was not going to be with Joseph in the manner that would cause her to get pregnant before they were married. She did not allow her thoughts to be filled with how things happened in the natural but she was trying to think of how God was going to do what Gabriel was telling her that was going to go beyond the natural. She was believing what she was hearing because she was told her Son would be the Son of God and she knew that did not mean Joseph. When she did ask and use her words, it was a faith-filled question. And when the question was answered, she again used her words to give a faith-filled response. Notice, the slightest of difference in the two responses: How can I be sure this will happen and how can this happen. Both questioned what they were hearing but one question was filled with doubt and unbelief and the other question was filled with faith trusting and believing in the message being heard. Words are important and convey whether we are trusting and believing God and His Word regardless of the vessel He chooses to deliver His message. Can God trust us with our words? Can we trust ourselves with our words? Do our words convey faith because we are trusting and believing God even if there is something else vying for our attention to try and sway us to trust and believe otherwise?

There was another who chose to walk by faith aligning his words, thoughts, and actions to be filled with faith. He walked in such a measure of faith that he is referred to as our father of faith. Galatians 3:6-8 TPT says: ***"Abraham, our father of faith, believed God, and the substance of his faith released God's righteousness to him. So, the true children of Abraham have the same faith as their father! And the Scripture prophesied that on the basis of faith God would declare gentiles to be righteous. God announced the good news ahead of time to Abraham: 'Through your example of faith all the nations will be blessed!'"*** We have the same faith as Abraham and when we walk in faith, we walk in all the blessings of Abraham. We have the blessings already just as we have all that our new life in Christ affords us. We walk in all we have been given when we walk in faith. It is like we are playing a video game and there are all these prizes you can pick up along the way and boasters that will help you play the game better. We can play the game and ignore the prizes and boasters and keep playing the game but the game seems harder that way. Or we can pick up the prizes and boasters as we play the game which makes the game easier and actually makes the game more fun. Walking by faith or not walking by faith is like we are standing at a cross road. One road has a sign that reads: faith go this way. The other road has a sign that reads: go this way. We have a choice over which road to take. Both roads have a sign that tells us to go this way but only one has added faith. When we choose to go with the road that has added faith to the sign, we are choosing to walk in the blessings of Abraham, our father of faith, left for us. He knew we inherited his blessings and they belonged to us so he left them for us on the road of faith. As we go down the road of faith, we see all the blessings all around us and all down the road as we walk. The further down the road we go the more blessings we find. We have to walk down this road ourselves but when we do we find it was worth it becomes we find what belongs to us and what is rightfully ours. Whenever God tells us something, especially in His Word, we can receive what He tells us by faith and receive all the blessings that come with it. Having faith-filled words and faith-filled thoughts helps us in our faith walk. We are better conditioned and in shape to make our faith walk. God does not reveal in His Word how old Zechariah was when John the Baptist was born; however, God does tell us Abraham was about one hundred years old when Isaac was born. God delivered another promise of a child being born and this time it was to Abraham. Abraham's response is revealed to us in Romans 4:19-20 NKJV: ***"And not being weak in faith, he did not consider his own body, already dead (since he was about a hundred years old), and the deadness of Sarah's womb. He did not waver at the promise of God through unbelief, but was strengthened in faith, giving glory to God."*** Abraham did not look at his circumstances or his and his wife's body. He did not walk by what he saw because He walked by what God told Him. He used his faith to believe and receive what God said because He chose to see himself as God saw him. He chose to walk by faith.

Even during times of testing and after Issac had been born, Abraham did not waiver in his faith. He did not waiver in how he thought or talked nor in how he walked by faith. Genesis 22:1-5 NLT says: ***"Sometime later, God tested Abraham's faith, 'Abraham!' God called. 'Yes,' he replied. 'Here I am.' 'Take your son, your only son - yes, Issac, whom you love so much – and go to the land of Moriah. Go and sacrifice him as a burnt offering on one of the mountains, which I will show you.' The next morning Abraham got up early. He saddled his donkey and took two of his servants with him, along with his son, Isaac. Then he chopped wood for a fire for a burnt offering and set out for the place God***

had told him about. One the third day of their journey, Abraham looked up and saw the place in the distance. 'Stay here with the donkey,' Abraham told the servants. 'The boy and I will travel a little farther. We will worship there, and then we will come right back.'" There is no mention of Abraham asking God why, or using his words at all, only that Abraham got up early the next day to carry out God's request. Sometimes, not speaking is walking in faith. I do not know if Abraham normally got up early or if he was considered a morning person as some people call themselves. Regardless, he chose to get up early rather than not getting up early. To me, this speaks of his willingness and how he was even thinking. He was not mulling over what God told him but he was preparing to go forth with what God asked him. There were some thoughts to what he had to do to get everything ready before he could sacrifice his son. He was fully surrendered and fully obedient to God. He was willing to give up his most prized possession, he was willing to give up his natural inheritance (his son), to do what God asked of Him. God is a good God and was testing Abraham's faith, testing how much Abraham believed in Him, and how much Abraham trusted Him. Abraham knew God had a plan for him and that it was good and it was for his future that was filled with hope. So much so, he told his servants when he was taking Isaac to sacrifice him as a burnt offering that they would be back. His words and thoughts remained full of faith. Abraham did not tell his servants about God's plan, about what he was about to do for God, he just went up as God directed prepared to carry forth God's instructions. He considered being obedient to God as an act of worship because he told his servants that is what he and his son were going to do. For him, it was intimate because he told the servants to stay behind while he and his son went on ahead. He knew his faith and he knew his son would follow his faith. And he had such faith in God, in God's goodness, in

Who God was, in God's Word that he knew God would raise his son from being dead. And not only raise him from being dead but from being ashes. God told him to offer Isaac as a burnt offering meaning he would have to sacrifice him and then burn the body to make the burnt offering in the same way they made animal sacrifices to God. Abraham had no idea in the natural how God was going to bring his son back from that but he knew God had promised him his son. And he knew God upheld His promises. He knew God would not give him his son to then take his son from him. He did not know why God was asking him to do what He was asking but he still trusted Him and did so without asking for a reason. Abraham was walking by faith and Abraham was talking by faith and Abraham was thinking by faith. And Abraham was establishing a pattern for all of us to walk by faith, talk by faith, and think by faith. Romans 4:17 NLT tells: ***"That is what the Scriptures mean when God told him, 'I have made you the father of many nations.' This happened because Abraham believed in the God Who brings the dead back to life and who creates new things out of nothing."*** NKJV says: ***"God, Who, gives life to the dead and calls those things which do not exist as though they did."*** Abraham was using his words for faith, he was using his words to trust and believe God. He was setting the example for his son, as well as us, on how to follow God, His Word, and His Ways. Genesis 22:6-14 NLT: ***"So Abraham placed the wood for the burnt offering on Isaac's shoulders, while he himself carried the fire and the knife. As the two of them walked on together, Issac turned to Abraham and said, 'Father?' 'Yes, my son?' Abraham replied. 'We have the fire and the wood.' The boy said, 'but where is the sheep for the burnt offering?' 'God will provide a sheep for the burnt offering, my son,' Abraham answered. And they both walked on together. When they arrived at the place where God had told him to go, Abraham arranged the wood on it. Then he tied his***

son, Isaac, and laid him on the alter on top of the wood. And Abraham picked up the knife to kill his son as a sacrifice. At that moment the angel of the Lord called to him from heaven, 'Abraham! Abraham!' 'Yes,' Abraham replied. 'Here I am!' 'Do not lay a hand on the boy! The angel said. 'Do not hurt him in any way, for now I know that you truly fear God. You have not withheld from me even your son, your only son.' Then Abraham looked up and saw a ram caught by its horns in a thicket. So he took the ram and sacrificed it as a burnt offering in place of his son. Abraham named the place Yahweh-Yireh (which means, 'the Lord will provide'). To this day, people still use that name as a proverb: 'On the mountain of the Lord it will be provided.' Abraham used his words to create a new thing out of nothing, to call those things which do not exist as though they did. He had his son to sacrifice as God had told him to; yet, when his son asked him where was the sacrifice, he told his son God would provide a sheep. And God did exactly as Abraham spoke, He had a ram caught waiting on Abraham. Abraham did not go up to the mountain looking for the ram but He did have faith to know God would provide. He went up the mountain carrying out the plan God had told him to carry out. And his son was following in his faith walk. He had heard his father say God was going to provide even though he could not see it in the natural. He knew what his father was preparing to do and he went along with his father because his father was going along with God. Isaac laid himself on the altar in faith. He let his father tie his hands and watch his father raise the knife to sacrifice him in faith. And then he saw God provide the ram for the sacrifice. They showed how God provides and He still does provide. God provided for them and He will provide for us. We have to keep our thoughts, our words, and our actions filled with faith knowing God will provide and He is always timely. We know God can be trusted and will provide what we need regardless of what others may be saying or doing and regardless of what our situation or circumstances may look or sound like. Abraham and Isaac were both demonstrating how God would later require another sacrifice. This time God would be asking His Son, Jesus, to be our sacrifice. And His Son, would be our Lamb, going to take our place because we deserved to die when He did not. He would do what no one else could do so we could live in the blessings and abundant life as God's children. John the Baptist would even announce Jesus as the Lamb in John 1:29 NLT: ***"The next day John saw Jesus coming toward Him and said, 'Look! The Lamb of God Who takes away the sin of the world!"*** Jesus would walk in faith knowing Who God is and understanding God's plan was a good plan.

When we talk and think how God wants us to talk and think, we honor Him and His Word, we honor Jesus. When we operate in our faith, we honor God and His Word, we honor Jesus. In doing so, we look like God's children are to look because we are thinking and talking and walking how God's children are supposed to. We can use our words to worship and praise God for Who He is and while we do, it reminds us of God and His goodness. We can then think on God and His goodness and Who He is to us as our Father and who we are to Him as His children. Our worship and praise positions us to see God and ourselves as He sees. Deuteronomy 32:3-4 NLT says: ***"I will proclaim the name of the Lord; how glorious is our God! He is the Rock; His deeds are perfect. Everything He does is just and fair. He is a faithful God who does no wrong; how just and upright He is!"*** And Psalms 100:1 NLT tells us: ***"Shout with joy to the Lord, all the earth!"***

CHAPTER 9

God's Kingdom in You

GOD HAS ALWAYS wanted us to follow Him, to listen to His voice for our daily instructions. He has wanted to have a people who would be obedient to Him so He could share His love and goodness, so He could share His Kingdom. He has known that following Him, following His side of the story is and will always be for our best. It was for Adam and Eve's best. Prior to listening to satan's side of the story and following his side, they were surrounded by God's glory so much so they did not recognize their nakedness. They could see God's glory in and on their lives and were able to experience God's glory daily until they decided to not be obedient to God. By not following God and His side of the story, the glory lifted off of them revealing their natural state and what it looked like without God. They began walking by sight rather than by faith, rather than by the supernatural side for which they were first created. They were created to rule and reign on this earth and use God's glory, use His authority they were given, to cause His Kingdom to cover the earth. They were to influence the world for God. God's plan was for the Garden of Eden to spread so His life, His ways, could be experienced all over the world. God knew the benefits and that it was for everyone's benefit for this to occur and so did satan. Thus, the reason satan moved in to spread his side of the story. Yet, God in His goodness and love had a plan to make everything right again and this time it was far superior and greater. Not only does God still want His Kingdom, His ways to cover the earth, He placed His Kingdom in all who are born again. With this new birth, God's Spirit, Holy Spirit, comes to live inside of every person who has received this new birth equipping all to be able to live like God's Kingdom on earth.

Even after Adam and Eve, God's plan never changed just as He never changes. He delivered His people, the Israelites, from Egypt and Moses was His vessel He used. However, God wanted to be able to speak directly to them and He did so when He was giving them His ten commandments. He was providing them with His instructions on how they needed to live which would be for their benefit and would enable His Kingdom to reign in their lives. Rather than seeing the goodness and power of God being displayed to them as a positive, they responded in fear. Instead of being thankful God was choosing to share some of His glory with them, giving them a glimpse that there was so much more, they turned away and looked to Moses, a man. God had already showed Himself strong by all He had done getting them to this point, which included having them walk unhindered and unimpeded through the Red Sea. However, when God wanted to speak to them, they did not respond appropriately. This is seen in Exodus 20:18-22 NLT: ***"When the people heard the thunder and the loud blast of the ram's horn, and when they saw the flashes of*** *lighting and the smoke billowing from the mountain, they stood at a distance, trembling with fear. And they said to Moses, 'You speak to us, and we will listen. But do not let God speak directly to us, or we will die!' 'Do not be afraid,' Moses answered them, for God has come in this way to test you, and so that your fear for Him will keep you from sinning!' As the people stood in the distance, Moses approached the dark cloud where God was. And the Lord said to Moses, 'Say this to the people of Israel: You saw for yourselves that I spoke to you from heaven.'"* Though the people had previously listened to Moses, they did not listen to him regarding how God wanted to talk directly to them and how they should have honor and reverence for Him, rather than fearing He would take their life. They failed to see God's goodness. They had failed to see what a privilege it was for God to want to communicate directly with them and how wonderful to know He was capable of speaking to multitudes and not just one person. They allowed themselves to be distracted by the manner for which He chose to speak. They made the focus on themselves and their will over God's and their wants over His. God had chosen one vessel, Moses, to speak through but His plan was for Him to be able to speak to all the people of Israel. His plan was for His side of the story to be carried forth in all the earth, for His Kingdom to be carried for in all the earth and He wanted His people to listen to Him and carry His Kingdom throughout all the earth. God had already been guiding them since delivering them from Egypt and the Egyptians. Exodus 13:21-22 NLT says: ***"The Lord went ahead of them. He guided them during the day with a pillar of cloud, and He provided light at night with a pillar of fire. This allowed them to travel by day or night. And the Lord did not remove the pillar of cloud or pillar of fire from its place in front of the people."*** God wanting to display more of Himself, more of His glory as He spoke to them should have been welcoming to them and a sign of how much He wanted to fellowship with them. This increase of God displaying Himself along with them hearing His voice should have been an encouragement and should have drawn them toward Him. They were already familiar with Him being with them day and night through the pillar of cloud and the pillar of fire. God was wanting to share more of Himself with them and they responded in fear. Not a fear that honored and reverenced God for Who He is and Who He wanted to be to them but a fear that He was going to do something bad to them. All based on Him wanting to talk to them and showing Himself to them the way He had chosen. They could not see past the natural and allow God to show them the supernatural, let Him show them firsthand more of His Kingdom. He had already been showing them how He can take care of them, how He can protect and deliver them, how He can provide for them. They had already seen miracle after miracle, sign and wonder after sign and wonder and still they did not want to speak directly to the One behind all they had previously experienced. Nothing He had done for them could man have done. He had shown them how His Kingdom was greater than the world they were living in. He had already shown them a glimpse of what He wanted for them and all He had shown them was good, good for, and good to them. Their response would set in motion a chain of events in which they would allow themselves to be enslaved to man's system, a worldly system set apart from God, over entrusting themselves to God's system. His system, His Kingdom that was far superior and greater.

Because of Israel's rejection of wanting to listen directly to God, it set up the precedent for God to use His prophet to speak to the people, to use His leader to deliver His justice. This was not God's best for them but He is only able to carry forth what man will accept and respond in kind regarding listening to Him and following in His plan and allowing for adjustments to be made as He provides the necessary correction. God had appointed such a person in Samuel and Samuel understanding he was getting older had appointed his sons to take his place. The people were not happy with this decision because Samuel's sons did not possess his same character. And they demanded to have a king. 1 Samuel 8:5 NLT tells us: ***"'Look,' they told him, 'You are now old, and your sons are not like you. Give us a king to judge us like all the other nations have.'"*** They were wanting to look like the world. Notice, they did not ask Samuel to talk to his sons nor did they try to make an appeal to God. Instead, they wanted to be under the control of the world's system. They thought their plan was better than God's. We see Samuel and God's response in 1 Samuel 8:6-9 NLT: ***"Samuel was displeased with their request and went to the Lord for guidance. 'Do everything, they say to you,' the Lord replied, 'for they are rejecting Me, not you. They do not want Me to be their king any longer. Ever since I brought them from Egypt, they have continually abandoned Me and followed other gods. And now they are giving you the same treatment. Do as they ask, but solemnly warn them about the way a king will reign over them.'"*** They were about to get what they wanted and thought was better for them and it was not going to be as good as they thought. God was warning them and letting them know they would not like their choice but it was of their choosing. 1 Samuel 8:10-18 MSG provides the warning: ***"So Samuel told them, delivered God's warning to the people who were asking Him to give them a king. He said, 'This is the way this kind of king you are talking about operates. He will take your sons and make soldiers of them – chariotry, cavalry, infantry, regimented in battalions and squadrons. He will put some to forced labor on his farms, plowing and harvesting, and others to making either weapons of war or chariots in which he can ride in luxury. He will put your***

daughters to work as beauticians and waitresses and cooks. He will conscript your best fields, vineyards, and orchards and hand them over to his special friends. He will tax your harvests and vintage to support his extensive bureaucracy. Your prize workers and best animals he will take for his own use. He will lay a tax on your flocks and you will end up no better than slaves. The day will come when you will cry in desperation because of this king you so much want for yourselves. But do not expect God to answer." Perhaps, some of this sounds familiar as to how governments in the world function today. God has His system and man has his. God has and continues to want His system, His Kingdom to be in place because He knows it is best for everyone when His Kingdom is in operation. God in His goodness has given us a free will to choose His Kingdom and choose to operate in His Kingdom. We have to first recognize His Kingdom as being best for us. We then accept and learn to operate in His Kingdom so His Kingdom can spread into the lives of others and across the world fulfilling God's plan.

We can operate in God's Kingdom with His wisdom because He has put His Kingdom and Spirit in us. Even before God provided His Spirit to all who would receive Jesus and to all who would receive even a greater measure of His Spirit, God had faithful followers. He had followers who knew Him and knew He would be sending Jesus as the world's Deliverer. They knew God and followed His ways over the worlds and they were able to impact the world around them for God's Kingdom. When the Israelites wanted a king, God gave them Saul who was raised to follow God's commands. Even though they wanted a king over listening to God and they wanted a king over listening to God's prophet, God was still trying to give them someone who would listen to Him. He knew anyone who would listen to and follow

Him would be best for them. However, Saul began to follow the people and what they wanted over God. His focus shifted from pleasing God, to pleasing people, and being seen as great in their eyes. Because Saul stopped following God's ways, God anointed David to succeed Saul as king. God was still wanting to establish His plan for His Kingdom to cover the earth because His plan was a better and greater plan. So, God sent Samuel to David's house to anoint him as king. Even though David's father did not think highly of him and considered him to be the lesser of his sons, God thought differently and still chose David. God is never swayed by man's opinions nor his preferences. 1 Samuel 16:13 NLT tells us: ***"So as David stood there among his brothers, Samuel took the flask of olive oil he had brought and anointed David with the oil. And the Spirit of the Lord came powerfully upon David from that day on. Then Samuel returned to Ramah."*** Notice it says, "the Spirit of the Lord came powerfully upon David from that day on." God's Spirit had already been lifted from Saul because of his continued disobedience and lack of reverence for God. Because Saul wanted to follow man and follow what he considered best, God was allowing him to do so in his own strength. Saul would complete his reign without God's help or anointing. We can see this being played out when Saul had to face Goliath. No physical fighting had yet to occur and still Saul and his men were in fear. 1 Samuel 17:10-11 NLT says: ***"'I defy the armies of Israel today! Send me a man who will fight me!' When Saul and the Israelites heard this, they were terrified and deeply shaken."*** Saul and his army were walking by sight and cowering to their enemy's voice. No one was seeking God for guidance and no one was acting like they were a part of God's army. They allowed this bombardment of the enemy's voice with no recourse of trying to stop the enemy. After the forty-day verbal assault, David arrives. The same David, who was already anointed to be king, while Saul still held the position of king. David had no worldly training on how to fight nor had he any worldly training on how to be a leader. He did have God's Spirit upon Him. David sees the situation according to how God's see it and David sees himself according to how God sees him. David is walking by faith. David wants to quiet the enemy and advance God's Kingdom. 1 Samuel 17:45-51 NLT: ***"David replied to the Philistine, 'You come to me with sword, spear, and javelin, but I come to you in the name of the Lord of Heaven's Armies – the God of the armies of Israel, Whom, you have defied. Today the Lord will conquer you, and I will kill you and cut off your head. And then I will give the dead bodies of your men to the birds and wild animals, and the whole world will know that there is a God in Israel! And everyone assembled here will know that the Lord rescues His people, but not with sword and spear. This is the Lord's battle, and He will give you to us!' As Goliath moved closer to attack, David quickly ran out to meet him. Reaching into his shepherd's bag and taking out a stone, he hurled it with his sling and hit the Philistine in the forehead. The stone sank in, and Goliath stumbled and fell face down on the ground. So, David triumphed over the Philistine with only a sling and a stone, for he had no sword. Then David ran over and pulled Goliath's sword from its sheath. David used it to kill him and cut off his head."*** David was able to defeat Goliath because David's trust was in God and what he would be able to do with God's help. God's Spirit was with David helping him. David only had God's Spirit upon Him and we have God's Spirit within. David took what God had given him and allowed God to work through him. Even though Saul was going to give David his battle gear, David stayed with the battle gear God provided for him. David's full reliance was on God. He defeated the giant, removing the enemy's obstacle, and advanced God's Kingdom. God used one man, who listened to Him, who was empowered by His Spirit, to do what a whole army and king were not able to do.

There were four others who were devoted to God and following Him. As a result, they made an impact in their world for God and His Kingdom. Each time when they followed God and His ways over mans, over the worlds, God delivered them and they had favor. Their focus never wavered from being on God and knowing Who He was to them and knowing who they were to Him. They always saw every situation through God's eyes and responded accordingly. Even when it came to eating, they still honored God. We first see Daniel wanting to honor God by eating and drinking as He had instructed them and not yielding to how the king wanted them to eat. His three friends, Hananiah [Shadrach], Mishael [Meshach], and Azariah [Abednego] followed his lead. There was no area of their lives where they did not look to honor God and follow His leading. God gave Daniel wisdom on how he could honor Him and Daniel followed the strategy given to him by God. We see the end result in Daniel 1:18-20 NLT: ***"When the training period ordered by the king was completed, the chief of staff brought all the young men to King Nebuchadnezzar. The king talked with them, and no one impressed him as much as Daniel, Hananiah, Mishael, and Azariah. So, they entered the royal service. Whenever the king consulted them in any matter requiring wisdom and balanced judgment, he found them ten times more capable than any of the magicians and enchanters in his entire kingdom."*** Not only were Daniel and his friends able to keep themselves pure, they were found to be far superior than anyone else in the king's kingdom. Four men willing to submit to God's Kingdom and God's ways were given all the favor, wisdom, and strength needed to live set a part for God in man's kingdom. We see Daniel and his friends being threatened with death, along with any other wise men, because the king was upset over no one being able to interrupt his dreams. Again, Daniel speaks up with authority and boldness because he knows he belongs to God Who is his King. Again, God gives Daniel the wisdom he needs and God tells Daniel the meaning of the king's dreams. Not only is Daniel and his friends not killed, Daniel gets recognition from the king. And God also gets recognition from the king who is able to see how God provided the answers needed. Daniel 2:47 NLT tells: ***"The king said to Daniel, 'Truly, your God is the greatest of gods, the Lord over kings, a revealer of mysteries, for you have been able to reveal this secret.'"*** When we operate and function in God's Kingdom, according to His ways, we bring His Kingdom to earth and others will take note, including leaders of this worldly system.

And sometimes the worldly system will set up their ways, which openly defy God's ways. They will do something that God does not approve of, including establishing laws. We see this happening first with Hananiah, Mishael, and Azariah. The king set up a statue of himself and expected everyone to bow down to his statue whenever a certain music was played. Hananiah, Mishael, and Azariah knew God's law, His commandment, and they honored God by not bowing. As a result, they were brought before the king and given a second chance but they remained firm in their conviction to follow God. The king had the furnace turned up seven times hotter and they were thrown in with their hands bound. God delivered them and we see how the king responded in Daniel 3:25-26 NKJV: ***"'Look!' he answered, 'I see four men loose, walking in the midst of the fire; and they are not hurt, and the form of the fourth is like the Son of God!' Then Nebuchadnezzar went near the mouth of the burning fiery furnace and spoke, saying, 'Shadrach [Hananiah], Meshach [Mishael], and Abed-nego [Azariah], servants of the Most High God, come out and***

come here.'" Not only had God delivered them completely unharmed but they did not even smell like smoke; God had sent Someone to be with them while they were in the fire. The king saw Him and referred to Him as being "like the Son of God." God was already demonstrating how He was going to send Jesus to go to hell so we could be spared from going. God was demonstrating His power over death and fire in the natural was greater because He was going to be demonstrating how His power over sin, death, and hell was greater. Jesus would stand in the gap between the natural and supernatural. Jesus would be our bridge from earth to heaven. Not only were they delivered from the king's law, the king changed the law to honor God. They honored God by upholding His law over the king's and now the king was establishing a new law to honor God. Daniel 3:28-30 NKJV tells us: ***"Nebuchadnezzar spoke, saying, 'Blessed be the God of Shadrach, Meshach, and Abednego, Who, sent His angel and delivered His servants who trusted Him, and they have frustrated the king's word, and yielded their bodies, that they should not serve nor worship any god except their own God! Therefore, I make a decree that any people, nation or language which speaks anything amiss against the God of Shadrach, Meshach, and Abednego shall be cut in pieces, and their houses shall be made an ash heap; because there is no other God Who can deliver like this.' Then the king promoted Shadrach, Meshach, and Abednego in the province of Babylon."*** Shadrach [Hananiah], Meshach [Mishael], and Abednego [Azariah] honored God and God's ways above the worlds and now God was being honored. God's Kingdom had touched earth and a new law was now put into place where no one could speak against God. God delivered them and the king promoted them. Later another worldly king was ruler. Daniel still had God's favor and wisdom on his life and the king was looking to promote Daniel over the whole empire. The king had taken note that Daniel was "faithful, always responsible, and completely trustworthy." This made others mad so they looked to sabotage the king's plan. They could find no fault with Daniel so they decided to use Daniel's devotion to God against him. They went to the king and got the king to make a law where no one could pray to anyone except the king for thirty days. If anyone did, they would be thrown into the lion's den. What would not praying to God for thirty days hurt? Could Daniel just forgo praying for thirty days? The law did not specify that you had to pray to the king for the next thirty days but specified that you could not pray to anyone except the king. After the thirty days, Daniel could have gone back to how he operated before the law. Just lay low for thirty days because surely God would understand and not expect Daniel to do something that would get him thrown into the lion's den. After all, God was using him so he could just pause and restart after thirty days. Daniel understood God and His ways, which are higher than man's. Daniel understood God and His thoughts, which are higher than man's. Daniel had an ongoing fellowship with God and he honored God above all. Daniel saw his situation through God's eyes and he was going to continue to pray to God and no other. He knew God gave him the wisdom and instructions he needed. Daniel knew God's Word. He knew Psalms 121:2-3 NLT: ***"My help comes from the Lord, Who, made heaven and earth! He will not let you stumble; the One Who watches over you will not slumber."*** Daniel knew Psalms 23:1-6 TPT: ***"Yahweh [God] is my best friend and my Shepherd. I always have more than enough. He offers a resting place for me in His luxurious love. His tracks take me to an oasis of peace near the quite brook of bliss. That is where He restores and revives my life. He opens before me the right path and leads me along in His footsteps of righteousness so that I can bring honor to His name. Even when Your path takes me through the valley of darkens, fear will never conquer me, for You already***

have! Your authority is my strength and my peace. The comfort of Your love takes away my fear. I will never be lonely, for You are near. You become my delicious feast even when my enemies dare to fight. You anoint me with the fragrance of Your Holy Spirit; You give me all I can drink of You until my cup overflows. So why would I fear the future? Only goodness and tender love pursue me all the days of my life. Then afterward, when my life is through, I will return to your glorious presence to be forever with You!" God provides His comfort, His love, His peace, His strength, and His Spirit to us and I believe Daniel knew this as well. I believe Daniel knew God would provide a way through this valley of darkness because Daniel was choosing to walk in God's authority and in His ways. Daniel was choosing to continue to fellowship with his God in prayer which he did three times a day. He did not try to hide because he knew Who the King of kings and Lord of lords was and was to him personally. People were watching hoping he would honor his God and when they saw he did, they ran to tell the king. The king, who did not want to see Daniel harmed or killed, had to abide by his own law. He hoped God would deliver Daniel as he had Daniel thrown into the lion's den. God caused the lion's mouths to be shut and no harm came to Daniel, not even a scratch was found on him. I actually picture Daniel laying down with the lions as he slept using them to keep him warm and from being on the ground. The next day the king went hoping to find Daniel unharmed and he did. He had all who were responsible for tricking him to create the law, to be thrown into the lion's den, along with their families. Not only did they receive the treatment they had meant for Daniel, so did their generations. Daniel remained respectful to the king and treated him the same as if he had never had him thrown into the lion's den. God's love keeps no record of wrong. Again, we see a worldly king changing a law giving recognition and honor to God because God had someone who stood in honor and recognition of Him and His ways and God was able to demonstrate His Kingdom on earth. Daniel 6:26-27 NLT tells us how the king responded: *"'I decree that everyone throughout my kingdom should tremble with fear before the God of Daniel. For He is the living God, and He will endure forever. His Kingdom will never be destroyed, and His rule will never end. He rescues and saves His people; He performs miraculous signs and wonders in the heavens and on earth. He has rescued Daniel from the power of the lions.'"* Not only did God rescue Daniel but God and His Kingdom got recognition and people knew God was able to perform miraculous signs and wonders on the earth. And Daniel prospered throughout the king's and the following king's reign. All because Daniel knew His King and lived his life in a manner showing others Who His King was and what His Kingdom was about. He lived not of this world but from God's Kingdom and how God sees.

If four men, who worked for a worldly king, could honor God and do what they did for God, how much more can God's children make an impact for Him and His Kingdom today? God knew because He was going to send One Man, Jesus, His Son, to make a way for all of God's sons and daughters to be able to make an impact for God and His Kingdom. Jesus was coming to reveal God's Kingdom to us and show us how God's Kingdom is to operate through us by making a way for God's Kingdom to be in us. Jesus came to deliver God's message in demonstration and power. He tells us in Mark 1:15 TPT: *"His message was this: 'At last the fulfillment of the age has come! It is time for God's Kingdom to be experienced in its fullness! Turn your lives back to God and put your trust in the hope-filled gospel!'"* The AMP says: *"The [appointed period of] time is fulfilled, and the Kingdom of God is at hand; repent [change your inner self – your old way*

of thinking, regret past sins, live your life in a way that proved repentance; seek God's purpose for your life] and believe [with a deep, abiding trust] in the good news [regarding salvation]." And 1 Corinthians 4:20 tells us: ***"For the Kingdom of God is not just a lot of talk; it is living by God's power."*** God was sending Jesus to do more than just talk about His Kingdom. God was sending Jesus to show us God's Kingdom. God was sending Jesus so we could see His Kingdom through His eyes so we would know what His Kingdom looked like. Mark 1:22 TPT tells us: ***"The people were awestruck by His teaching, because He taught in a way that demonstrated God's authority, which was quite unlike the religious scholars."*** Jesus came in the authority of God's Kingdom to show us we too can operate in the authority of God's Kingdom. And Jesus only did what God, His Father, told and showed Him what to do. And He will do the same for us. We can have our identity so firmly established in being God's children we operate just like Jesus did. When the enemy rises up, we can use the same authority as Jesus because Jesus has given us His authority. Mark 1:23-27 TPT tells us: ***"Suddenly, during the meeting, a demon-possessed man screamed out, 'Hey! Leave us alone! Jesus the victorious, I know Who You are. You are God's Holy One and you have come to destroy us!' Jesus rebuked him, saying 'Silence! You are bound! Come out of him!' The man's body shook violently in spasms, and the demon hurled him to the floor until it finally came out of him with a deafening shriek! The crowd was awestruck and kept saying among themselves, 'What is this new teaching that comes with such authority? With merely a word He commands demons to come out and they obey Him!'"*** Jesus was demonstrating God's Kingdom by using His authority over demons. Even though they followed satan, they had to obey Jesus and they did. As God's children, Jesus was showing us we have the same authority over demons.

There were three parts to Jesus' ministry when He was on earth: preaching God's Kingdom, teaching God's Kingdom, and demonstrating God's Kingdom. And He did so as God directed Him. Jesus lived His life yielded to God and His Spirit and Jesus lived His life by yielding to His Own Spirit over His soul and flesh. And God, through His Spirit, instructed Jesus to go see a man who held many in terror due to the torment he was in. And Jesus went to see this man and introduce him to the Kingdom of God and set him free from his torment. Mark 1 5:2-13 NLT tells us: ***"When Jesus climbed out of the boat, a man possessed by an evil spirit came out from the tombs to meet Him. This man lived in the burial caves and could no longer be restrained, even with a chain. Whenever he was put into chains and shackles – as he often was – he snapped the chains from his wrists and smashed the shackles. No one was strong enough to subdue him. Day and night he wondered among the burial caves and in the hills, howling and cutting himself with sharp stones. When Jesus was still some distance away, the man saw Him, ran to meet Him, and bowed low before Him. With a shriek, he screamed, 'Why are You interfering with me, Jesus, Son of the Most High God? In the name of God, I beg you, do not torture me!' For Jesus had already said to the spirit, 'Come out of the man, you evil spirit.' Then Jesus demanded, 'What is your name?' And he replied, 'My name is legion, because there are many of us inside this man.' Then the evil spirit begged him again and again not to send them to some distant place. There happened to be a large herd of pigs feeding on the hillside nearby. 'Send us into those pigs,' the spirits begged. 'Let us enter them.' So, Jesus gave them permission. The evil spirits came out of the man and entered the pigs, and the entire herd of about 2,000 pigs plunged down the steep hillside into the lake and drowned in the water."*** Again, a demon (a legion of demons) recognized Jesus for Who He was and understood the authority

He had. The demons knew that Jesus had the power to send them and all the others to some place that was not good because even they did not want to go. So, they asked to be allowed to enter the pigs that were nearby. Jesus had such authority and authority over the demons, He had to give them permission to do so. Jesus was identified by His authority He had over demons, even by the demons themselves. And He wants us to be identified by our authority we have over demons. We should know who we are as God's children and walk in all the authority been given to us by Jesus, that demons know our names. Jesus not only demonstrated God's Kingdom by setting the man free from the demons and their tormenting him but Jesus demonstrated God's Kingdom by fully restoring the man as seen in Mark 5:15 NLT: ***"A crowd soon gathered around Jesus, and they saw the man who had been possessed by the legion of demons. He was sitting there fully clothed and perfectly sane, and they were all afraid."*** The man was now fully restored. Not only was the man no longer tormented but he would no longer be tormenting others. One man freed through God's Kingdom caused a whole area to be freed. There is no mention of Jesus bringing clothes but the man was fully clothed. They failed to see the entirety of the miracle Jesus did by demonstrating the power of God's Kingdom because their focus was on themselves. They failed to see God's Kingdom standing before them. They could have started praising and worshiping Jesus and what He had just done. Yet, they remained in fear and asked Him to leave. God wants to touch lives for His Kingdom and He wants His children to demonstrate His Kingdom just like Jesus did.

Jesus, still listening to God and following His lead, quietly left. And as He went, He met someone who did want what God's Kingdom could offer. He met a father whose daughter was dying and he had come to Jesus for help. He had come to Jesus for her to be healed. Mark 5:22-24 NLT tells us: ***"Then a leader of the local synagogue, whose name was Jairus, arrived. When he saw Jesus, he fell at His feet, pleading fervently with Him. 'My little daughter is dying,' he said. 'Please come and lay Your hands on her; heal her so she can live.' Jesus went with him, and all the people followed, crowding around Him."*** But before Jesus could get to Jairus' house, a woman found Him because she was looking to God's Kingdom for help, she was looking to Jesus as God's Kingdom representative, she was looking to receive healing. Mark 5:25-29 NLT tells us: ***"A woman in the crowd had suffered for twelve years with constant bleeding. She had suffered a great deal from many doctors, and over the years she had spent everything she had to pay them, but she had gotten no better. In fact, she had gotten worse. She had heard about Jesus, so she came up behind Him through the crowd and touched His robe. For she thought to herself, 'If I can just touch His robe, I will be healed.' Immediately the bleeding stopped, and she could feel in her body that she had been healed of her terrible condition."*** The NKJV says: ***"For she said, 'If only I may touch His clothes, I shall be made well.'"*** She lined up her thoughts and words to match God's Kingdom and His ways. She lined up her words and thoughts with faith. She knew there was nothing the world's system through man could do for her. She had tried and only grew worse. However, God knew what she needed and God knew He could provide her healing and complete restoration. God knew and He sent Jesus, walking down the road where she could touch Him and receive from God's Kingdom. She had heard God's Kingdom had come to earth and was being demonstrated through Jesus. Now that she had touched God's Kingdom because she had touched Jesus, she received her healing. Because Jesus remained focused on God's Kingdom, He knew someone had touched Him by faith and had made a withdrawal of God's Kingdom healing power. However,

God had not revealed who. So, He stopped as we see in Mark 5:30 NLT: ***"Jesus realized at once that healing power had gone out from Him, so He turned around in the crowd and asked, 'Who touched My robe?'"*** I believe Jesus stopped because He had reverence and honor for God's Kingdom and what His Kingdom could do for people. I believe He stopped because He was moved with compassion to want to know who needed such a touch and He wanted to give God honor by acknowledging someone had just touched God's Kingdom and the need had been met. The woman had gone out to touch God's Kingdom and in doing so broke the law held by the religious system. She knew she could have been stoned because she was not supposed to go out in public based on her unhealthy condition. She was considered unclean, unsanitary. But she went anyway and received what no other system could or would be able to give her. When no one responded, Jesus remained persistent as we see in Mark 5:32-34 NLT: ***"But He kept on looking around to see who had done it. Then the frightened woman, trembling at the realization of what had happened to her, came and fell to her knees in front of Him and told Him what she had done. And He said to her, 'Daughter, your faith has made you well. Go in peace. Your suffering is over.'"*** When God's Kingdom touches people's lives, their suffering is over. God wants His children to use their faith to touch His Kingdom for themselves as well as others. In God's Kingdom, there is health and wholeness, there is complete restoration. His Kingdom is a fear free zone where His love and His peace reign. Jesus stopped even though He was headed to help someone else and the matter was time sensitive. God still had Him stop because God does not operate according to the world's time-frame. Jesus was operating according to God's time-frame and according to how God was leading Him. We see how this unfolds more in Mark 5:35-36 NLT: ***"While He was till speaking to her, messengers arrived***

from the home of Jairus, the leader of the synagogue. They told Him, 'Your daughter is dead. There is no use troubling the Teacher now.' But Jesus overheard them and said to Jairus, 'Do not be afraid, Just have faith.'" Jesus knew the power of God's Kingdom and He knew faith would draw from God's Kingdom. Jarius had just witnessed firsthand the woman use her faith and receive her healing. Jesus was letting Jarius know how he needed to respond according to God's ways and God's Kingdom. And Jarius chose to walk by faith and did not get into fear. Jesus knowing the power of faith and the importance of not responding in fear, left the crowd and only took three of His disciples to Jairus' house. Once He got to his house, He sent everyone who was there away, except the child's mother. They were all seeing the situation through the eyes of the world and had already began mourning the girl's death. Jesus was seeing the situation through God's eyes. Before He sent all of the people away, He spoke to them from God's Kingdom perspective in Mark 5:39 NLT says: ***"He went inside and asked, 'Why all this commotion and weeping? The child is not dead, she is only asleep.'"*** Jesus was letting everyone know that He was walking by faith and not by sight, He was walking by God's Kingdom and not the worlds and that He was sent to demonstrate God's Kingdom. Mark 5:41-42 NLT: ***"Holding her hand, He said to her, 'Talitha koum,' which means 'Little girl, get up!' And the girl, who was twelve years old, immediately stood up and walked around! They were overwhelmed and totally amazed."*** Jesus Who was full of Holy Spirit (Who was full of God's Kingdom) was fulfilling God's plan by demonstrating God's Kingdom on earth.

When God does something, He has a purpose and reason. He wants us to seek Him, to ask of Him, to want to know what He knows because He is giving by nature. The girl who Jesus raised from the dead was twelve, and the woman, who touched

Jesus and was healed, had suffered and been ill for twelve years. Numbers have significance with God and the number twelve in Hebrew means perfect government – God's government, divine order. God sent Jesus to bring His Kingdom so His government and divine order could be established on earth. He sent Jesus to demonstrate His divine authority and for Jesus to become the very foundation for our spiritual completeness. Jesus paved the way for us to become God's children and for us to continue on establishing God's Kingdom, for us to continue on establishing God's government and divine order in the world. Jesus was making a way for our new identity to be fully established in Him where our spirits would be made complete. Jesus was providing us with complete restoration. Jesus was showing us how to be God's children on earth. 2 Corinthians 5:17-20 ESV tells us: ***"Therefore, if anyone is in Christ, he is a new creation. The old has passed away; behold, the new has come. All this from God, Who, through Christ reconciled us to Himself and gave us the ministry of reconciliation; that is, in Christ God was reconciling the world to Himself, not counting their trespasses against them, and entrusting to us the message of reconciliation. Therefore, we are ambassadors for Christ, God making His appeal through us."*** These are not just stories about Jesus, these are our stories too. God made His appeal through Jesus so He could then make His appeal through us for His Kingdom to come on earth. We are to be God's ambassadors on earth just as Jesus was. Being an ambassador for God is a part of our identity where we establish God's Kingdom wherever we go. Philippians 3:20 NLT tells us: ***"But we are citizens of heaven, where the Lord Jesus Christ lives. And we are eagerly waiting for Him to return as our Savior."*** As a citizen of heaven, we have the same rights and privileges of heaven right here on earth. We are to obey God's laws, the laws of heaven by living the life Jesus provided for us. Because of Jesus, He made a way for us to be citizens of heaven right now. Even though He will one day return, we are to be actively awaiting His return by serving as ambassadors for God's Kingdom. If I were an ambassador for the United States and was sent to another country, I would not forget that I am a citizen of the United States. I know one day my assignment as ambassador will come to an end and I will return back to the place of my citizenship, the United States. However, while I am in the other country, I will fully engage myself as being an ambassador. I will not just sit back awaiting the day I finally get to go back because that would defeat the purpose of my being an ambassador. Instead, I would live and operate in the country where I was an ambassador, the same as I would live and operate if I were still living in the United States. We are to live and operate here on earth as if we were living in heaven. Jesus told us in John 17:16-18 NLT: ***"They do not belong to this world any more than I do. Make them holy by Your Truth; teach them Your Word, which is Truth. Just as You sent Me into the world, I am sending them into the world."*** Jesus was sent to the world to bring God's Kingdom, to bring God's Word in life form to earth. Jesus functioned as a citizen of heaven while He lived on earth. Now, He is sending us to function the same. We are to think and act like ambassadors and fulfill the duties of an ambassador on God's behalf and for His Kingdom, which is in heaven. As God's ambassadors: we are to be God's point of contact here on earth representing His Kingdom government and His interests; we are to act as His highest-ranking official presenting His Kingdom ways to others and gaining recognition for Jesus; we are to advance His Kingdom on the earth; we are to build relationships for God and His Kingdom; we are to coordinate our efforts to ensure the safety and well-being of God's children; we are to provide valuable insight and negotiations on behalf of God and His Kingdom in all arenas of life including social, political, and economic; we are to promote God's image and His Kingdom's image; we are to coordinate efforts and activities among other sons and daughters to ensure they remain aligned with God and His Kingdom. We are to bring God's Kingdom life to this earth and to those He sends us to or to those He sends to us. Proverbs 13:17 NKJV tells us: "***A wicked messenger falls into trouble, but a faithful ambassador brings health.***" And TPT says: "***An undependable messenger causes a lot of trouble, but the trustworthy and wise messengers release healing wherever they go.***" As God's ambassadors, we are to bring health, wholeness, and restoration wherever we go just as Jesus did. We are to let people know Jesus provided a life and a life more abundant and then demonstrate what that is to them. We are to be the ones people can come to when they need to touch God's Kingdom and receive their healing. We are the ones people can come to when they are being tormented by demons and need to be set free. We are the ones people can come to when someone has died and need to be brought back to life. We are the ones people can come to when the world has no answers and is unable to help them. We, as God's children, have His Kingdom in us and are to be operating in His Kingdom to a world in great need of His Kingdom. We have the answer to how people can live in a state of complete physical, mental, and social well-being. In bringing the health of God's Kingdom, we are providing people with the ability to function effectively in every area of their daily life. People can then fully experience the *sozo* life that was purchased by Jesus and they can believe in and follow Him themselves. They can become God's ambassadors because they have become His children.

God provided us with His own Ambassador, Holy Spirit Who is within us to help us be God's ambassadors on earth. Holy Spirit is the ultimate representative of heaven for us because He originated in heaven and is from God Himself. He knows God and Jesus personally, He knows how They think and act and He knows how we need to think and act like Them. Holy Spirit listens to God with pristine focus and attention and is able to deliver God's messages in the same manner. He can help teach us what it means to be God's ambassador and how to put into action what we learn. Our faith provides us with the means to access what is in heaven and bring it to earth. It allows us to travel between the seen and unseen realms just as Jesus did. Matthew 6:10 TPT tells us: ***"Manifest Your Kingdom realm, and cause Your every purpose to be fulfilled on earth, just as it is in Heaven."*** For something to manifest, it has to be made known, made evident by show or display. Jesus made known, made evident God's Kingdom by showing and displaying God's Kingdom here on earth. In 1 Corinthians 2:4 NLT, Jesus lets us know: ***"And My message and My preaching were very plain. Rather than using clever and persuasive speeches, I relied only on the power of the Holy Spirit. I did this so you would trust not in human wisdom but in the power of God."*** And 1 Corinthians 2:5 GNT tells us: ***"Your faith, then does not rest on human wisdom but on the power of God."*** As God's children, we are to trust in God's power and the teachings of Jesus by relying on the help and power of Holy Spirit. We are to trust in who we are in Him and that we have His faith to carry out His assignments, to see His Kingdom come into operation on the earth through us, His ambassadors. Philippians 4:13 NLT tells us: ***"I can do everything through Christ, Who, gives me strength."*** The GNT says: ***"I have the strength to face all conditions by the power that Christ gives me."*** And TPT says: ***"And I find that the strength of Christ's explosive power infuses me to conquer every difficulty."*** While the AMPC lets us know: ***"I have strength for all things in Christ Who empowers me [I am ready for anything and equal to anything through Him Who infuses inner strength***

into me; I am self-sufficient in Christ's sufficiency]. We have the strength and are empowered by Christ to do the same works on earth as Jesus did. We have all the sufficiency in Him we need to live in God's Kingdom and to demonstrate God's Kingdom on earth. We have the ability in Christ to see ourselves as God sees us and to see the world as God sees. We have the same anointing as Jesus, we have the same Holy Spirit to go forth as God leads us for His glory and the expansion of His Kingdom. Jesus told us in Acts 1:8 NLT: ***"But you will receive power when the Holy Spirit comes upon you. And you will be My witnesses, telling people about Me everywhere – in Jerusalem, throughout Judea, in Samaria, and to the ends of the earth."*** Once we get born again and have God's Spirit within us, Jesus was letting us know there was even more of God's Spirit we could get so He could empower us to do God's work on earth just like He empowered Jesus. Before Jesus went back to heaven, He instructed His disciples to wait, before they went to do anything else for Him, for Holy Spirit. He had already informed them He had to go so Holy Spirit could come to help them and now He was telling them He was sending Him and for them to wait until they received Him. Jesus tells them in Luke 24:49 NLT: "***And now I will send the Holy Spirit, just as My Father promised. But stay here in the city until the Holy Spirit comes and fills you with power from heaven.***" Jesus was letting them know Holy Spirit was a promise from God to them and now the promise was going to be fulfilled. All they had to do was stay where Jesus told them and receive God's promise, receive Holy Spirit. He was letting them know in receiving Holy Spirit they would be receiving God's power from heaven. It was a package deal because God's power from heaven comes with Holy Spirit. He was letting them know how they were to go about doing their Father's business just as Jesus did. Jesus disciples had listened to His instructions and were obedient. And as they waited, per His instructions, we see the outcome in Acts 2:1-4 NKJV: ***"When the day of Pentecost had fully come, they were all with one accord in one place. And suddenly there came from heaven, as of a mighty wind, and it filled the whole house where they were sitting. Then there appeared to them divided tongues, as of fire, and one sat upon each of them. And they were all filled with the Holy Spirit and began to speak in other tongues as the Spirit gave them utterance."*** They received power from heaven because they received Holy Spirit and God is still providing His power from heaven to all who receive His Holy Spirit. Holy Spirit is our power Source just as He was for Jesus. God wants us to have His Spirit to the fullest measure, which includes being able to speak in Holy Spirit, being able to speak in tongues.

Holy Spirit came to help us firmly establish our identity as God's children so we could live by His Kingdom and not the world's. Holy Spirit came to help us live as God's children reflecting our big Brother, Jesus' image everywhere we go. 1 Corinthians 2:12 NLT lets us know: ***"And we have received God's Spirit (not the world's spirit), so we can know the wonderful things God has freely given us."*** Holy Spirit reveals all the wonderful things God has given us and He is One of the wonderful gifts God has given us. He can let us know the enemy's plans while providing us with the strategy to advance God's Kingdom. John 16:13-15 NLT says: ***"When the Spirit of Truth comes, He will guide you into all truth. He will not speak on His own but will tell you what He has heard. He will tell you about the future. He will bring Me glory by telling you whatever He receives from Me. All that belongs to the Father is mine; that is why I said, 'The Spirit will tell you whatever He receives from Me.'"*** Jesus was here on the earth, working One on One with Holy Spirit to bring God's Kingdom on earth and now Holy Spirit is here to work One on one with us to bring God's

Kingdom on earth.

Jesus tells us in Matthew 18:18-20 NLT: ***"I tell you the truth, whatever you forbid on earth will be forbidden in heaven, and whatever you permit on earth will be permitted in heaven. I also tell you this: If two of you agree here on earth concerning anything you ask, My Father in heaven will do it for you. For where two or three gather together as My followers, I am there among them."*** God is giving us instructions on how to pray and letting us know the authority we have through our prayers. He is letting us know, as we understand who we are as His children and begin to operate in the same authority given to us as Jesus, our prayers can bring what is in heaven to earth and prevent what is on earth that is not in heaven. Our prayers are a way for God's Kingdom to spread across the earth. When we and our brothers and sisters come together, there is power in unifying our authority, which can cause a mighty power surge coming from heaven to earth. When all of God's children understand who they are in Him, collectively we are more powerful for making an impact for His Kingdom. God answers our prayers just as He did with Jesus. Jesus knew Who He was and He knew how to ask the Father for what He wanted and needed on earth. He walked in the ultimate understanding of His authority and the power of His words when He spoke. And we can do the same. God is wanting us to know there is power in agreement but there is power when we pray ourselves just as there was power when Jesus prayed. Jesus not only died for us but He went to hell for us and He took back all authority that Adam and Eve had given to satan. Jesus made a way for us to gain access and it is up to us to do our part and access what is in heaven so God's Kingdom can be on the earth. Jesus told us He did this in Matthew 16:19 NLT: ***"And I will give you the keys of the Kingdom of Heaven. Whatever you forbid on earth will be***

forbidden in heaven, and whatever you permit on earth will be permitted in heaven." Keys have the power of access to lock and unlock, to let in or not let in. In a company, those who need access to the building are given keys. And even within a particular building you may have a master key where you have full access to the building and others may have keys that limit their access. Jesus gave us the master key to heaven where we have full access to everything that is in heaven so we can allow what is in heaven to come here on earth. Jesus tells us in Matthew 6:10 NKJV to pray: ***"Your Kingdom come. Your will be done on earth as it is in heaven."*** We should always be praying and expecting our prayers to come to pass. Our prayers should match God's will that His Kingdom will come to earth because that is His will. We should know Him through our fellowship and time in His Word to know His will so His will comes to pass on earth. We should know His Spirit within us and be listening for His instructions and leading because He knows God's will for heaven to come to earth. We can have God's thoughts regarding prayer. We can realize how powerful are our prayers and pray reaching heaven and bringing heaven to earth. I remember going to a church when I was still in high school. We would stand up and recite Matthew 6:9-13 as a congregation. I had it memorized much like anything else I had to memorize when in school. Though I could recite it by memory, I did not have the revelation of this Scripture, especially verse 10. I do not ever recall anyone explaining it, teaching on it, nor preaching about it. I just knew it was a part of what we did each Sunday at this particular church. I did not even fully understand this was an actual passage of Scripture in God's Word. It had just become a tradition that you recite as part of the Sunday ritual during service. We would stand, say it together, and then sit back down. It seemed so remote it was like checking a check in a box or putting a mark on a list after you had completed something before going to the next thing on the list. I have no idea what impact this may or may have had on anyone else nor do I know where this ritual first started. I just know it did not make an impact on me that it was God's will for His Kingdom to come on earth and I had a role to play. Nor did I understand this was one of Jesus' primary purposes when He was on earth; however, Jesus fully understood. I also did not understand God had given me His Spirit to help me in carrying this out. I failed to realize I had been given the same authority as Jesus and I could come to God with my prayers, as His child, rather than some beggar. I was just following a ritual of man. Even though it was God's Word, I had no revelation of how this was to apply to me nor how I was supposed to be impacting this world for God's Kingdom. I had it memorized but that is all I had. Thanks to Holy Spirit, I now have the revelation.

Holy Spirit is our Helper to help us know how to pray (even how to pray using God's Word), what to pray, and when to pray. He is God's anointing and power within us and He will even give us His language to pray in when needed. He is within us to help us and not to control us. He is here to reveal God's will but just like Jesus, we have to submit our will to God's and submit to following Holy Spirit, including when we pray. We remain in the driver's seat, fully in control of how we drive and where. Holy Spirit is in us helping show us how to drive and where to go as we are driving. He helps us know when to drive but we still have to be willing to get in our vehicle and drive and do so with Him leading us. I had no concept, no understanding, nor any teaching regarding praying in tongues, praying in Holy Spirit. I had never even heard anyone praying in Holy Spirit and had no exposure growing up. If someone did, it was never where I could hear. Jude 1:20 NKJV tells us: ***"But you, beloved, building yourselves up on your most holy faith, praying in the Holy Spirit."*** One of the benefits of praying in Holy Spirit, is our faith is built up. It is like exercising with weights and the more you do, the stronger you get. The more we pray in the Spirit, the stronger our faith gets. The more we pray in the Spirit, the more we will be able to reach into the spiritual realm to bring what is needed to the natural realm, the more we will bring heaven to earth. Romans 8:26 NKJV tells us: ***"Likewise the Spirit also helps in our weakness. For we do not know what we should pray for as we ought, but the Spirit Himself makes intercession for us with groanings which cannot be uttered."*** I have learned the value of praying in Holy Spirit, praying in tongues. There have been times I knew I was to pray but did not know how to pray, so I was able to pray in Holy Spirit. As I did, He let me know when I was released from praying. Other times, while praying in Holy Spirit, my spirit will pick up what to pray for so I begin praying in my own language. And there are times when Holy Spirit will let me know in my own language what I had been praying when praying in tongues. When we pray in Holy Spirit, it is like our spirit reaches up and directly touches God's Spirit. Paul tells us in 1 Corinthians 14:18 NLT: ***"I thank God that I speak in tongues more than any of you."*** Holy Spirit is God's Spirit in us and He knows how to honor and follow God, even in prayer.

Not only has God equipped us by His Spirit being within us, but He has given us His armor and provided us with His fighting strategy. Ephesians 6:11-18 NLT tells us to: ***"Put on all of God's armor so that you will be able to stand firm against all strategies of the devil. For we are not fighting against flesh-and-blood enemies, but against evil rulers and authorities of the unseen world, against mighty powers in this dark world, and against evil spirits in the heavenly places. Therefore, put on every piece of God's armor so you will be able to resist the enemy in the time of evil. Then after the battle you will still be standing firm. Stand your ground,***

putting on the belt of truth and the body armor of God's righteousness. For shoes, put on the peace that comes from the Good News so that you will be fully prepared. In addition to all of these, hold up the shield of faith to stop the fiery arrows of the devil. Put on salvation as your helmet, and take the sword of the Spirit, which is the Word of God. Pray in the Spirit at all times and on every occasion. Stay alert and be persistent in your prayers for all believers everywhere." We have God's armor He wants us to put on and He wants us to fight according to His way of fighting. Before David defeated Goliath, Saul wanted him to use his armor. David put it on and it did not fit. He was able to defeat Goliath after he took off Saul's armor and went into battle with the armor God had provided for him. We must not try and fit into the armor the world may try and get us to wear nor must we fight like the world will want us to fight. We must fight as God tells us. We must show His Kingdom on earth so His Kingdom can spread to all the earth. We must see our enemy as satan. We must understand the influence he has over this world and the people who choose to follow in the ways of the world. We must understand he is our enemy and not the people. Operating in God's Kingdom, demonstrates how far superior and better for us are God's ways. Utilizing His armor helps us accomplish this. The more we put on His armor, the easier and more natural it becomes. We will learn how to become proficient in using His armor as our own. Praying is a part of our armor and how we wage war for God. And how God tells us to pray is to pray in Holy Spirit and also to pray for our brothers and sisters. Our big Brother, Jesus, is even praying for us. Romans 8:34 ESV tells us: ***"Who is to condemn? Christ Jesus is the One Who died – more than that, Who was raised – Who is at the right hand of God, Who indeed is interceding for us."*** Jesus came to save us and gives us a life more abundant rather than condemn us. Now, He sits by our Father in heaven praying for us. He wants us to succeed and we should want our brothers and sisters to succeed. He wants us to fully live here on earth as God's children and we should want this for our brothers and sisters. It is a part of God's Kingdom coming to earth, which can, because we have a part of His Kingdom in us, we have Holy Spirit.

Understanding how we are to fight God's way, as His children, helps us in advancing His Kingdom. Whenever people go into war in the natural world, they prepare and train so they are battle fit. God has His own way for us to be battle fit and ensure our body, our flesh, is ready to fight for Him and how He wants us to fight. God wants us to follow His orders and represent His Kingdom. We carry His flag and are a part of His bigger army. However, we are responsible for ensuring we remain battle ready and meet the standards for His army as He sets them. We can only do our part as any solider but we must be willing to do our part. God lets us know how to make our bodies battle fit for His army in Romans 12:1 NLT: ***"And so, dear brothers and sisters, I plead with you to give your bodies to God because of all He has done for you. Let them be a living and holy sacrifice – the kind He will find acceptable. This is truly the way to worship."*** We are to give God our bodies as a form of worship to Him and allow Him to set the standards on what we do and what we do not do with our body. We are enlisted in His army and we are to follow His commands on what is pleasing and not pleasing to Him. We are not to follow the world's standards. People should see God's children as being set apart and battle fit for His Kingdom. When we do this, it is seen as an act of worship by God. We are to see our bodies through His eyes and how our bodies are to honor Him. 1 Corinthians 6:19-20 NLT says: ***"Do you not realize that your body is the temple of the Holy Spirit, Who, lives in you and was given to you by God? You do not belong to yourself, for God bought***

you with a high price. So, you must honor God with your body." God thought of and valued us so much that He gave us His Spirit to live in us. He wanted us to be empowered to be able to be in His army and do what Jesus did. Galatians 5:16 TPT tells us: ***"Let me emphasize this: As you yield to the dynamic life and power of the Holy Spirit, you will abandon the cravings of your self-life."*** And the NLT says: ***"So I say, let the Holy Spirit guide your lives. Then you will not be doing what your sinful nature craves."*** Holy Spirit will help us in knowing what to do and not to do with our bodies. The more of ourselves we yield to Him the more of His power we have access to.

Holy Spirit is in us helping us see as God sees. He helps us remain firm in living from our spirit rather than living from our soul and flesh so we can fully represent God's Kingdom on earth. 2 Corinthians 3:16-18 NLT tells us: ***"But whenever someone turns to the Lord, the veil is taken away. For the Lord is the Spirit, and wherever the Spirit of the Lord is, there is freedom. So, all of us who have had that veil removed can see and reflect the glory of the Lord. And the Lord – Who is the Spirit – makes us more like Him as we are changed into His glorious image."*** Holy Spirit helps us see Lordship as God sees Lordship so we can function properly in spreading God's Kingdom. He helps us to make the distinction between Lordship, according to God and lordship, according to man. He reveals to us the freedom we have when we are under God's Lordship, just like Jesus, when He was on earth. He helps us know being under God's Lordship is a part of our identity as God's children. And Holy Spirit helps us realize this is how we are transformed more and more into God's image so we can portray His image to the world, so we can portray His Kingdom to the world.

One of our roles as God's children and as Jesus' siblings, is to be Jesus' disciples. We are to follow His teachings by following His example as His brothers and sisters. We are to live like Him in every way showing others Who He is and how they can know Him and begin following Him. He tells us in John 8:31-32 NLT: ***"Jesus said to the people who believed in Him, 'You are truly My disciples if you remain faithful to My teachings. And you will know the truth, and the truth will set you free.'"*** We hold steadfast to Jesus' teachings by not believing any other teaching over His. When we do, we live in the freedom His teachings provide for us and we can then teach and show others how to do the same. Any time we hear or see something different from what Jesus teaches, we believe Jesus and follow Him regardless of the topic. We never waiver nor consider any other teachings except Jesus'. One of God's ways of showing us His ways and thoughts are higher is through Jesus because Jesus' ways and thoughts are the same as God's. Jesus presented to us, a living example, in the flesh on earth, God's ways and thoughts. Holy Spirit helps us to believe and hold steadfast to Jesus' teachings. God's Kingdom is like taking a lab class along with a regular class. You talk about it in class and then you go to the lab to demonstrate what was just talked about. You hear and then you demonstrate what you were taught. Jesus tells us in Luke 4:43 NLT: ***"But He replied, 'I must preach the Good News of the Kingdom of God in other towns, too, because that is why I was sent.'"*** And then He tells us in Luke 11:20 TPT Jesus said: ***"But if I am casting out demons by God's mighty power, God's Kingdom is now released upon you."*** And the NLT says: ***"But if I am casting out demons by the power of God, then the Kingdom of God has arrived among you."*** Right after Jesus said this, a woman in the crowd was listening to Him and said "God bless Jesus' mother, Mary." Though Mary was highly favored of God and chosen to have a supernatural conception giving birth to Jesus, Jesus responded to the woman in Luke 11:28 NLT: ***"But***

even more blessed are all who hear the Word of God and put it into practice." The GW says: ***"Rather, how blessed are those who hear and obey God's Word."*** We are blessed, and more so, by hearing, obeying, and demonstrating God's Word. Our lab is our lives and the world. We hear God's Word and then we demonstrate His Word in our own lives and then demonstrate His Word to the world. We hear God's Word and receive His blessings as we walk according to His Word and then we have His blessings to show the world the outcome of hearing and walking in God's Word. While on earth, Jesus was talking about God's Kingdom and then He was showing people God's Kingdom through demonstrating heaven's power with Holy Spirit as His Helper. Jesus is now wanting us to do the same but even greater than He did. He ran His race and now is telling us to run ours even better, even greater than He did. Jesus has provided us with the training on how we are to run like Him but even greater. And He has provided us with the One Who helped Him run, He has provided us with Holy Spirit. Because Jesus tells us in John 14:12-14 NLT: ***"I tell you the truth, anyone who believes in Me will do the same works I have done, and even greater works, because I am going to be with the Father. You can ask for anything in My name, and I will do it, so that the Son can bring glory to the Father. Yes, ask Me for anything in My name, and I will do it."*** This is Jesus Himself speaking to anyone who follows Him, to anyone who is His disciple. Jesus wants us to carry on in His footsteps, He wants us to pick up where He left off and go on and do even greater than He did. And He wants this all for the glory of His Father, our Father, and all for our Father's Kingdom.

CHAPTER 10

Established in God's Love

LOVE HAS BEEN in existence for as long as God has been in existence. To attempt to separate God from love, would be an attempt to separate God from Himself. In knowing God, we know love. The more of God we know, the more of love we know. For love does not lie, love does not sin, and love does not change because God does not. God's love is not like the world's, so we are not to love like the world. 1 John 4:8 TPT tells us: ***"The one who does not love has yet to know God, for God is love."*** God knows love better than anyone because God knows Himself better than anyone. We were created by love because we were created by God. Therefore, we were created to love. God knew we needed help so He sent us Jesus to save us by His love and then to establish His love in us through Jesus. All who receive Jesus receive God's love. No matter what anyone may have done previously, God's love is still extended to them. We can see God extending His love to Saul, who was a Jewish Pharisee and a Roman citizen. He had been thoroughly trained in Jewish law by the top Rabbi and Pharisee during that time. Saul had already watched a follower of Jesus be killed. This marked the first time someone was killed because he followed Jesus. Now, Saul had a zeal to persecute all who followed Jesus, including killing them. And he was given the authority to do so without measure. Yet, God had another plan. God had His love that He wanted to show and establish in Saul, which is the same love He wants to show and establish in us. We see in Acts 9:1-6 NLT: ***"Meanwhile, Saul was uttering threats with every breath and was eager to kill the Lord's followers. So, he went to the high priest. He requested letters addressed to the synagogues in Damascus, asking for their cooperation in the arrest of any followers of the Way he found there. He wanted to bring them – both men and women – back to Jerusalem in chains. As he was approaching Damascus on this mission, a light from heaven suddenly shone down around him. He fell to the ground and heard a voice saying to him, 'Saul! Saul! Why are you persecuting Me?' 'Who are You, Lord?' Saul asked. And the voice replied, 'I Am Jesus, the One You are persecuting! Now get up and go into the city, and you will be told what you must do.'"*** Jesus is asking Saul why is he opposing, mistreating, bringing hardship, and suffering to Him (Jesus). Saul is going after anyone who is following Jesus and Jesus' teachings but Jesus sees this as an attack on Himself. When Jesus spoke to Saul, He was letting him know that whatever he was doing to His brothers and sisters, He was doing to Him. Jesus was establishing a precedent that if you go after God's children, you are going after Jesus. In John 17:18 TPT, He tells us: ***"I have commissioned them to represent Me just as You commissioned Me to represent You [God the Father]."*** Jesus was telling Saul that the people he was going after were doing the same work that He had done. He was telling Saul that just as God had sent Him to do God's work, to do God's Kingdom work, Jesus had now sent these people (His brothers and sisters) to do His work, to do His Kingdom work. Jesus was letting Saul know what John 17:21 TPT says: ***"I pray for them all to be joined together as One even as You and I, Father, are joined together as One. I pray for them to become One with Us so that the world will recognize that You sent Me."*** All of God's children are One with Jesus. Jesus was letting us know whenever we go against our brothers and sisters (God's children), we are going against Him. He is wanting us to operate in God's love, which is His love, just as He did when He was on earth, and this includes how we are to love our brothers and sisters.

To do God's commands is to do what God asks. To do God's commands is love. Saul would be going on to do God's commands, he would be going on to do God's love. But before he could, God was going to use someone named Ananias to help him. Ananias would first follow God's command and he would first demonstrate God's love. Saul was on his way to Damascus to bring followers of Jesus back to Jerusalem in chains. He was going to persecute them and his plans for them were far from pleasant. And Ananias was one of Jesus' followers in Damascus where Saul was headed to possibly arrest. But God had other plans for both of these men. Acts 9:10-18 NLT tells us: ***"Now there was a believer in Damascus named Ananias. The Lord spoke to him in a vision, calling 'Ananias!' 'Yes, Lord!' he replied. The Lord said, 'Go over to Straight Street, to the house of Juda. When you get there, ask for a man from Tarsus named Saul. He is praying to Me right now. I have shown him a vision of a man named Ananias coming in and laying hands on him so he can see again.' 'But Lord,' exclaimed Ananias, 'I have heard many people talk about the terrible things this man has done to the believers in Jerusalem! And he is authorized by the leading priests to arrest every-***

one who calls upon your name.' But the Lord said, 'Go, for Saul is my chosen instrument to take My message to the Gentiles and to kings, as well as to the people of Israel. And I will show him how much he must suffer for my name's sake.' So, Ananias went and found Saul. He laid his hands on him and said, 'Brother Saul, the Lord Jesus, Who, appeared to you on the road, has sent me so that you might regain your sight and be filled with the Holy Spirit.' Instantly something like scales fell from Saul's eyes, and he regained his sight. Then he got up and was baptized." God provided both men with a vision letting them know His plan for Saul. God was letting them know His thoughts for Saul were good and He had a hope filled future for Saul. Saul had to be willing to receive from Ananias and Ananias had to be willing to go to Saul. Before Saul's ministry could start, Ananias had to first be obedient in following God. He had to first know God's love and understand God was wanting to put His love into action for Saul. And he had to be willing to be God's chosen vessel so God could put His love into action for Saul. Whenever God speaks to us, we must be obedient in doing what He tells us. For when He speaks and tells us something, He is giving us a commandment. He is Lord, He is King, and when He speaks, He commands. The choice to follow His command is ours. The choice to do so with a good attitude, with a good heart, is ours. And it was the same choice for Ananias, who chose to listen and follow God over listening to himself or man. He had heard the stories of what Saul was doing but He followed what God was saying. Ananias was demonstrating God's love and Saul was receiving God's love. Saul, who had done some bad things to God's children, was now receiving through one of God's children, God's love, His healing, His Son, and His Spirit. And Ananias, was God's child, Who God had chosen, to accomplish this. God and Jesus saw Saul as being worthy to receive God's love, to be healed, be born again, and to be filled with God's

Spirit. They saw Saul through Their eyes and responded in kind by implementing Their plan for him. Even though Saul's plan for God's children involved bringing them harm and even death to some, God's plan for Saul was for him to become God's child and go on to preach, teach, and demonstrate God's Kingdom to others. More importantly, God saw Saul worthy of being His son and Jesus saw Saul as worthy of being His brother.

1 John 5:2-3 ESV tells us: ***"By this we know that we love the children of God, when we love God and obey His commandments. For this is the love of God, that we keep His commandments. And His commandments are not burdensome."*** Ananias did not find it burdensome to go do what Jesus wanted Him to do. He showed His love through following God's commandment. And Saul would go on to do the same. Then in Acts 8:19-20 NLT we see: "***Afterward he [Saul] ate some food and regained his strength. Saul stayed with the believers in Damascus for a few days. And immediately he began preaching about Jesus in the synagogues, saying, 'He is indeed the Son of God!'"*** Saul was now changed forever and was one of God's children and rather than persecute God's children, he was going around preaching about Jesus and that Jesus was God's Son. Saul was telling others about Jesus and was now a follower of Jesus himself. Saul began demonstrating God's love as seen in Romans 1:14-15 TPT when he tells us: ***"Love obligates me to preach to everyone, to those who are among the elite and those who are among the outcasts, to those who are wise and educated as well as to those who are foolish and unlearned. This is why I am so excited about coming to preach the wonderful message of Jesus to you in Rome!"*** Saul, now known as Paul, was showing love by preaching Jesus' message, preaching God's Kingdom and he saw that everyone was worthy of hearing and receiving the message of Jesus. He saw God's love as being

worthy to be given for anyone who would hear and receive His love, who would hear and receive His Son, Jesus, who would receive His message and become His follower. He saw God's love as needing to be shared because he had learned to love like God. He had learned to love others and understood the importance of others needing to know Jesus and His message. Saul understood that operating in God's love means walking in God's love, which includes following God's commands. 2 John 1:6 NLT tells us: ***"Love means doing what God has commanded us, and He has commanded us to love one another, just as you heard from the beginning."*** The AMPC says: ***"And what this love consists in is this: that we live and walk in accordance with and guided by His commandments (His orders, His ordinances, percepts, teaching). This is the commandment, as you have heard from the beginning, that you continue to walk in love [guided by it and following it]."*** God has given us His commands by giving us His Word and by speaking directly to us, just like He did with Ananias. This has always been His plan, even when the Israelites rejected His plan, because they did not want to listen to God speak directly to them. Ananias did not reject God's plan because He listened to God and then did as God told him. In doing so, he walked in God's love. Loving others and doing God's commands are the same. Loving others is a command from God but also following all of God's commands is following God Who is love. God understood how destructive people are without Him and how they distort what love is because they do not know His love. God wants us to listen to Him and follow what He tells us, including in His Word. How good of a listener are you? Are you aware of how God wants to speak to us? Is God telling you something? If He is, are you doing it? Did you know this includes doing what He says in His Word? Whenever someone is talking, we are either listening to what is being said or we are not. This holds true for when God is speaking. We have His Spirit to help us recognize and listen to God. We should be listening to God every day and wanting to hear what He is saying because He is wanting to express His love to us by communicating and conversing with us which is a part of fellowship. We should hear every Word He says, both spoken (Rhema) and written (His Word). Notice, Ananias actually conversed with God. God told him to do something but Ananias had questions and was able to speak to God. He honored God because he called Him Lord but he did not fear being able to converse with God, unlike the Israelites. And God did not mind Ananias speaking to Him in this manner because God answered Ananias and He will answer us; He wants to answer us. He welcomes our questions. We have to be willing to accept His answers but He will never turn us away for wanting to talk to Him, even when it is in the form of a question. God wants to be the One we can go to and talk things through, to have someone to listen to us. The best thing about talking to God is He will always provide the correct advice. When we want Godly advice, Who better to provide than God Himself. He remains willing and is accessible twenty fours hours a day, each and every day. He wants to share His love with us by listening and conversing with us. He wants to provide us with the advice, the answers we need. God wants to share His plans with us and what He knows is His best for us. He wants us to know the good thoughts He is thinking about us and the good, hope filled plans He has for our future. John 14:21 NKJV Jesus tell us: ***"He who has My commandments and keeps them, it is He who loves Me. And he who loves Me will be loved by My Father, and I will love him and manifest Myself to him."*** Jesus is telling us that we love Him by having and keeping His commandments. In order to have and keep something, we first have to know it exists. Second, we have to realize it's value and worth. After which, we can obtain what we know exists because we find it worthy and valuable enough to obtain it. Not only do we show our love for Jesus by having and keeping His commandments but we receive God's love as well as Jesus' love. As we do, Jesus will make Himself real to us, He will make Himself known to us. Notice, it is Jesus Himself doing this. He is displaying His love to those who display their love for Him by having and keeping His commandments just as He displayed His love for God by keeping God's commandments. By keeping Jesus' commandments, we are keeping God's.

God sent Jesus to openly display His love for us so we could see His love, through His eyes. He sent Jesus so we could experience His love and become established in His love. He sent Jesus so we could love like Him and believe His love over any others. 1 John 4:10 TPT tells us: ***"This is love: He loved us long before we loved Him. It was His love, not ours. He proved it be sending His Son to be the pleasing sacrificial offering to take away our sins."*** And the NLT says: ***"This is real love – not that we loved God, but that He loved us and sent His Son as a sacrifice to take away our sins."*** Before God sent Jesus, He loved us. He loved all who were not lovable, all who rejected Him and His ways, all who did not think He existed, all who worshiped false gods, and all who did not think they needed Him or needed saving. However, God still loved them because He gave them Jesus. He sent Jesus as an act of love to the world. He wanted anyone and everyone to be able to fully receive His love because He knew their true value. He wanted them to be able to see and experience their true value by receiving His love and obtaining their freedom from sin. John 3:16 NLT tells us: ***"For this is how God loved the world: He gave His One and only Son, so that everyone who believes in Him will not perish but have eternal life."*** God loved us by giving. God loved us by giving His most priceless and precious of all possessions, His Son. God loved us so much that He gave us His Son so we would not have to die. God loved us so much He made a way for us to not die but be able to have an eternal life with Him. God loved us so much He choose to save us rather than judge us. John 3:17 NLT says: ***"God sent His Son into the world not to judge the world, but to save the world through Him."*** Jesus was not sent here to point out our sin but to make a way for us to be free from sin. You can point out a problem and talk about the problem discussing all the details involved or you can point out the solution and talk about the solution discussing all the details involved. God gave us His solution by giving us His love through giving us His Son. Through Jesus, God gave us our way to break free from sin and death, our way to secure an eternity with Him, our way to be able to fellowship with Him, and our way to operate in His Kingdom just like Jesus.

God was showing us a new way of doing things through Jesus. God was wanting to actively display His love for others and He did so by displaying Jesus Who was God's love in action. Jesus trusted God and His plan because Jesus knew God and His love and He wanted us to know God and His love. And Jesus knew He was God's way for this to happen. Jesus was willing to show His love by being obedient to God's command, to follow God's plan for Him. Jesus was giving Himself to us. And Jesus followed God's commands everywhere He went, in every situation, because He only did what He saw God doing and He only said what He heard God saying. Jesus was expressing His love for God through His obedience to God. He even did so when others tried to trick Him as we see in John 8:1-11 NLT: ***"Jesus returned to the Mount of Olives, but early the next morning He was back again at the Temple. A crowd soon gathered, and He sat down and taught them. As He was speaking, the teachers of religious law and the Pharisees brought a woman who had been caught in*** *adultery. They put her in front of the crowd. 'Teacher,' they said to Jesus, 'this woman was caught in the act of adultery. The law of Moses says to stone her. What do you say?' They were trying to trap Him into saying something they could use against Him, but Jesus stooped down and wrote in the dust with His finger. They kept demanding an answer, so He stood up again and said, 'All right, but let the one who has never sinned throw the first stone!' Then He stooped down again and wrote in the dust. When the accusers heard this, they slipped away one by one, beginning with the oldest, until only Jesus was left in the middle of the crowd with the woman. Then Jesus stood up again and said to the woman, 'Where are your accusers? Did not even one of them condemn you?' 'No, Lord,' she said. And Jesus said, 'Neither do I. Go and sin no more.'"* Here Jesus was showing that He did not come to judge but to save because God had sent Him not to judge but to save. And even though He had not gone to the cross, He was still showing those who were able to see that He was there to save, He was there to provide them with life and a more abundant life. Jesus knew through God's wisdom, God's help, that not one of those who were wanting to stone the woman for her sin, was without sin. He knew He was there to express God's love over judgment. And He knew that stoning her, bringing her to be judged for her sin was not the reason He was there. And just as He told her to go and sin no more Jesus wanted the woman and everyone else to know He was there to set people free from their sins. He wanted them and He wants us to focus on Him and His love for us. He wants us to focus on Him Who is our promise and freedom from sin, rather than focusing on the problem and sin. He wants us to focus on Him so we can receive all that comes with being God's children. Jesus wants us to focus on Him, our big Brother, so we can fully walk in our identity as God's children just like He did. Here was the woman caught in the sin of adultery, a sin that required two people to commit. Those who brought her before Jesus wanted judgment but only for her. The world's system will always be unjust and unfair when God's system is not in place. Those who brought her to Jesus had another motive and their motive was to trick Jesus. They were looking to find some fault with Him so they were using her in an attempt to prove their point. They were in the midst of love Himself and were unable to see Him as being God's love on earth because their focus was in the wrong place. Their focus was on their ways and how they were trying to justify their ways. All the time, God's ways was standing before them as a witness and living testimony of how God was trying to show them His ways, which were higher than theirs. When the trick did not work, the opportunity remained for them to shift their focus to Jesus, God's love in the flesh, and begin to learn of His ways, which would have been learning God's ways. Yet one by one, each person who was there wanting to have the woman killed because of her sin, left the presence of the One who came to free them from their sin. Their focus was now on how they were themselves sinners and they walked away from Jesus unchanged. The woman would be able to walk away from Jesus changed, changed for God's Kingdom and His ways. She would be able to receive God's love and His plan for her. Notice, there were two different ways Jesus was identified. First, Jesus was identified as Teacher by those who brought the woman to Him. They never changed how they addressed Him. Second, the woman called Him Lord. After everyone had left, she addressed Him as Lord when He spoke to her. She was verbally signifying her recognition of Jesus and His authority. She was honoring Him by how she was now identifying Him. She was recognizing His rulership on earth and in her life. And now she was the one who would be walking away free from sin, free from death. She had received Jesus' love which compelled her to move from where she was in sin to where Jesus was sin free. Because God's love, expressed through Jesus, transforms people from darkness to light, from sin to freedom, from death to life.

Right after Jesus finished speaking to the woman, He returned His attention to those He had previously been teaching. He shifted His focus back to teaching God's ways. And in John 8:12 NLT it tells us: ***"Jesus spoke to the people once more and said, 'I am the light of the world. If you follow Me, you will not have to walk in darkness, because you will have the light that leads to life.'"*** Jesus was letting them know He was the light sent to lead them out of darkness, to lead them out of sin, to lead them to life. And those who had brought the woman to Jesus could have stayed to hear what Jesus would say next. Jesus asked them if they had not sinned to be the first to throw a stone. He did not ask them to leave rather they left on their own. They could have stayed and listened to Jesus and learned about God's ways. They could have stayed in the presence of God's love and learned how to see themselves and others through God's eyes. They could have stayed to hear a way out of their sin, to hear how they could be free, to hear how they could be free from judging and being judged. They could have gained an understanding of what Jesus had already spoken in John 3:18-21 NLT: ***"There is no judgment against anyone who believes in Him. But anyone who does not believe in Him has already been judged for not believing in God's One and only Son. And the judgment is based on this fact: God's light came into the world, but people loved the darkness more than the light, for their actions were evil. All who do evil hate the light and refuse to go near it for fear their sins will be exposed. But those who do what is right come to the light so others can see that they are doing what God wants."*** They could have stayed to allow Jesus' light to shine on their darkness bringing the much needed freedom to their lives. After which, they could have then brought people to Jesus so they could gain freedom from their sins over judgment. Because 1 John 4:9 TPT tells us: ***"The light of God's love shined within us when He sent His matchless Son into the world so that we might live through Him."*** God wanted to send His love, to send Jesus, so we could receive His love, so we could receive Jesus and then we could live in His love by living through Jesus. God wants us to live a life of love according to how He sees, according to His side of the story.

God was establishing His plan for our future that encompassed His hope through giving us the light of His love, His One and only Son, Jesus. Romans 5:5-8 NLT says: ***"And this hope will not lead to disappointment. For we know how dearly God loves us, because He has given us the Holy Spirit to fill our hearts with His love. When we were utterly helpless, Christ came at just the right time and died for us sinners. Now, most people would not be willing to die for an upright person, though someone might perhaps be willing to die for a person who is especially good. But God showed His great love for us by sending Christ to die for us while we were still sinners."*** Holy Spirit can help us understand and receive God's love. We can become so full of God's love that His love spills over onto others just by us walking by them. Have you ever been by a pool when someone got out? And the person getting out of the pool had so much water on him that is just splashed onto you? God wants us so full of His love that is just splashes onto others wherever we go so they are then impacted by God and His love. He wants us to be so full of His love that, no matter what is going on around us, His love is what is splashing out of us. Ephesians 3:17-20 TPT: ***"Then by constantly using your faith, the life of Christ will be released deep inside you, and the resting place of His love will become the very source and root of your life.***

Then you will be empowered to discover what every holy one experiences – the great magnitude of the astonishing love of Christ in all its dimensions. How deeply intimate and far-reaching is His love! How enduring and inclusive it is! Endless love beyond measurement that transcends our understanding – this extravagant love pours into you until you are filled to overflowing with the fullness of God! Never doubt God's mighty power to work in you and accomplish all this. He will achieve infinitely more than your greatest request, your most unbelievable dream, and exceed your wildest imagination! He will outdo them all, for His miraculous power constantly energizes you." God wants us, His children, to fully experience Him for ourselves so we can share His love with others so they can fully experience Him for themselves. God wants us to be in a continual overflow of His love and we can by continually accepting Jesus and His commands whereby we are accepting God and His commands. God knew if the woman who had been brought to Jesus was stoned, she would have died in her sin. God did not provide her a free pass to sin but freedom from sin through Jesus. He provided her with the freedom to no longer sin, no longer be held in sin's grip. God was not identifying the woman with how she had sinned because He was identifying her through His Son Who would free her from her sin. In receiving Jesus as her Lord, she received her freedom from sin by identifying herself as being a servant to Him and His ways, by being obedient and belonging to Him and His ways.

God provides us with His definition of love in 1 Corinthians 13:4-8a AMPC: *"Love endures long and is patient and kind; love never is envious nor boils over with jealousy, is not boastful or vainglorious, does not display itself haughtily, it is not conceited (arrogant and inflated with pride); it is not rude (unmannerly) and does not act unbecomingly. Love (God's love in us) does not*

insist on its own rights or its own way, for it is not self-seeking; it is not touchy or fretful or resentful; it takes no account of the evil done to it [it pays no attention to a suffered wrong]. It does not rejoice at injustice and unrighteousness, but rejoices when right and truth prevail. Love bears up under anything and everything that comes, is ever ready to believe the best of every person, its hopes are fadeless under all circumstances, and it endures everything [without weakening]. Love never fails [never fades out or becomes obsolete or comes to and end]. God demonstrated His love as enduring long, as being patient, and as being kind when He sent Jesus. He had watched what man was able to do without Him, all the sin and the death it caused. God wanted man to experience His love and all the fullness of life that is in His love. God wanted man to experience life without sin. Thanks to Holy Spirit, God's love is in us so we can love like Him. It is in His love that we learn how to love and then choose to love. We love from His love when we choose to walk in the spirit and not in the flesh or soul. God's love in us helps us receive God's love for ourselves and then love others with the same love of God. We gain an understanding of God's love for us when we realize what He has done for us and what Jesus did for us. Psalms 11:7 NIV tells us: ***"For the Lord is righteous, He loves justice; the upright will see His face."*** God so loves justice that He wanted us to be just and Jesus was the only way for this to occur. He knew He would need to establish His righteousness in us and Jesus was the only way. He knew the difference and what injustice would cause, what sin would cause. God knew the price for having a king over having Him as King. He knew the cost of having a system that was not set up by Him and was not run according to His ways. He knew what would happen when man took things into his own hands and ran something without God being the focus, without bringing God into the mix, without doing things according to God's ways. He knew there would be many stories, many news reports, many forms of love, many strategies, many sides on what is right and wrong, all because man was choosing to do things apart from Him, apart from His Son, Jesus.

God knew His Kingdom needed to come on earth so He sent Jesus to show us how to bring His Kingdom here and how to spread His Kingdom. His plan was for us to carry on in bringing His Kingdom to earth and spreading His Kingdom. God knew His love was a part of this and He wanted to establish His love in us. He knew Jesus would be able to carry His love and be our example of how we could carry God's love. Jesus was letting us know about God's love so we would be able to receive and give God's love which is a commandment. He tells us in Matthew 22:37-39 NLT: ***"Jesus replied, 'You must love the Lord your God with all your heart, all your soul, and all your mind. This is the first and greatest commandment. A second is equally important: Love your neighbor as yourself."*** The MSG says: ***"Jesus said, 'Love the Lord your God will all your passion and prayer and intelligence.' This is the most important, the first on any list. But there is a second to set alongside it: 'Love others as well as you love yourself.'"*** We are to first love God with our whole self, with our whole being, withholding no part of ourselves or life from Him and our loving Him. He is to be first in our life and in every area of our life. Then we are to love ourself and loves others the same as we love ourselves. Our neighbor includes anyone outside of ourself. We can love our neighbor as we are to love when we first accept God's love for us and then love ourselves as God loves us. We love ourselves by seeing ourselves as God sees us. In Luke 10:25-36, Jesus was asked how does someone inherit eternal life. And Jesus referred the person to the first and second commandments. He told the person to do both commandments and he would live.

But the person responded by asking Jesus, "Who is my neighbor?" And Jesus replied with a parable of the Good Samaritan. In this parable, Jesus tells of a Jewish man who was attacked and left half dead. Two people passed up the Jewish man and both were Jews. First, a priest and then a priest's helper. Then a third man, who was a Samaritan, stopped and helped the man. He took care of his wounds and took him to an inn. Cared for him there and then paid for the keeper of the inn to continue his care. He told the keeper he would return to pay any remaining balance so that the man could receive all the care needed for a full recovery. He felt compassion, which means He was moved to make a difference, He was moved to bring restoration to this man, who was in need. The Samaritans and Jews would not have seen each other as being neighbors nor worthy of helping each other. They had allowed their differences to bring a division among them and normally did not even associate with each other. But Jesus was making a point in this parable. He was letting people know that He was establishing a new way, God's way of doing things. He was letting us know we are to love people even if they are somehow different in appearance, in culture, in how they are seen by others or even themselves, if they live somewhere different or if they believe differently. Jews and Samaritans believed differently but Jesus just told a parable showing a Samaritan helping a Jew. And at the end of the parable Jesus asked the person which of these had been a neighbor to the man attacked. His response was "the one who had showed him mercy." And in Luke 10:27 NLT it tells us: ***"Jesus said, 'Yes, now go and do the same.'"*** And it was not just Samaritans that Jesus was wanting the Jewish man to see as his neighbor but the whole world. For God so loved the world, He saw the whole world as His neighbor, who needed His love, who needed saving, who needed healing, who needed restoration, who needed to be set free from themselves so they could experience His love and His ways. He was moved with compassion so He sent His love in the form of His Son Who was the only One Who could accomplish this. Jesus so loved the world, He saw the whole world as His neighbor, so He came to accomplish all God sent Him to accomplish. Jesus came revealing to us our neighbor, the world, who we are to love as He and God loves. Jesus came revealing God's love changes people for His Kingdom and changes the world's system into His Kingdom. Jesus came revealing God's love transforms lives so people can see how God sees them and live accordingly.

Loving others the way Jesus loves is loving others with His love, which is God's love. His love changes people for God's Kingdom. His love changes people into God's children. His love keeps God's commands and God's ways. His love shares Himself with others so they can be free from sin. His love makes people right with God. His love is giving. His love sees how God sees. His love restores and redeems. His love prays for others. His love meets people's needs. His love loves like God loves. His love is moved by compassion to see people's lives changed by God's Kingdom. Jesus Himself came into contact with a Samaritan. He saw her as His neighbor and her encounter with Him changed how she believed into her believing how He believed. She exchanged how see saw herself into seeing herself how Jesus saw her, how God saw her. She saw Who Jesus was and her life was changed by God's Kingdom. We can see how this transpired in John 4:1-42. Jesus had journeyed through Samaria on His way to Galilee. He was tired and hungry so He sent his disciples to get some food while He remained at a water well known as Jacob's well. A Samaritan woman came to get some water and Jesus asked her for a drink. She was surprised because Jews were known for not wanting anything to do with Samaritans. She asked Him why was He asking her since she was a Samaritan. He responded to her in verse 10 NLT: ***"If only you knew the gift God has for you and Who you are speaking to, you would ask Me, and I would give you living water."*** She did not see how Jesus could give her water because He had nothing with him to draw water from the well. She could only see what He was talking about from the natural standpoint. He again responded to her in verse 13 NLT: ***"Anyone who drinks this water will soon become thirsty again. But those who drink the water I give will never be thirsty again. It becomes a fresh, bubbling spring within them, giving them eternal life."*** She asked Him for this water because she no longer wanted to go to the well. Again, she was not able to see beyond the natural. Jesus was giving her supernatural responses letting her know there was more to be seen than she was able to see in the natural. Jesus was letting her know there was another well, His well, where you can obtain an eternal life, which is far more sustaining than this natural life. Jesus demonstrated God's Kingdom to the woman by giving her a word of knowledge. He was able to tell her something that He could have only known had God told Him. It was then she recognized Him as a prophet because prophets were known by God revealing information to them about other people. Again, she responded in the natural because she wanted to know why Samaritans and Jews choose different places to worship. Her focus was still on man's ways rather than God's. Rather than engaging in a debate or history lesson, Jesus remained focused on God's Kingdom. He explained how God sees worship and how we are to worship Him. He was opening her eyes from seeing naturally to seeing spiritually, from seeing how man sees to seeing how God sees. He let her know in verse 24 NLT: ***"For God is a Spirit, so those who worship Him must worship in spirit and truth."*** This caused her focus to shift and she told Him she knew the Messiah was coming, the One called Christ and that He would be able to explain. Jesus replied to her in verse 26 NLT: ***"I Am the Messiah!"*** This caused her to run back to tell people in her village that she may have met the Messiah. Before she left, Jesus' disciples returned and could not understand the reason He was talking to a Samaritan. They were not able to see her as their neighbor like Jesus. They were still not able to see like God saw and how Jesus was showing them how. They urged Him to eat but He had been fully sustained because He was sharing spiritual food with the Samaritan. Jesus was so focused on God's Kingdom, His body yielded. He told his disciples in verse 34 NLT: ***"My nourishment comes from doing the will of God, Who sent Me, and from finishing His Work."*** Jesus was operating from His Spirit rather than His flesh and soul. He was showing us a new way to operate and a new way to worship. He was showing us how we are to function from our spirit, how we are to live from our spirit, how we are to worship God from our spirit, over our flesh and soul. And He was letting us know doing God's work is fulfilling and will even sustain our flesh when needed. Jesus' natural hungry had yielded when Jesus was fully operating in His Spirit. When the woman told the people in her village about her encounter with Jesus, many believed. And they returned with her to see Jesus. They asked Jesus to stay with them and He did for two more days. While He was there, He continued telling them about God's Kingdom and they believed Jesus was the Savior of the world. Jesus saw His neighbor, as God saw. He spoke with His neighbor about God's Kingdom as God directed Him on what to say. His neighbor then believed He was the Messiah; He was the Savior of the world and many in her town also believed. They all now knew about God's Kingdom and how God's Kingdom was on the earth. And now God's Kingdom had spread to and throughout the town. Even though Jesus had been experiencing hunger in His natural body, He yielded to His Spirit and was able to see a neighbor who needed to be impacted by God's Kingdom. All because Jesus understood God's two greatest commandments and then He was putting those commandments into operation. He was showing God how much He loved Him and how much He loved His neighbor as Himself. In loving His neighbor and yielding to love, His natural hunger was overtaken by His spiritual hunger to see people know God's love, to see people know God's Kingdom.

God loves with His love which is set apart from how the world and man loves. He sent His love to reach all of the world, to reach all who are in this world. He sent His love to the unlovable so they could become loveable by receiving His love. He sent His love for all sinners regardless of their sin. Jesus came as God's love in demonstration to provide the way for God's love to be fully received. Jesus came so we could be established in God's love. Jesus came so we would carry on God's commandment of love. Jesus came so we would be carriers of God's love spreading His love across the earth. 1 Peter 4:8-9 NKJV tells us: ***"And above all things have fervent love for one another for love will cover a multitude of sins. Be hospitable to one another without grumbling."*** God wants us so immersed in His love that we spread His Kingdom throughout the earth. To know Jesus, to know God, is to know love. To love Them is to love like Them. We just have to receive the love God has for us and realize He loves us with an everlasting love. His love will not run out because He will not run out. None deserved Jesus; yet, God sent Him anyway because that is what His love does. 1 John 4:7-16 NLT says: ***"Dear friends, let us continue to love on another, for love comes from God. Anyone who loves is a child of God and knows God. But anyone who does not love does no know God, for God is love. God showed how much He loved us by sending His one and only Son into the world so that we might have eternal life through Him. This is real*** *love – not that we loved God, but that He loved us and sent His Son as a sacrifice to take aways our sins. Dear friends, since God loved us that much, we surely ought to love each other. No one has ever seen God. But if we love each other, God lives in us, and His love is brought to full expression in us. And God has given us His Spirit as proof that we live in Him and He in us. Furthermore, we have seen with our own eyes and now testify that the Father sent His Son to be the Savior of the world. All who declare that Jesus is the Son of God have God living in them, and they live in God. We know how much God loves us, and we have put our trust in His love. God is love, and all who live in love live in God, and God lives in them."* When we live in God's love, we live in God and God lives in us. It is a love that is His and only comes from Him but He willingly shares with us. He is the One Who is love and He shows us His love and how to live in His love. As His children, we are to grow up in His love by growing in His love. 1 John 4:17-21 NLT says: *"And as we live in God, our love grows more perfect. So, we will not be afraid on the day of judgment, but we can face Him with confidence because we live like Jesus here in this world. Such love had no fear, because perfect love expels all fear. If we are afraid, it is for fear of punishment, and this shows that we have not fully experienced His perfect love. We love each other because He loved us first. If someone says, 'I love God,' but hates a fellow believer, that person is a liar; for if we do not love people we can see, how can we love God, Whom we cannot see? And He has given us this command: Those who love God must also love their fellow believers."* God has provided us with His command to love our brothers and sister in Christ. He did not place a condition on this love. He did not say love them if they are believing like you or if they go to your church or if they are behaving themselves. He said love them. He said love them when they have a need, love them because they need His love. He said love them with

His love. Love them so others who do not know Him can begin to know Him. Love them so others can be drawn to Him. Love the world with His love like He loves the world. Love so full of His love that it spills over into their lives so they can know Jesus, so they can become God's children. Love like Jesus seeing people as God sees them. 1 Corinthians 13:13 NLT tells us: ***"Three things will last forever – faith, hope and love – and the greatest of these of love."*** God and His love will last forever. Jesus came so we can last forever with Him and God. He came so we can live in God's love on earth by living in His love and not sin. Jesus came so we can carry His love to all the world. Jesus came to give us His love commandment for us to live by as seen in John 13:34-35 TPT: ***"So now I am giving you a new commandment: Love each other. Just as I have loved you, you should love each other. Your love for one another will prove to the world that you are My disciples."***

CHAPTER 11

One God, One Family, No Race

I REMEMBER HEARING STORIES from my paternal grandmother regarding growing up in Ohio before moving to Florida. She lived in a town that had a high population of people who were originally born in other countries. They had all come into the country (United States) through the proper channels of entrance and had gotten their citizenship. However, the town remained predominately divided up according to where each people group had come from. My grandmother's family lived in an area of town made up of people who had come from Greece. However, that was not the case prior to her parents marrying. Her father, my great-grandfather, was born in Greece and had come to the States when he was eighteen. Her mother, my great-grandmother, was born in Whales and had come to the

States with her parents when she was thirteen. Prior to knowing each other, both had settled into neighborhoods that matched the origin of their birth country. Even though they were now in another country, had obtained citizenship, they were still living surrounded by other people from the country of their birth.

They were living around people that looked like them, sounded like them, shared the same customs, and ate the same food. After marrying, my great-grandmother moved to the area of town where my great-grandfather had been living and they started their own family. Though I did not get the opportunity to meet my great-grandfather, I did get the opportunity to meet my great-grandmother. She was small in stature but big in character and big in how she loved. Everyone called her mom, those inside the family and outside the family. Her home always felt warm and comfortable, the door always open, to family and friends, and she always had fresh bread she was willing to share. Had I not known her background, because she did not tell of it, I would not have known she had been disowned by her own family just for marrying my great-grandfather. She had not seen her family since that time when they told her if she followed through with marrying him, she would no longer see her parents or any of her family. She followed through marrying the one that was for her and she never saw any of her birth family. There would be no one from her family sitting on the bride's side at the wedding because there would be no one from her family at her wedding. All contact abruptly stopped and it was as if her family had never existed or rather, she never existed to them. They said they would disown her and they did. It was like she had been put up for adoption at birth to never know anything about her birth family nor them knowing anything about her. But I could never tell any of this by knowing my great-grandmother. All I saw when I saw her was love. She loved her family well and loved others well. She had been grafted into his family who accepted her as their own. She may have lost a birth family but through marriage she gained another family. His family had taken her in as their own, had accepted her marrying one of their own, and saw her as being a part of their family. They treated her like they treated him. And his family was close and tight-knit. They had moved to Florida at the request of one of his brothers who needed help. So, my great-grandfather packed up his family and moved to help his extended family because to him family was family and you helped family when needed. I remember seeing my great-grandmother as just that my great-grandmother who I loved and enjoyed spending time with. I did not even see her as being old even though she lived to be ninety-nine. I did not see her according to her past. To me, she was full of life and always making bread. She was full of love and always took time to sit and talk with me, especially over a piece of bread. And I knew she knew the One Who was the Bread of Life, Jesus. Her real citizenship was in heaven where she now resides.

As a believer in and follower of Jesus, we belong to God's family. When we belong to His family, we are all His children and we should see each other as brothers and sisters. We should see each other through His eyes because when God looks at us, He sees His children, He sees us as Jesus' younger brothers and sisters. When God looked at my great-grandmother, He saw her as His child. He did not look at her as someone who was Welch or Greek or anything else. He saw His child, Jesus' younger sister, who was covered by Jesus' precious blood. Her saw her as being a part of His family's bloodline and that is how He sees all of His children. God sees His children as being one big family spread across the earth. One of the ways we are to ensure God's Kingdom covers the earth is in how we follow Jesus' example in the way we pray for, talk about, think about, see, and treat our brothers and sisters. And He gave all of His children the same Holy Spirit to help us. And He gave all of His children His Word so we can learn more of His ways and His thoughts regarding how we are to live as one family. In His family, we are all connected by one bloodline and it is Jesus'. We are to see ourselves connected through Jesus' bloodline just as God does. We have to receive our new family and bloodline with our faith and then function accordingly. Picture all of God's family going to get a blood test. And each family members' blood type comes back saying blood of Jesus. We get a blood type card with our name on it and by our blood type is blood of Jesus. Picture each family member taking a paternity test. The results for everyone would come back verifying God is our Father. Picture God taking a census and there would be two categories, each having two check boxes. The first category would say male, according to how God created you and female, according to how God created you. And then please check one. The second category would say God's child or not God's child. And then please check one. In writing about the second category, I found myself being a little hesitant because the thought came up saying, "that is harsh." And then I realized that thought did not come from God. When I slapped that thought out of the way, I was able to see how God was wanting to ensure that got written because the harsh part of that sentence is those who are not God's child are headed for an eternal separation from God and living in a hell that was meant only for satan and his demons. The world, through satan's influence, would want us to be so sensitive we miss one of the key functions of God's family, which is ensuring others learn of Jesus and His ways, so they can choose Him and become a part of the family. When we see ourselves as God's children and being a part of His family, we will see and do as He does, by being about God's business just like Jesus. We then want others to be able to check God's child and live in all the benefits, blessings, and birthrights afforded them the same as us. It will keep our focus on the prize of increasing our family just as Jesus was focused on. He knew He had to do what He was to do (before the cross, on the cross, going to hell, and being raised from the dead) so we could become God's children and be a part of His family. We are to not compromise our identity as God's children, which includes being a part of His family, just like Jesus did not compromise.

In seeing through God's eyes, we realize He does not want us to compartmentalize, categorize, or generalize others, especially regarding skin tone. For me, one of the best things about being a part of God's family is how vastly different are all the skin tones. It is like God created this big bouquet of skin tones because He is that creative. And while the world and man, along with satan's influence, would want to look at and define people according to outward appearances, God is looking at the heart. God is looking to see if His children have an understanding of who they are in Him and are they walking in a manner that others will recognize them as His. We should never adopt an ideology or system that sets something up which goes against God and His ways and how He sees. I must see the value in people the same as God. He saw the value in people because He sent Jesus. He sent Jesus into the world because He loved the world, who did not love Him back, did not understand Him, who were doing things their own way, and their way was leading them to death and hell. And yet, He saw them as being valuable enough to become His children, independent of skin tone or any other outward appearance. When God and Jesus are conversing about us, God is saying, "look at My child" and Jesus is saying, "look at My brother, look at My sister." They are not making a distinction regarding skin tone nor should we. They are not saying, "look at My dark skin toned child" and "look at My dark skin toned brother and sister." They are not saying, "look at My light skin toned child" and "look at My light skin toned brother and sister." This includes Them not addressing those who are not a part of the family (but can still become a part of the family) by skin tone. God's ways are higher and this includes how He speaks about people and how He describes them. We are to follow His example and the only other example He provided for us is Jesus.

We follow the example of our brothers and sisters, when our brothers and sisters are following Jesus' example. If our brothers and sisters are not following Jesus' example, we are not to follow them. As God's children, our example is and will always be Jesus, including how we are to live as being a part of His family, how we are to see each other, and how we are to refer to each other. God has given us a free will. We can use our free will to see ourselves and refer to ourselves however we want. We can use our free will to see others and refer to others however we want. We can use our free will to line up with the world, with satan, and others according to how they refer to people. Many have made those choices and many problems have followed which can still be seen in operation across the world. God wants us to use our free will to refer to others how He and Jesus do, which does not include seeing people or talking about people using skin tone. This includes telling stories and referring to people by skin tone. When we do, we are aligning ourselves with the world and its system rather than God and His Kingdom. I do not believe anyone in heaven is going around looking at people and making a distinction based on skin tone. We are to live as heaven on earth, with Jesus being our example, so we do not need to be going around looking at people and making a distinction based on skin tone, even if others choose to do so. God's children are to be setting the example according to God and His Kingdom. I believe a part of bringing heaven on earth is seeing and living together as if we are already in heaven, which includes making no distinctions based on skin tones. Do people treat people differently, badly, look down on them, bring harm to them, and even kill them based on skin tone? Yes. Has this occurred in the past? Yes. Is this is still occurring? Yes. As God's children, are we ever to do any of those? No. Would Jesus? No. Is God love? Yes. Does love see skin tone? No. We belong to God and we are His children because we accepted Jesus as our Lord and Savior, we have chosen to follow and believe Jesus. When we do, we choose to follow His ways. We learn about His ways as we grow in being God's children. We grow up spiritually, we use our faith, and Holy Spirit helps us. Skin tone has no role in this equation so it should not play a role in our lives. God is not in heaven with Jesus trying to decide how They are going to separate or categorize us based on skin tone. We should not be on earth trying to separate or categorize others based on skin tone. We are to be about our Father's business and pick up from when Jesus went back to heaven. Looking at people based on skin tones or any other outward appearance is not moving God's Kingdom forward and picking up from when Jesus went back to heaven.

Collectively, we are to show God's Kingdom as much as we are individually. We are to show the world how a family is supposed to operate according to God's ways. Each one of His children represent His church. We often talk about church as being each individual meeting places with their own members. However, if we are God's children, He sees us as being one body which represents His church. Each person is responsible for his or her own fellowship with God and all that goes with being one of His children. However, God never meant for anyone to live in isolation but for

His children to function like a body would function. 1 Corinthians 12:12 NLT says: ***"The human body has many parts, but the many parts make up one whole body. So it is with the body of Christ."*** How many of us would agree with giving up a part of our body just for the sake of giving it up? We should be as fervent in seeing each other as equally important. No matter where we all end up congregating at we are all still brothers and sisters and that is how we should see each other. And by no other characteristics, especially skin tone. We should allow God to plant us in which congregation we need to be in with the help of Holy Spirit's leading. And each congregation is to be learning about Jesus and God's Word with Holy Spirit helping. Jesus is the head of the body, He is the head of the church. We should always be making Him the focus. Colossians 1:18 NLT says: ***"Christ is also the head of the church, which is His body. He is the beginning, supreme over all who rise from the dead. So, He is first in everything."*** Jesus is first and then we follow. We may be at different places in our following Him but we still are all brothers and sisters who have the same Father, God, and the same big Brother, Jesus. We need to understand that once we are a part of God's family, we belong to Him. Even if other brothers and sisters may let us down, He will not and we must maintain our focus just like Jesus. We must still do our part as being a part of the family even if it does not appear like anyone else may be or at least not that we can currently see. We have someone, satan, who is always trying to make sure we see each other differently and respond to each other accordingly but we must remain firm in seeing as God sees. For when we do, it is easier for our actions to follow how we see and keep us focused on God and His Kingdom. When we understand we are God's children, we understand we belong to Him. And when we belong to Him, we belong. If others do not see us like He does, we still belong to Him. We gain a security that can not be shaken or taken from us because once we are His children He does not abandon us or give us up for any reason. If we choose to be disobedient, we are still His children. If we walk away from Him, we are still His children and He waits for us to return to Him. We are His children and we fit into His family and into His Kingdom. He wants us to see ourselves as He does. He wants us to use our faith so we see ourselves as connected as He sees us because we are connected. I recently had a battle where I was not feeling like I fit in, I was feeling left out, and feeling ignored. I had not always felt like this but I did on this particular day. I had to go somewhere and I really did not want to go. The only reason I did was because I believed God wanted me to. So, I was going in obedience to Him. When I got there, other people were already there. I knew they all had a deeper connection to each other than I did. And when I saw how they were interacting it only deepened how I felt. Notice, how many times I have made reference to feelings. I went ahead and found a seat. As I was sitting down, I heard God speak to me in His loving Father's tone, "you belong because you belong to Me." Something clicked deep within me as I firmly grabbed a hold of that revelation. I realized I had gone because He told me to go and no matter who else was there or their connection with each other, I belonged to God. I knew I was His daughter, His child. I knew He loved me and knew I did not have to do anything to obtain His love. I knew we had an ongoing fellowship and I had a deep connection with Him. But something just clicked in me that needed to click. He knew exactly what I needed to hear, how I needed to hear it, and when I needed to hear it. Instantly, it was like I was in the room all by myself with Him. There was such a love and warmth of His embrace I felt. I know I have Holy Spirit in me, but at that moment I felt His presence so intense it was like He had stepped out of heaven and was sitting right next to me as close as He could get. Even while writing, I can sense it all over again, His presence and Him sitting next to me as if He had stepped out of heaven and was sitting next to me, as close as He can get. I realized I had gotten over into my emotions and had allowed my emotions to run amuck. I was all into my feelings because I had allowed my thoughts to reel through my mind going unchecked. And now my thoughts had spilled over into how I was feeling. I finally took back control of my thinking and my emotions and started yielding to my spirit and Holy Spirit. Now, wherever I go, I am reminded I belong because I belong to Him. It is not wherever I go that I belong rather I go wherever He sends me knowing I belong to Him, so I can go focused on Him and His love for me, yielding to my spirit over my soul or flesh. When we realize we are His child and we are a part of His family, we realize our connection to Him and that it runs deep. So deep, no one can sever it even if they see us differently, or judge us by our outward appearance, including skin tone. Someone forgets us, He will not. Someone does not include us, He will not. Someone shuts us out to let someone else in, He will not. Someone looks at us and decides our skin tones do not match so we get ignored, He will not. We are His and we belong to Him.

It is so important we see as God sees and function accordingly. God is not categorizing us and then making generalizations about us. We are His children and that is how He sees us. Regardless of any similarities we may or may not have with each other, we are all unique. Psalms 139:14 NLT tell us: ***"Thank you for making me so wonderfully complex! Your workmanship is marvelous – how well I know it."*** And TPT says: ***"I thank you, God for making me so mysteriously complex! Everything you do is marvelously breathtaking. It simply amazes me to think about it! How thoroughly You know me, Lord!"*** The MSG lets us know:

"I thank you, High God – You are breathtaking! Body and soul, I am marvelously made! I worship in adoration – what a creation! You know me inside and out, You know every bone in my body; You know exactly how I was made bit by bit, how I was sculpted from nothing into something." We are to see how marvelously and wonderfully we are made. When we look at our eyes, we should think we have the perfect eye color rather than thinking our eye color needs to be different or that one eye color is better than another. God made our eyes and all the different colors displayed in people's eyes. He made our skin and all the different shades of skin tones displayed on people's skin. When we look at ourselves and others, we should be thanking God for how He made us and we should be worshiping Him for how wonderful He is for creating people. And remind ourselves He did so in His image. We should be thanking Him for how wonderfully and mysteriously complex we are, how marvelous His workmanship is, and how marvelously we are made. We should be thanking Him for how thoroughly He knows us inside and out. We should be thanking and worshiping Him for how He created us. We must not allow ourselves to come into agreement with the world's system for it is a trap and the world uses categorizations and generalizations. The world will not see as God sees until we, as God's children, begin to influence the world the way God's sees. For us to influence the world, we must be solid in seeing like Him. Before I was in fellowship with God and had made the commitment to follow and believe in Jesus, I did not want anything to do with church or what I thought Christianity was about. I had taken hurt and disappointment that had piled up and piled up and allowed it to skew my perception and my understanding. I had categorized all Christians as being hypocrites and then generalized if anyone was a Christian it meant being a hypocrite. I wanted nothing to do with church because my focus was on people and not Jesus.

Had Jesus focused on people He would not have seen people as worthy of being saved. Jesus focused on His Father's love He had for the world and how He wanted to see people saved. People were sinning by being influenced by satan and through the world's systems. Jesus came influenced by God and His Kingdom and focused on doing what was needed so people could become God's children. Jesus did not categorize or generalize people and see or think only certain people deserved or could become God's children. He did not have a skin tone chart out looking to see who He thought were worthy enough and then provide His data to God. He was not grading people according to some standard He had set for how people would qualify. Jesus came to qualify for us and all who accepted Him qualified regardless of any outward appearance or sin. I changed how I saw Christians and how I saw church when I changed my focus to Jesus and began seeing how God sees. I allowed the change to occur in me by receiving Jesus, Who sees like God, and now I had gained clarity in my vision so I could start seeing like God.

When we follow the world's system, we will follow how the world sees, acts, talks, including race. If you look up the word *race* in Wikipedia, the title reads: Race (human categorization). Race is a social construct that was created through the world's system and is not based on God's Kingdom. Not only is race not essential, not necessary, for humans to live and thrive, it is not essential or necessary for God's children nor it is how God sees or wants us to see. There is no biological or scientific basis for race. People can categorize race differently and make changes which we can see through history and across the world. People are still people. Yet, race has taken on different categorizations. God is the same and He has not taken on any worldly categorization nor will He, this includes race. Originally, Greeks were categorized differently than they are now according to the US Census. However, my great-grand father was still my great-grand father regardless of any race categorization created through the world's system. And he was still my great-grandmother's husband, who she loved regardless of how someone wanted to categorize him based on his place of birth or based on his skin tone or for any other reason. Yet, a human is still a human, with the same biological make-up, same DNA structure, and created in God's image regardless of how the world's system may say otherwise. As a follower and believer of Jesus, why have we followed such categorizations? An eye is still an eye regardless of color and God still made the eye. Skin is still skin regardless of the skin tone and God created skin. Someone may have a preference on eye color or skin tone but that does not make one eye color or skin tone better than another. We are never to take our preferences and project those as being the correct preferences for everyone else. We are never to set up a system where anyone appears dominate over others because that is not the way of God's Kingdom. Human skin is different from animal skin because humans were created in God's image and animals were not. God is wonderfully creative to have created our bodies and our soul and we look so differently and yet be the same. Our enemy, satan, has used race, through the world's system, to create identities for people. Identities created to lure people away from God and their true identity as found in Him and being His children. Identities created to bring discord, distrust, and separation, which do not line up with God and His ways, nor with Jesus. Race is a platform built to draw attention to itself, attention to the world's system influenced by satan. Race is a platform to draw attention away from God, away from His Kingdom, away from how He created humans, and for what purpose He created them. Race focuses on differences, with the goal being to bring division rather than unity. When my paternal great-grandparents moved to the United States and settled in Ohio, they and anyone else living there, could have seen themselves as American. They could have seen their moving to the United States and changing citizenship as their common ground and new shared identity. They could have chosen to see each other through their new identity as American citizens rather than through their differences based on their original country of origin. They could have learned what it meant to be an American citizen and made that their focus over any differences. God wants us to learn what it means to be His children and then what it means to live as one big family on earth. He wants us to live in unity seeing each other how He sees us, living from our identity in Him, and how He created us. He does not see race nor should we.

I have a best friend who was generalized when she was younger. She grew up not thinking she was any different than anyone else just because her skin tone was darker. Her parents had not taught her to like or not like people based on their skin tone. She did not realize that this was not always the case until her path crossed another little girl who had a lighter skin tone. This little girl refused to play with my friend at school because the girl's mother had told her to not interact with anyone who had a darker skin tone. My friend went home and told her mother what had happened. Her mother explained how the girl had not been taught to see people like God sees. My friend's parents had taught her to see how God sees. Her mother reassured her that she was still loved by her parents and God. I do not know how this made my friend feel when she went through this as a child. I do know her now as an adult and she loves people well and sees them like God sees them. My husband and I have been generalized as to what some people think being a Lopez is supposed to look like. I remember when we were traveling on our honeymoon, we had several people tell us we did not look like a Lopez. We have had other similar encounters since. When told that, I always think what is a Lopez supposed to look like? I gave it no thought when marrying my husband. My husband looks like my husband, the man I wanted to marry and did marry. What is a Glaros, my great-grandfather's name, suppose to look like? My great-grandfather looked like the man my great-grandmother wanted to marry and did marry. How different would the world be if God's children did not categorize or generalize people, especially regarding skin tone? Perhaps, more like God's Kingdom? God understands the importance of influence and knows we are either influencing or being influenced. God wants us to realize how we are to be the ones influencing this world for His Kingdom, rather than us being influenced by the world. The more we know who we are in Christ Jesus and who we are as God's children, the stronger our foundation in our identity will be so we will be influencing rather than being influenced. God tells us what to do in establishing relationships, which includes marriages, in 2 Corinthians 6:14-18 NLT: ***"Do not team up with those who are unbelievers. How can righteousness be a partner with wickedness? How can light live with darkness? What harmony can there be between Christ and the devil? How can a believer be a partner with an unbeliever? And what union can there be between God's temple and idols? For we are the temple of the living God. As God said: 'I will live in them and walk among them. I will be their God, and they will be my people. Therefore, come out from among unbelievers, and separate yourselves from them, says the Lord. Do not touch their filthy things, and I will welcome you. And I will be your Father, and you will be my sons and daughters, says the Lord Almighty.'"*** God mentions two types of people: believers (His children) and unbelievers (those who are not His children). He does not mention skin tone or any other characteristic. He understands the importance of a covenant and how it binds people together. He does not want His children to be bound to this world, including people who are entrenched in the world's ways. When we our bound to someone, it establishes a relationship with a set of expectations and promises that have outcomes attached. God wants us to be in covenant with and bound to Him, so we obtain all His promises and we are the ones who are influencing others for His Kingdom.

1 Corinthians 14:33 TPT tells us: ***"For God is the God of harmony, not confusion, as is the pattern in all the churches of God's holy believers."*** Where there is confusion, God is not involved, including when people are operating in confusion. When God's children are having church, they are to be operating according to His ways, which will always line up with His Word, Jesus, and Holy Spirit. God remains the same and because He does, He will never operate in confusion because it is not in His nature. There is no peace, which is a fruit of His Spirit, in confusion. He wants us to lean on His understanding because in Him will be harmony and all the fruits of His Spirit. God wants us to function in His Kingdom because His Kingdom is led by Him and His ways. And God expects His children to take His Kingdom, His pattern, His ways outside of His meetings (His church) because we are to be His representatives spreading His pattern, His ways into the world. This includes how people are to be seen and treated. When I worked for an agency that worked with children and families, I worked with a family that had two children who were twins (a boy and a girl). The mother had a lighter skin tone and the father had a darker skin. The girl was lighter skin toned and the boy was darker skin toned. Aside from their skin tone and gender, the siblings had a close resemblance to each other as twins. It was noted according to their own personal account to me that they were treated by others based on their skin tone, even within their

extended family and even by others at school, including teachers. Each sibling told me they had begun to see themselves based on their skin tone, they had begun relating to others who shared their same skin tone, and they had chosen to hang around those whose skin tone matched theirs. And when asked what race they were, the girl said she was the same race as affiliated with her light skin tone and the boy said he was the same race as affiliated with his darker skin tone. I remember thinking how odd and how sad that such a system had been set up where you have two siblings (twins) who ended up with two different skin tones, who had the same parents, but were seen differently all because of skin tone, and now they saw themselves differently. There was no choice given to say biracial or anything else to say they are both due to their parents representing each skin tone. Could they not just check both? They were a combination of the two rather than one or the other. Where did all these check boxes originate and for what purpose? Does this impact God's Kingdom and His Kingdom going into all the earth? Do these check boxes bring people together or further apart? More check boxes have been added and people have more options. Aside from what we can see by our skin, does anyone really know their natural heritage? Where did seeing people based on outward appearance originate? None of this originated from God. God would not check anything because He does not see race and He wants us to see as He sees. God's form would not have a race section. His form would indicate if you were His child or not. And regardless of which one was checked, He would expect His children to see and treat people as He does, as Jesus does. He would expect His children to remember their identity and to Whom they belong. He has already told us in 1 Peter 2:10 NLT: ***"Once you had no identity as a people; now you are God's people. Once you received no mercy; now you have received God's mercy."*** Our identity is in being God's people, in being His children and not according to a race categorization or any other categorization, because through God's eyes there is no race and He wants us to see through His eyes.

In God's Kingdom, there are no divisions or separations. He wants everyone to become His children and He set up a way for it to happen. He did not discriminate according to who can become His child. You only have to get born again, born anew, and there is only one way that occurs and it is through accepting Jesus as Lord and Savior. We only get born in the natural through one way. Jesus Himself was born in the natural through the same way, except He was not born with a sin nature. A man did not cause a woman to get pregnant in His case. Holy Spirit caused a woman, who had not known a man, to get pregnant. One way to be born in the natural. One way to be born in the spiritual, the supernatural, to become God's children. And by becoming His children, we are to allow our spiritual nature, our spiritual self, rule and reign in our lives. Even though the family I just mentioned was one family, they had been set up by the world's system to be divided solely based on skin tone. The siblings had started to treat each other differently and according to how others were treating them, all based on skin tone. One family, variations in skin tone, still one family. God sees us as one family with variations in outward appearances, including skin tone; yet, He does not see race because in His Kingdom, according to His ways, there is no race. Galatians 3:26 NLT let us know: ***"For you are all children of God through faith in Christ Jesus."*** And TPT says: ***"You have all become true children of God by faith in Jesus Christ! Faith immersed you into Christ, and now you are covered and clothed with His life."*** In Galatians 3:28-29 MSG it says: ***"In Christ's family there can be no division into Jew and non-Jew, slave and free, male and female. Among us you are all equal. That is, we are all***

in a common relationship with Jesus Christ. Also, since you are Christ's family, then you are Abraham's famous descendant, heirs according to the covenant promises." And the NKJV says: ***"For you are all sons of God through faith in Christ Jesus. For as many of you as were baptized into Christ have put on Christ. There is neither Jew nor Greek, there is neither slave nor free, there is neither male nor female for you are all one in Christ Jesus."*** And TPT says: ***"And we no longer see each other in our former state – Jew or non-Jew, rich or poor, male or female – because we are all one through our union with Jesus Christ."*** We are all one with Jesus Christ, we are all one family thanks to Jesus Christ. When we "put on Christ," it is Him we are to see when we look at each other, we should look like our big Brother. When God looks at us, it is as if He is saying, "Hey, you look like My Son Jesus!" When we look at others who follow and believe Jesus, we should say, "Hey, you look like my Brother Jesus!" When others look at us because we follow Jesus, they should say, "Hey, you look like your Brother Jesus!" Change should always start with God's children and the change should always reflect God's Kingdom and God's ways. This is to include how we tell stories, especially regarding others. When we see as He does, how we refer to others should line up. We should tell a story the same as He would, the same as Jesus would. They would not tell a story and mention someone's skin tone nor refer to anyone based on their skin tone. This means we are not to reference anyone based on skin tone, even when we are telling stories. It is not imperative nor relevant to the story to denote someone's skin tone. It is verbiage, we as God's children, need to take out of our speaking, especially when telling stories. I have heard stories being told, even in churches and from pastors, where someone in the story would be referred to by a darker skin tone. I have not noticed when hearing stories any other skin tone being referenced or pointed out, except darker skin tones. Where and when did this start? Why are God's children participating? We are to be influencing according to God and His Kingdom. I have pointed it out to people when I have had the opportunity and have gotten mixed responses. Some agreed with me that they should make a change, while others seemed to not realize they needed to make a change nor did I believe they would. As God's children, we should make any needed changes to how we speak so it lines up with how God speaks, how Jesus speaks, how Holy Spirit speaks, and according to God's Word. If God nor Jesus would say it, why would we? If God nor Jesus would be talking about us and then mention our skin tone, why are we? We are to bring heaven to earth even in how we tell stories and how we reference others.

My husband and I are soccer fans. My enthusiasm for the sport has grown since marrying him. I have gained a good understanding of the game, though it does not match his, and I enjoy watching the game. One thing that has continually stood out is the soccer world's stance on fighting racism. I have noticed certain leagues across the world have some mention of there being no place for racism or no tolerance for racism and you can see banners on the side lines depicting this. They even display the slogan where they have the score and time shown on the television, so when you are looking at the score and time, you are looking at the slogan: no place for racism. Some teams have had special jerseys made and even specialized the numbers on the back of jerseys to display solidarity in overcoming racism. Some athletes and previous athletes have taken up the cause to bring a stop to racism through various platforms. They have now extended the platform in fighting racism to go beyond skin tone. The enemy has gotten in the fight against racism to bring confusion. Racism comes from the root word *race*. Choosing to identify in a manner other than how God created people has nothing to do with skin tone. We have watched games where they have had a moment of silence before the game starts to bring awareness to racial injustice. We have even seen games stopped over racial remarks to players that was demeaning in nature. We have seen games rescheduled and played without the fans being able to watch in person. Soccer is a world-wide sport where there has been and still remains a problem with racism and it extending beyond the soccer pitch (field). I think awareness to problems has its place. It can bring attention to an area where attention needs to be brought. It can let people know there is a problem needing solving. The solution is to bring the Light of Jesus to those caught in the lie of racism. We are to help people see how God sees by bringing them to the Light of Jesus. True freedom from racism is when people accept the Light of Jesus and begin walking in His Light themselves. John 1:4-5 TPT says: ***"A fountain of life was in Him, for His life is Light for all humanity. And this Light never fails to shine through darkness – Light that darkness could not overcome!"*** The MSG says: ***"What came into existence was Life, and the Life was Light to live by. The Life-Light blazed out of the darkness; the darkness could not put it out."*** It is God's Light, the Light of Jesus, that needs to shine into any darkness, especially racism, so that those caught in that trap of the enemy, caught in his lie that seeing others differently based on skin tone, can have the opportunity to change how they see and begin believing in Jesus and following in His ways. In Jesus' ways, there is no form of hate but love, there is no darkness but Light. Darkness stays dark when there is no light to bring to its attention that it is dark. The Light of Jesus is eternal, is from heaven, is supernatural, is spiritual, and brings the needed change that is lasting. The Light of Jesus brings God's Truth to eradicate and replace the lie with God's Truth. The Truth and Light are One, and the One is Jesus.

He brings God's Kingdom onto the scene letting those in darkness know how God sees others and they are to see others as He does. It brings the change in their heart, true change, that can only happen when one truly turns their lives over to Jesus, over to believing in Him and His ways and following Him and His ways, so the change can occur. And then make their life about learning more about Jesus and His ways and then following in His ways. Learning how to line up their thinking and words to match Him and His ways. This brings a real and lasting change and will stop racism in their lives and how they respond to others. People can see the change and be drawn into the Light of Jesus so they can be changed. To stop racism, we bring people to the Light of Jesus where there is no race, where they can become a part of His family, where they can live as one big family of God. In John 8:12 TPT Jesus says: ***"I Am light to the world, and those whose embrace Me will experience life-giving light, and they will never walk in darkness."*** In the NLT, Jesus says: ***"I am the light of the world. If you follow Me, you will not have to walk in darkness, because you will have the light that leads to life."*** Walking in His Light causes us to no longer walk in darkness. His Light directs and guide us and He leads us to Himself, He leads us to God's Word. Psalms 119:105 NLT tells us: ***"Your Word is a lamp to guide my feet and a light for my path."*** Embracing Jesus and embracing God's Word causes us to walk in His life-giving light which will produce life-giving light thoughts, life-giving light speech, and life-giving light actions towards others regardless of their outward appearance, including skin tone.

CHAPTER 12

Seeing Through God's Eyes

GOD WANTS US to see the world's news as an opportunity to change its news into His Good News. God's Word is our news coverage, which is our influence for how we receive and respond to any other news. God wants us so grounded in our identity as His children and in Christ Jesus that we are able to see ourselves through His eyes at all times. Our image should be the same image as God's image of us so nothing will move us but His Spirit and His Word. For every question and every problem, God has the answer. He wants us, His children, to always go to Him, knowing He will provide the answers we need each and every time. Then we will have the answers to provide to the world each and every time. God's News is always trustworthy and dependable. It is a news free of fear, bondage, doubt, discouragement, hate, separation or anything else considered negative, destructive or affiliated with death. It's Good News providing just the opposite. Good feelings come and go just as easily as bad feelings. Both based on circumstances and temporary things. The world's news can move our feelings to either good or bad, anything in between the two, or even fluctuating back and forth, all to create a worldly response. God's News moves our spirit which does not fluctuate but moves with God's Spirit, moves with God's power, moves according to God's Word. A power that brings world change just like Jesus did. When we know who we are as seen by God, we can help others see as God sees, including worldly news.

There has been a lie that has made its way around in society and it has seeped into the spheres of influence such as government, business, education, media, entertainment, families, and even into some churches. And the lie is that we are to keep Jesus to ourselves, we are to keep His teachings and His way of life out of every sphere of influence and out of society. The lie builds itself by implicating if we are believers and followers of Jesus, we are to not have an impact on society but let society have an impact on us. Because when we do not go forward in advancing God's Kingdom and living the way Jesus did, the way He teaches, we are being influenced by omission. Jesus spoke as He heard His Father speak, He did as He saw His Father doing, and we are to do the same. Holy Spirit is in us helping us. Sometimes, not saying something is what is needed and Holy Spirit will prompt us. When we are confident in our identity as seen through God's eyes, we are confident in making an impact in society, making an impact in the world for God and His Kingdom. It is a confidence that is not drawn from our own ability but drawn from Jesus as our example and Holy Spirit as our Helper. Jesus did not keep God and God's Kingdom to Himself. His purpose was to share and show God's Kingdom and to lead us to do the same. God's Kingdom was Jesus' lifestyle and He wants God's Kingdom to be our lifestyle. John 21:25 ESV tells us: ***"Now there are also many other things that Jesus did. Were every one of them to be written, I suppose that the world itself could not contain the books that would be written."*** Jesus kept His focus on God's Kingdom and doing the work of God's Kingdom and He is our example. All He did for God could not be written down but God saw Him. Jesus' focus was on God and in God being His audience to Whom He wanted to please. What will be written about us? Will it match what was written about Jesus? Can people say we are God's children; we are Jesus' brothers and sisters? Can we be linked to God's Kingdom; can people come to us for God's News?

We are Kingdom carriers for God. Where we go, God's Kingdom goes. We take ground for His Kingdom in living by Jesus' ways right where we are, each day and every day. We carry His Kingdom into the stores where we shop, we carry His Kingdom into our homes, we carry His Kingdom into our workplace, we carry His Kingdom into our relationships, we carry His Kingdom because as we go His Spirit goes with us. We have His Word, His Good News, as we go His Word, His Good News goes with us. As we yield to His will, as we go His will goes with us. Our lives are a platform for Jesus and His ways to everyone we come in contact with. If every child of God knew their identity in Him to the degree as Jesus, think of the ground that would be taken for God's Kingdom? Literally, as we stand in a line waiting to be checked out at a store, where we stand is ground taken for God's Kingdom. The woman who approached Jesus to touch His garment, ground taken for God's Kingdom. She heard of Jesus and how He healed, ground taken for God's Kingdom. She went to where Jesus was and received her healing, ground taken for God's Kingdom. She went back from whence she came with her testimony of how Jesus healed her, ground taken for God's Kingdom. She lived her life in complete health, ground taken for God's Kingdom. When we stand our ground in knowing who we are, just as Jesus knew Who He was, ground taken for God's Kingdom. Jesus was mocked, made fun of, spat on, His beard pulled out, He was beaten beyond recognition, and He was nailed to a cross where He died and went to hell before being raised again, all because He stood firm in knowing He was God's Son, sent by God to save us. Ground taken by Jesus for us so we could take ground for God's Kingdom, first by being able to become God's children and then going forth as Jesus advancing in ground being taken for God's Kingdom.

Jesus followed His King, His Father, Who He bowed to, Who He revered and honored, Whose laws He upheld. He carried His King's authority with Him everywhere He went looking to spread His King's Kingdom, because He was empowered by His King to do so. Acts 10:38 NLT inform us: ***"And you know that God anointed Jesus of Nazareth with the Holy Spirit and with power. Then Jesus went around doing good and healing all who were oppressed by the devil, for God was with Him."*** And Mark 6:56 NLT tells us: ***"Wherever He [Jesus] went – in villages, cities or the countryside – they brought the sick out to the marketplaces. They begged Him to let the sick touch at least the fringe of His robe, and all who touched Him were healed."*** Jesus never was influenced by the world's systems or the world's power but remained focused on God and the power He received from Him. He remained focused on telling and showing people, what God and His Kingdom could do for them, that the world was unable to do for them. He touched every sphere of influence, including the government. So much so, a Roman officer (centurion), who was considered a part of the governmental structure of the Roman empire that ruled when Jesus was on earth, came to Jesus for help. The Roman officer knew where to go for help because he knew the Roman empire where he served nor anyone else could help him, except Jesus. Jesus Who served His Father's empire, His Father's Kingdom, was where this governmental authority figure found what he needed. And Jesus provided the help as seen in Matthew 8:5-10,13 GW tells us: ***"When Jesus went to Capernaum, a Roman army officer came to beg Him for help. The officer said, 'Sir, my servant is lying at home paralyzed and in terrible pain.' Jesus said to him, 'I will come to heal him.' The officer responded, 'Sir, I do not deserve to have You come into my house. But just give a command, and my servant will be healed. As You know, I am in a chain of command and have soldiers at my command. I tell one of them, 'Go!' and he goes, and another, 'Come!' and he comes. I tell my servant, 'Do this!' And he does it.' Jesus was amazed when He heard this. He said to those who were following Him. 'I can guarantee this truth: I have not found faith as great as this in anyone in Israel.' Jesus told the officer, 'Go! What you believed will be done for you.' And at that moment the servant was healed."*** Jesus was so known for demonstrating God's Kingdom, the Roman officer, who was a Gentile, knew his servant would receive healing at Jesus' command. He recognized the authority Jesus walked in and His authority was different than the world's. All because Jesus knew His authority as God's Son and He was already walking in His authority outside and inside of the temples as He went about preaching, teaching, and demonstrating God's Kingdom. As Jesus went, so did God's Kingdom. Jesus was showing us there is no separation from God's Kingdom and the world because the world needs His Kingdom. Jesus was showing us we are His church and He is our leader. Jesus was showing us He shared God's Kingdom wherever He went and we are to share God's Kingdom everywhere we go. People caught in the world's systems should be seeking out God's children just like they did

Jesus. We, as God's children, have what they need and we need to see ourselves as capable of meeting their needs just like Jesus. Holy Spirit helps us.

Jesus remained focused on God and His Kingdom even when they came to arrest Him. He knew what He was about to face but His focus on God's Kingdom never wavered. He was with His disciples, minus Judas. Judas was with those who were going to arrest Jesus because Judas was going to let them know which person was Jesus. When the rest of the disciples realized what was going on, they wanted to respond in the natural. However, Jesus remained in the supernatural, He continued operating from His Spirit, and was operating according to God's Kingdom. Jesus kept His focus on what He needed to do for God and He continued following God's way of doing things. Luke 22:49-51 GW tells us: ***"The men who were with Jesus saw what was going to happen. So, they asked Him, 'Lord, should we use our swords to fight?' One of the disciples cut off the right ear of the chief priest's servant. But Jesus said, 'Stop! That is enough of this.' Then He touched the servant's ear and healed him."*** Even on His way to the cross, Jesus was still demonstrating God's Kingdom, He was still showing God's side of the story even while being arrested. And in going to the cross and going through all He went through on the way to the cross, Jesus remained Kingdom minded, He remained Kingdom powerful. When He told those who came to arrest Him that He was "I Am" they all fell to the ground under the power of Jesus' words. John 18:6 NLT says: ***"As Jesus said 'I Am He,' they all drew back and fell to the ground!"*** Jesus was still walking in God's power and those who came to arrest Him experienced this power just by Jesus declaring Who He was. The Jewish leaders wanted Jesus arrested and crucified but only the Romans by law could execute someone and by law they found no fault in Him.

Jesus remained pure even in the eyes of the law. When brought before Pilate, the Roman official in charge, John 18:36 NLT tells us: ***"Jesus answered, 'My Kingdom is not an earthy kingdom. If it were, My followers would fight to keep Me from being handed over to the Jewish leaders. But My Kingdom is not of this world."*** Jesus was still proclaiming God's Kingdom while arrested and headed to be crucified as an innocent man. John 19:6-7 NLT says: ***"When they saw Him, the leading priests and temple guards began shouting, 'Crucify Him! Crucify Him!" 'Take Him yourselves and crucify Him," Pilate said. 'I find Him not guilty.' The Jewish leaders replied, 'By our law He ought to be because He called Himself the Son of God.'"*** Jesus was the Son of God and the Jewish leaders, as well as other Jewish people, could not see Who Jesus truly was. There was no basis to crucify Jesus, no crime He had committed except He declared His identity, He demonstrated His identity and those who could not see Him for Who He was, wanted Him to die. John 19:15-16 NLT says: ***"'Away with Him,' they yelled. 'Away with Him! Crucify Him!' 'What? Crucify your King?' Pilate asked. 'We have no king but Caesar.' The leading priests shouted back. Then Pilate turned Jesus over to them to be crucified."*** The Jewish leaders, those who lead their temples, their synagogues, looked to Caesar and his way of doing things over Jesus and His way of doing things. They turned to man's system which is still happening today. God sent Jesus so we would turn to His system and we would spread His system across the earth. Pilate, who would be considered a Gentile, could even see the truth because in John 19:19-22 NLT it tells us: "***And Pilate posted a sign on the cross that read, 'Jesus of Nazareth, the King of the Jews' The place where Jesus was crucified was near the city, and the sign was written in Hebrew, Latin, and Greek, so many people could read it. Then the leading priests objected and said to Pilate, 'Change it from 'The King of the Jews' to 'He said, I am King of***

the Jews.' Pilate replied, 'No, what I have written, I have written.'" Jesus was announced as being King even by a Roman leader. Jesus continued to keep His focus on God's Kingdom all the way to the cross and even while on the cross. He was between two thieves, who were guilty, while He was innocent. Yet, He was still seen as God's Son by one of the thieves. As long as there was breathe in His body, Jesus was still emanating God's Kingdom and His Sonship. Luke 23:39-43 NLT tells us: ***"One of the criminals hanging beside Him scoffed, 'So you are the Messiah, are you? Prove it by saving yourself – and us too, while you are at it!' But the other criminal protested, 'Do you not fear God even when you have been sentenced to die? We deserve to die for our crimes, but this man has not done anything wrong.' Then he said, 'Jesus, remember me when you come into Your Kingdom.' And Jesus replied, 'I assure you, today you will be with Me in paradise.'"*** Even on the cross, someone was able to see Who Jesus was and realize His innocence, realize He was from another Kingdom, God's Kingdom. Jesus continually reflected God's Kingdom and He is wanting us to do the same. Wherever we are and whatever may be going on around us, God's wants us operating according to His Kingdom. Even before Jesus gave up His last breath on the cross, He was still operating according to God's Kingdom. Luke 23:34 NLT tells us: ***"Jesus said, 'Father, forgive them, for they do not know what they are doing.'"*** He spoke forgiveness, He spoke God's Kingdom into the situation because He was seeing His situation through God's eyes. He knew they were immersed in the world's ways and they did not know God's ways. He knew He was sent to save them but they would need to receive Him as their Savior. He knew His death was first needed as a part of the salvation process and He did not want their part in His death held against them. Jesus was still demonstrating God's Kingdom up until His death. He was speaking God's love because God's love keeps no record of wrong but is patient and kind and upholds God's Truth. He wanted them to know God's Truth because He knew it would bring them out of the world's system into God's. We as God's children are empowered to bring people out of the world's system into God's.

As we go forward for God's Kingdom, reflecting who we are as God's sons and daughters, just as Jesus reflected Who He was as God's Son, we make an impact on the world, we make an impact on the societies of the world. Jesus tells us more about ourselves in Mathew 5:13-15 NLT: ***"You are the salt of the earth. But what good is salt if it has lost its flavor? Can you make it salty again? It will be thrown out and trampled underfoot as worthless. You are the light of the world – like a city on a hilltop that cannot be hidden. No one lights a lamp and then puts it under a basket. Instead, a lamp is placed on a stand, where it gives light to everyone in the house."*** As God's children, He wants us to be like salt and light for the world. God wants us to enhance and bring balance in the earth according to His Kingdom, according to Jesus' ways. He wants His children to establish His Kingdom so others can experience the benefits and abundance His Kingdom provides. God wants us to bring His Kingdom on earth to thwart corruption, destruction, and death that the world brings. God wants us to establish His justice in the world because He is a just God. Psalms 37:28 NLT tells us: ***"For the Lord loves justice; and He will never abandon the godly. He will keep them safe forever, but the children of the wicked will die."*** God Who is love tells us in 1 Corinthians 13:6 NLT that His love: ***"It does not rejoice about injustice but rejoices whenever the truth wins out."*** The truth that wins out over injustice is God's Truth, His Word, His ways. God's Kingdom replaces the injustices of the world by bringing Jesus and His example onto the scene, so people can become His children and learn to replace the unjust ways of the world for the just ways of His Kingdom. God understands the damage darkness does and He wants His children to spread His Light, which is filled with His love and His love contains His justice. John 1:5 NLT says: ***"The light shines in the darkness, and the darkness can never extinguish it."*** Light rules over darkness on the earth and it began the moment God spoke His Light into existence in the earth. His Light is waiting to join with God's children just as His Light joined with Jesus. Now it is Jesus' Light we are to shine so the world can see and be drawn to Jesus, so the people can come to know Jesus and exchange their ways for His, bringing them out of darkness into His Light. As we show Jesus, they can begin to experience John 8:12 TPT: ***"Then Jesus said, "I Am Light to the world, and those who embrace Me will experience life-giving Light, and they will never walk in darkness again."***

Before Jesus was born, God used salt as a reminder of His eternal covenant to His people. Leviticus 2:13 NLT tells us: ***"Season all your grain offerings with salt to remind you of God's eternal covenant. Never forget to add salt to your grain offerings."*** God sent Jesus to establish His eternal covenant with us so we could go forth living in God's eternal covenant. He wants us to know and live out that eternal covenant for ourselves now and in a way that it brings others into His eternal covenant. God wants us to shine His Light into the world by how we live for God and by directing and guiding others toward God and His Kingdom so they can shed their darkness for His Light. Where God's Light shines, darkness is unable to stay. The more of His Light gets spread to the world, the more the darkness yields. God wants us to see how He sees so we can focus on our part and doing what we need to do for His Kingdom. He wants us focused on being His salt and His Light for the earth and if any justice is needed, He knows how to obtain it. His ways and thoughts are higher so we continue to trust His ways and thoughts even about justice. He tells us in Romans 12:19-21 NLT: ***"Dear friends, never take revenge. Leave that to the righteous anger of God. For the Scriptures say, 'I will take revenge; I will pay them back,' says the Lord. Instead, 'If your enemies are hungry, feed them. If they are thirsty, give them something to drink. In doing this, you will heap burning coals of shame on their heads.' Do not let evil conquer you, but conquer evil by doing good.'"*** We must seek God and His side of the story and what He wants us to do when we see bad things happening. He does not want those bad things to continue or even happen in the first place which is why He needs us to spread His Kingdom on earth. His Kingdom is the answer for how bad things stop happening on the earth. His Kingdom stopped Stephen Morin from being a serial killer and His Kingdom can stop others from all manner of darkness and sin, which sin is darkness. God needs His children to do their part in bringing His Kingdom to earth and when His children know who they are it is powerful and satan knows it.

God wants us to see the value of people as He does. The world sees the value of its systems and will lure people into thinking other people are less valuable because that is what satan wants. The world sees gaining power and wealth as important regardless of the cost to others. As God's children, we are to be setting up His Kingdom on earth which includes valuing people and knowing God always provides for His children. This includes setting up God's Kingdom way of handling and obtaining money. In 1 Timothy 6:10 NLT, God tells us: ***"For the love of money is the root of all kinds of evil. And some people, craving money, have wandered from the true faith and pierced themselves with many sorrows."*** Money is not evil. It is the focus being on money and getting money even if others are hurt, harmed, or even killed that is evil. It is a snare of satan that entraps people into thinking gaining money is worth more than people because satan wants to see people destroyed, he hates God's creation. Hebrews 13:5-6 AMPC tells us: ***"Let your character or moral disposition be free from love of money [including greed, avarice, lust, and craving for earthly possessions] and be satisfied with your present [circumstances and with what you have]; for He [God] Himself has said, I will not in any way fail you nor give you up nor leave you without support. [I will] not, [I will] not, [I will] not in any degree leave you helpless nor forsake nor let [you] down (relax My hold on you)! [Assuredly not!] So we take comfort and are encouraged and confidently and boldly say, The Lord is my Helper; I will not be seized with alarm [I will not fear or dread or be terrified]. What can man do to me?"*** We should be as focused on God's Kingdom as Jesus that nothing of this world will entice us into being distracted from our identity as God's children and living like we are His children.

As God's children, we are to love God's creation and see people as He sees them, valuable and worthy of saving. The world takes and God gives. How different if one of God's children had given up their seat on the bus because they saw the value of people like God? How different if the one addicted can be brought to one of God's children for deliverance? How different if the family is about to be evicted and one of God's children pays off their mortgage? How different when people are touched by God's Kingdom through God's children? When we demonstrate God's Kingdom to the world, people are valued above all else, especially money. When we know who we are as God's children, we know He will always take care of us because He is a good Father. We can then let people know how much God values them and how much He will take care of them. We can focus on Him like Jesus knowing He will meet our every need, including leading us to others who need what God's Kingdom can provide. Matthew 17:24-27 MSG tells us: ***"When they had arrived at Capernaum, the tax men came to Petter and asked, 'Does your teacher pay taxes?' Peter said, 'Of course.' But as soon as they were in the house, Jesus confronted him, 'Simon, what do you think? When a king levies taxes, who pays – his children or his subject?' He answered, 'His subjects.' Jesus said, 'Then the children get off free, right?' But so we do not upset them needlessly, go down to the lake, cast a hook, and pull in the first fish that bites. Open its mouth and you will find a coin. Take it and give it to the tax men. It will be enough for both of us.'"*** There was an immediate need and Jesus told Peter how God was going to meet the need and God did. Peter had to follow what Jesus said, he had to walk by faith and trust in what Jesus was telling him to do. Jesus was showing God would do the same for us as His children. We are to walk by our faith in every area of our lives as God's children, including our provision, knowing what we need God will make it happen. He wants us to lean on His understanding and not our own following Him by doing as He instructs. He wants how we see money, how we handle money, how we value money like He sees. He wants us to show the world how to operate in His Kingdom, even regarding money, so people can be free from evil and not become rooted in evil. God wants us living free from sin and living free in every area of our lives, so we can demonstrate how others can do the same, we can demonstrate the power of God's Kingdom. Philippians 4:19 AMPC says: ***"And my God will liberally supply (fill to the full) your every need according to His riches in glory in Christ Jesus."*** God wants us to understand He will meet our every need and His supply comes from His riches, which He established for us through His Son and His anointing. Jesus saved us and a part of Him saving us was to save us from the world's way of making money to God's way of meeting our every need. He wants us to fully understand Matthew 6:31-33 GNT that says: ***"So, do not start worrying" "Where will my food come from? Or my drink? Or my clothes? (These are the things pagans are always concerned about). Your Father in heaven knows that you need all these things. Instead, be concerned above everything else with the Kingdom of God and with what He requires of you, and He will provide you with all these other things."*** God wants our focus to be on Him and His Kingdom and what He wants us to do. He wants our focus to be on Him and His Kingdom and how He wants us to see and treat others. As we focus on Him and trust Him, He will ensure our needs are completely taken care of because He takes care of His children.

When we understand who we are as God's children, we understand God's Good News is for us and we can accept God's Good News as our own. Our Father said it, we believe it, it is ours, we take it, we live it. Psalms 146:4-6 MSG tells us: ***"Do not put your life in the hands of experts who know nothing of life, of salvation life. Mere humans do not have what it takes; when they die, their projects die with them. Instead, get help from the God of Jacob, put your hope in God and know real blessing!"*** We are God's children and when we fully realize we are, we will no longer want to go to man or the world's system regarding anything. Instead, we will always want to go to God, look to Him for what we need, look to Him for our answers, and always believe His side of the story over any others. We will realize only God can truly bless us and only God is Who we are to put our trust in. He will remain for all eternity and we will remain with Him as His children, while the world and all its ways fade away. I came to a point in my life where I realized no amount of education, no amount of training, and no amount of credentials provided by the world can ever compare to

God's Word, Jesus' ways, and Holy Spirit's help. We can begin living like we are already in heaven with God, where everything we need, we have. He said it in His Word and by faith we settle it in our hearts as being so. As God's children, when we realize the world has nothing to offer, we then begin to understand we have everything to offer the world because we have God's Kingdom. The world could not do what God could do for us through Jesus and when we accepted Jesus was have something the world needs. 1 Peter 2:24 TPT tells: ***"He Himself carried our sins in His body on the cross so that we would be dead to sin and live for righteousness. Our instant healing flowed from His wounding."*** As God's children, sin lost its control over us thanks to Jesus. When we fully embrace what Jesus did for us, we can equally embrace the healing He provided for us and sickness lost its control over us. Anything holding us back from being all God created us to be and all Jesus enabled us to be, washes away because we understand the power of what He did for us and we can then walk in all the power He gave us, including walking free from being hurt. We can walk free from sin and free from hurt, enabling us to carry on His Kingdom, without any hindrance. We can then be free to live out Matthew 5:43-48 MSG which tells us: ***"You are familiar with the old written law, 'Love your friend,' and its unwritten companion, 'Hate you enemy' I am challenging that. I am telling you to love your enemies. Let them bring out the best in you, not the worst. When someone gives you a hard time, respond with the supple moves of prayer, for then you are working out of your true selves, your God-created selves. This is what God does. He gives His best – the sun to warm and the rain to nourish – to everyone, regardless: the good and bad, the nice and nasty. If all you do is love the lovable, do you expect a bonus? Anybody can do that. If you simply say hello to those who greet you, do you expect a medal? Any run-of-the-mill sinner does that. In a word, what I am*** *saying is, Grow up. You are Kingdom subjects. Now live like it. Live out your God-created identity. Live generously and graciously."* We can live out our God-created identity as He always planned for us, living our lives by displaying His character to others. Living our lives according to His Kingdom showing people what His Kingdom looks like. We can live our lives knowing God's love He has for us and how dearly precious we are to Him. When we know who we are as God's children, we can know Colossians 3:12-17 TPT which tells us: ***"You are always and dearly loved by God! So, robe yourself with virtues of God, since you have been divinely chosen to be holy. Be merciful as you endeavor to understand others, and be compassionate, showing kindness toward all. Be gentle and humble, unoffendable in your patience with others. Tolerate the weaknesses of those in the family of faith, forgiving one another in the same way you have been graciously forgiven by Jesus Christ. If you find fault with someone, release this same gift of forgiveness to them. For love is supreme and must flow through each of these virtues. Love becomes the mark of true maturity. Let your heart be always guided by the peace of the Anointed One, Who, called you to peace as part of His One Body. And always be thankful. Let the Word of Christ live in you richly, flooding you with all wisdom. Apply the Scriptures as you teach and instruct one another with the Psalms, and prophetic songs given to you spontaneously by the Spirit, so sing to God with all your hearts! Let every activity of your lives and every word that comes from your lips be drenched with the beauty of our Lord Jesus, the Anointed One. And bring your constant praise to God the Father because of what Christ has done for you!"*** When we fully receive God's love He has for us as His children, we can fully love others through His love living holy as in His sight. We can understand others and treat them as He tells us because we are able to see them as He does. His Word will be established deeply in us so the fruit of His Word will be what comes forth out of us. People can then come to us and experience God's Kingdom. When we understand who we are as God's children, we will know He has chosen us to be His priests who are to be set apart and devoted to Him so we can present His Kingdom as He commands. We will be willing to set ourselves apart just as Jesus did. We can fully understand how He sees us as told in 1 Peter 2:9 TPT: ***"But you are God's chosen treasure – priests who are kings, a spiritual "nation" set apart as God's devoted ones. He called you out of darkness to experience His marvelous light, and now He claims you as His very own. He did this so that you would broadcast His glorious wonders throughout the world."*** The MSG says: ***"But you are the ones chosen by God, chosen for the high calling of priestly work, chosen to be a holy people, God's instruments to do His work and speak out for Him, to tell others of the night-and-day difference He made for you – from nothing to something, from rejected to accepted."*** Just like an instrument is played and the instrument presents the music according to who is playing the instrument, we will present God's music to a world in need of His melody. We can present His Word to a world who needs to hear His Word as we present His Word according to Him because we are His instrument and He is the One Who is playing His music through us. We can become the solid foundation for God's Kingdom, being a solid foundation for Jesus' body on earth by being moved only when and how He tells us to move. And all for His glory and His Kingdom coming to the earth. Matthew 16:18 MSG tells us: ***"Now I am going to tell you who you are, really are. You are Peter, a rock. This is the rock on which I will put together My church, a church so expansive with energy that not even the gates of hell will be able to keep it out."*** Jesus was talking to Peter but He was foretelling what was going to happen with His church. Peter was going to be one rock, among many, that Jesus was going to put together by others joining Jesus' church, by others joining Jesus' family. This is who you are as God's child, as seen through His eyes, you are a rock on which He has put together His church. You are one of many rocks, who are so expansive with energy, empowered by Holy Spirit, not even the gates of hell will be able to keep you out. You are God's child, a member of His Godly family, who He has equipped to fight like Jesus. You are a sibling of Jesus, the same Jesus Who went to hell for you and hell could not keep. Hell had to watch as He stayed there three days all the while He knew Who He was and His authority and He knew what was about to happen. Hell had to watch as Jesus swiftly left because the time He spent in hell had paid the price for us not to go to hell and even satan himself had no power except to watch. Now your big Brother has passed all of His authority to you and now hell and its gates tremble knowing it is out matched by you. Only by you not knowing who you are is any darkness in this world safe, including hell itself. Now go on telling God's Good News and demonstrating His Kingdom to a world in need. Go storm the gates of hell and take back those stolen by satan. Nothing can hold you back, but you, so do not let yourself get in the way but see yourself as God sees you. You are not alone, because we are not alone. We belong to a family with many brothers and sisters, we belong to God Whose love will never run out. We have our big Brother, Jesus Who is cheering us on and made a way for us to follow Him in doing what He did on earth. He knows we are capable because through Him and Holy Spirit we are able. We only need to believe who we are as God's children by living out our identity as His children here on earth. We need to keep ourselves encouraged knowing we are on God's side and He is on our side. We need to remain diligent in seeing everything according to how He sees and always responding the same, in thought, word, and action.

Prayer of Salvation

Y**OU ARE THE ONE GOD** so loved that He sent His Son, Jesus, for because He did not want you to perish. God wants to spend eternity with you and He wants you to begin receiving all the love He has for you right now. He wants to enter into fellowship with you and you can by receiving Jesus and the gift of life and life more abundant He provided for you. God sees you as worthy and so does Jesus. Jesus was thinking of you when He went to the cross and He took every sin with Him so you can be set free from sin. All you have to do is believe in your heart and confess with your mouth Who Jesus is and what He did for you by saying this prayer:

Father God I realize I am a sinner in need of saving and that You sent Jesus, Your Son, to save me. I believe Jesus died on the cross to take away my sins and He was raised from the dead so that I can be made right with You. God, I believe You forgive me of my sins because of what Jesus did for me and I receive this gift by receiving Jesus as my Lord and Savior. I choose to follow Jesus Christ as my Lord and Savior and begin following in His Ways. I choose to turn away from a life of sin and turn to a life filled with Jesus and learning of Him and how I am to live my life devoted to Him. Thank You for hearing me and I receive my new life by faith and commit my life to believing in and following Jesus. Amen.

Now that you prayed this prayer, I encourage you to begin taking your new birth seriously and start learning more about who you are by getting into God's Word daily. Ask God to direct you to the right church where you can grow with others who love Jesus and are living their lives for Him. I know He will guide and direct you as needed because He is that good and loving and He wants you to grow in your fellowship with Him. Now that your spirit has been made alive learn to listen to your spirit, with Holy Spirit's help, and learn to nurture your spirit with the things of God.

John 3:16, Romans 10:9, Ephesians 2:8-9

Prayer to be Filled with the Holy Spirit

IF YOU WANT TO BE EMPOWERED in your life just as Jesus was, you can receive the baptism in Holy Spirit. It will take your walk with Jesus to a deeper level and help bring more revelation of God's Word and how you are to live just as Jesus when He was on earth. Holy Spirit is a precious gift given by God and Jesus Himself said Holy Spirit would be your Helper. Receiving Holy Spirit in a greater measure will equip you to live the victorious and powerful life Jesus provided for you. You can develop a more intimate fellowship with Holy Spirit and learn to listen and follow His lead at a greater level in your daily life. If you would like to be filled with Holy Spirit (baptized in Holy Spirit) with evidence of speaking in tongues, say this prayer:

Father God I thank You for giving me Holy Spirit

as My Helper and I ask you to fill me with Holy Spirit right now. I thank You that as I am filled with Holy Spirit, I have my new prayer language of speaking in tongues. Thank You for hearing me and for filling me with Holy Spirit and for my new prayer language. I receive this by faith and commit my life to being fully empowered by Holy Spirit and will actively use my new prayer language of speaking in tongues. I realize this will help me to walk as Jesus walked when He was here. Amen.

Now that you prayed this prayer, I want to encourage you to not allow yourself or anyone else talk you out of this wonderful gift God has provided for you. Pray each day in your prayer language. Ask Holy Spirit to fill you fresh and new each day so you remain filled and full of Him. Listen to your spirit and not your soul or flesh and know Holy Spirit is your Helper and Encourager.

John 16:7-8, Acts 1:8, Acts 2:1-4, Jude 1:20

— My — Encouragement & Prayer for You

I **WANT TO ENCOURAGE YOU** that it does not matter where you have come from, what you may have done, or even what may have been done to you, God loves you greatly and His love does not nor will not change. Allow yourself to journey on in growing deeper into fellowship with Him regardless of where you may be on this journey. Time to God is a matter of yielding yourself to Him and then seeing yourself as He does. Learning each day more of how He sees and how He wants you to see like Him. It will be an ongoing life change for the betterment of your life personally and for all who will cross your path. You will see with such clarity that will only become more and more clear as you realize more and more who you truly are as God's precious child. It will help you to receive the fullness of God's love for you and help you give God's love to others. You will see the importance of God's Kingdom on earth and the impact His Kingdom makes on earth. You will come to understand how much satan fights against this because he knows and does not want anyone else to know this powerful truth. Jesus knew so He came to tell and show you just how much God's Kingdom is in you as God's child and how much of a threat you are to satan. You win. Jesus won it for you. You just have to realize this and then walk it out. You won the race already and the prize is yours. Now you just have to run but you are running as the winner you truly are. Chin up, shoulders back, eyes locked on Jesus because He is cheering you on knowing you can do what He did and even greater. Know I am cheering with Him.

> ***Father God I want to thank You for (insert your name) who has read this book. I ask You to reveal more of Yourself and how much love You have for (insert your name). I pray (insert your name) comes into a deeper and greater fellowship with you and experiences all the fullness this affords. I plead the blood of Jesus over (insert your name) and decree that (insert your name) will finish strong the race you have before (insert your name). I decree (insert your name) will come to know more of who (insert your name) is in You as Your beloved and that (insert your name) grows more in sonship and in understanding that (insert your name) identity is found in You. I speak health and wholeness into (insert your name). May Your joy be (your name's) strength and may (insert your name) be continually filled with Your peace that passes all understanding. May (insert your name) gain more and more revelation of Your Word as being the Good News it truly is. Amen.***

Genesis 1:1 through Revelation 22:21

Please feel free to contact Michelle Lopez via email at:

michellelopez.hearts4444@gmail.com

We carry this confidence in
our hearts because our union
with Christ before God.
Yet we do not see ourselves as capable
enough to do anything in our own strength,
for our true competence
flows from God's empowering presence.
He alone makes us adequate minsters
who are focused on an
entirely new covenant. Our ministry
is not based on the letter of
the law but through the power of the Spirit.
The letter of the law kills, but the
Spirit pours out life.

2 Corinthians 3:4-6 TPT

BUY ONE SOW ONE

Available on
amazon

WHAT IMAGE DO YOU CONVEY?

What image do you WANT to convey?
Are you influencing or being influenced?

We are constantly shaped by people, places, and platforms telling us who we should be. Even influencers are influenced. At any moment, we are influenced by either God, the Father of Jesus Christ, or satan, the ruler of this world. Discover who you are through His eyes. Start now, let Him reveal more to you, and if you already know, go deeper into your journey with Him.

MICHELLE LOPEZ loves the Lord with all her being and wants you to love Him just as much. She values God above all else, finding her identity in being His daughter. Learning about Him and His Word has ignited a deep passion that only grows stronger. Worldly accolades mean nothing compared to knowing who she is in Christ. She follows God in obedience, no matter how it looks to others. This book is an act of that obedience, written to glorify Him. She longs for deeper fellowship with God and hopes to inspire you to do the same. Whether you're just beginning or already walking with Him, He is calling you to go deeper.

Made in the USA
Coppell, TX
08 December 2025

64604326R00177